Offbeat Museums

The Collections and Curators of America's Most Unusual Museums

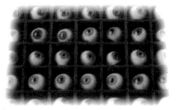

Saul Rubin

Offbeat Museums

Published by:
SANTA MONICA PRESS
1-800-784-9553
P.O. Box 1076
Santa Monica, CA 90406-1076

Printed in the United States

Library of Congress Cataloging-in-Publication Data

Rubin, Saul.
Offbeat museums: the curators and collections of America's most unusual
museums / by Saul Rubin.
p.   cm.
ISBN 0-9639946-4-6 (pbk.)
1. Museums—United States—Guidebooks. 2. Curiosities
and wonders—Museums—United States—Guidebooks.
3. Eccentrics and Eccentricities—Museums—United States—Guidebooks.
4. Popular culture—Museums—United States—Guidebooks. 5. United States—Guidebooks.
6. Museum curators—United States—Biography.
I. Title.
AM11.R83   1997
069'.0973—dc21   97-16766
                                            CIP

10 9 8 7 6 5 4 3 2 1

Book design by Ad Infinitum, Santa Monica, CA

SANTA
MONICA
PRESS

Contents

Introduction

In the 17th century—an age of exploration and scientific inquiry—Europe's parlor set entertained themselves by musing over private collections known as "cabinets of curiosities." Collectors gathered items for their educational as well as shock value. The result was haphazard, sensational displays featuring everything from art treasures to such exotic knickknacks as shrunken heads and dried kidney stones. Before newspapers and steamships, let alone computer networks and jet travel, this was how the world's marvels became known.

Many of these early collections formed the basis for the world's first museums. Charles Willson Peale opened the Philadelphia Museum in 1786, presenting the tradition of curiosity cabinets to a much wider audience. In his self-portrait "The Artist and His Museum," Peale depicts himself as a conjurer lifting up a curtain and presto!—a magical world appears stocked with mastodon bones, stuffed animals and a live porcupine.

Early museums were, in a word, fun. The dawn of the 20th century, however, marked a sobering period for America's exhibit halls. Museums were increasingly perceived as solemn places designed to educate the public in a somber manner, a concept that persists today. America's most cherished institutions are marble-lined mausoleums, presided over by high-minded boards of trustees and guarded by uniformed sentinels armed with attendance clickers.

Thankfully, hundreds of more homespun American museums are not burdened with such lofty concerns. Instead, by seemingly subverting the role of the modern museum, they recapture the spirit of America's early collections. By stepping outside the mainstream, these offbeat institutions fulfill the traditional promise of the world's first great collections: To amaze, inspire and enlighten the public.

It is to these remarkable museums that we turn our attention. This book presents 50 of the most offbeat museums in America, institutions that defy conventional wisdom by their very existence. Their names alone are enough to trigger puzzlement and curiosity. The Museum of Menstruation? The Madison Museum of Bathroom Tissue? In Pennsylvania there's The Shoe Museum, where you can examine the pumps that shod former First Ladies. In Massachusetts there's the American Sanitary Plumbing Museum, which began with the surprising discovery in 1956 of a Colonial-era spigot.

Common sense says that the words "banana" and "museum" should never appear together, but then sure enough you come across a listing for the International Banana Club® and Museum. It's in Altadena, California, and on the Internet, too, with a bright yellow web page.

These museums invite us to ponder the significance of diverse artifacts, such as a table setting from the doomed Hindenburg airship and dentures from the mouth of the father of our country, George Washington. Curators at these museums have taken items such as hair jewelry, spinning tops and obsolete U.S. spy equipment, and displayed them just as proudly and naturally as fine art museums hoist Van Goghs.

Just who is mounting these exhibits? It's a reasonable question to ask. They are courageous people. In the era of the Shopping Channel, when dozens of curious items fly across television screens hourly, these modern-day Peales dare to say that there's room in contemporary society for genuine amazement.

There is Elizabeth Tashjian, a charming Connecticut woman with a lilting voice and an unusual obsession. In her 20-room Victorian mansion, she's fashioned a reverent tribute to the nut. There is Charles Gandolfo, who opened a voodoo museum in New Orleans to dispel negative myths about the religion. He was motivated by family history—his great-grandfather was cured

of lockjaw by a Voodoo priestess named Mama Midnight. In Chicago, John Urbaszewski exhibits his wondrous creations made from household trash, including a replica of the Taj Mahal. If visitors to his traveling museum care to listen, Urbaszewski will tell them of his grand vision to revive urban America by building mile-high residential complexes, anchored by bustling casinos.

We've selected some museums for the provocative way they transform everyday items into fascinating objects worthy of careful study. The National Museum of Dentistry, the National Lighter Museum and the Hamburger Hall of Fame come readily to mind. Others, including The Museum of Death, the Tragedy in U.S. History Museum, and the American Funeral Service Museum, bravely shine a light upon dark, but deserving, subjects.

In the age of cable television and the World Wide Web, it's easy to smugly believe that we've seen it all. The Kansas Barbed Wire Museum, The Museum of Questionable Medical Devices, and The Great Blacks In Wax Museum suggest otherwise. There's much to learn and surprise is still possible. This is especially true when viewing items normally taken for granted, such as cakes, cockroaches, clocks and toothbrushes—all subjects deemed worthy of scrutiny by the museums in this book.

We submit Offbeat Museums as a modern cabinet of curiosities. Let them be your trusted guide on a journey of unexpected wonder and discovery.

— Saul Rubin

International Banana Club® and Museum

2524 El Molino Avenue
Altadena, California 91001

818-798-2272

BananasTB@AOL.com
http://www.Banana-Club.com

By appointment only to
members and their guests.

$10.

From Downtown
Los Angeles, take the 110
Freeway north. When it
ends at Colorado
Boulevard, turn right. Make
a left on Lake Avenue and
travel about three miles
north to El Molino Avenue.

Ken Bannister knew how dull business conventions could be. So while attending one in 1972 as a representative for a photo supply company, he decided to liven things up by handing out Chiquita Banana stickers. People took pride in sticking them on their convention badges as a mirthful emblem. Bannister noticed how the simple gag elevated everyone's mood and brightened up the event.

The convention ended, but Bannister's banana fun was just beginning. He began receiving banana-themed tokens in the mail from the people he had pinned with banana stickers. He encouraged the donations, as long as they weren't "crude or lewd," he says. Before long his office was overflowing with yellow-tinted items and he was compelled to open a museum. He now has more than 17,000 banana artifacts.

The banana is the number one selling fruit in the world, so a tribute to it seems fitting. Bannister praises it for its nutritional values and its user-friendly design.

"It doesn't squirt, squeak or leak," he observes.

Once the museum opened, a banana club seemed inevitable. Bannister says there are now 9,000 members from 23 countries, who vie to earn "BMs" or "banana merits," on their way toward two banana degrees issued by the club.

Members are encouraged to adopt appropriate banana titles. Bannister is "TB," or "Top Banana." Member Pat Curry is known as "Banana Laugh Director," because Bannister is greatly amused by his high-pitched chuckle.

Mostly, though, it's others who are amused by Bannister's banana antics. He offers his bright yellow collection to the public as an amusing antidote to a world gone bananas.

"I've used the museum as a morale builder and vehicle to keep people's spirits up for many years," he points out.

Banana Literature

"I eat one finger the minute I get up."

What is Woddis?

Bannister publishes a banana newsletter called "Woddis," which is a nonsense word he created with the help of one of his three daughters. It's published, he says, "occasionally and rarely."

More frequent are picnics hosted by the museum that feature banana-related food and games. Chess is played with banana halves. There is a "Peel and Draw" contest which determines the fastest person to yank a banana from a pocket and expose a peeled fruit. Not a remarkable talent, to be sure, but a skill that members find challenging just the same.

A Few Fingers a Day

As you might expect, Bannister doesn't just honor bananas. He eats them, too. Savors them, actually.

"I eat one finger the minute I get up," he says, using the slang reference for the fruit. "I usually have a finger at three or four in the afternoon to keep up my spirits and get that potassium blast and energy boost."

Bannister's family gobbles its way through three or four hands (bunches) a week. The average American consumes 28 pounds of the yellow fruit annually.

The banana's appeal, Bannister observes, extends to the very young and old, especially when a lack of teeth is a concern.

Top Banana Ken Bannister in banana heaven

Collection of stuffed banana toys

Hanging on a wall, but probably belonging in the "hard" section, is the "Petrified Banana." Long past ripeness, it was discovered in a severely decomposed state after five years of accidental storage in a friend's closet.

In the "soft" section there are items ranging from banana slippers to a banana Muppet designed by Jim Henson.

Elsewhere there are banana cards, photographs and a variety of banana foods, from baby mixes to banana-flavored popcorn. Bannister's critique of the fruity popcorn is that "it's no big banana."

"It's the first fruit you eat when you come into this world," he muses, "and the last fruit you eat on your way out."

Museum Highlights

The opening section includes banana clothing, from hats to T-shirts. Banana Club® T-shirts feature its logo, a smiling banana, partially peeled, hands on hips. Bannister himself owns two tuxedos that sport bananas on the lapels. He also owns quite a bit of yellow clothing, he says with pride.

A "hard" section of the museum includes a variety of banana-themed items, including drinking glasses, clocks, lamps, salt-and-pepper shakers, squirt guns and jewelry.

A banana well past its prime

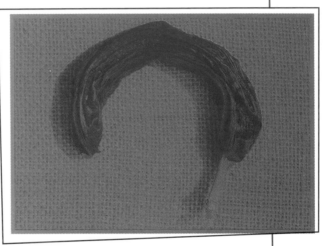

Musical Tributes

The banana has been celebrated in many songs, and the museum exhibits sheet music and albums featuring banana music. When the museum is open, a tape of 40 banana songs plays continuously. The tunes range from the classic "Yes, We Have No Bananas," to more obscure titles such as "My Wife Left Town with a Banana," and "I Like Bananas Because They Have No Bones."

The Top Banana
goes formal

"It's the first fruit you eat when you come into this world, and the last fruit you eat on your way out."

Bananas...

Are shaped like a smile
Have no bones
Contain no cholesterol
Don't leak
Have no seeds
Come in their own wrappers
The peels shine tan shoes
One is called a finger
A bunch is called a hand
Ripen off the plant
Are fun to play with
Come from a giant herb plant
Reduce stress
Make great pets
99.8% fat free
Contain fiber and vitamins
Are a natural diet food

Smiling...

Is the first step to laughing
Is shaped like a banana
Makes us look good
Makes others feel good
Is "appealing"
Stretches out the lips
Makes wrinkles vanish
Takes fewer calories than frowns
Leaves a good impression
Is contagious
Shows off your beautiful teeth
Is a "bunch" of fun
Reflects your positive attitude

Bannister likes to peel away the skin of his bananas in one motion, folding the skin away "like Superman's cape."

How Do You Peel a Banana?

Many people prefer to peel a banana by first breaking the stem, and then peeling away the skin in three motions: pulling down first to the left, then to the right, and then back to the left. Bannister likes to peel away the skin of his bananas in one motion, folding the skin away "like Superman's cape," he says. "You make a little incision with your fingernail on the back side and pull the skin back with two fingers on each hand, and it folds back like a cape."

A Most Delicious Drink

The museum, of course, contains cookbooks that feature favorite banana recipes, from banana bread to banana cream pie. Here's Bannister's own recipe for a refreshing banana shake:

"I fill a blender half-full with low-fat vanilla ice cream and a little bit of milk. I don't measure things. You add one whole banana and a couple of drops of vanilla and let it rip. That's probably the most delicious drink in the world. Those who wish can add alcohol."

INTERNATIONAL
Banana Club INC.®

This is to Certify that

_____

is an official member

★ ★ ★

Signed and Certified This _____ Day of _____
In The Year 19_____

Ken Bannister T.B.
Top Banana

The Mütter Museum

19 South 22nd Street
Philadelphia, PA 19103-3097

215-563-3737

http://www.collphyphil.org

10 A.M. to 4 P.M.
Monday through Saturday.

$8 adults, $4 children 6–18,
students with college ID, senior
citizens, groups with prior
reservations.

From the airport, take
Route 76 and exit at
30th Street (Exit 37).
Go to the second light
and turn right on Market
Street to 21st Street.
Turn right for parking.
The entrance to the
college is on 22nd
Street between Market
and Chestnut Streets.

The College of Physicians of Philadelphia boasts esteemed colonial roots and the noble purpose of increasing public awareness about medical science and the doctor's role in society. While the College's Mütter Museum offers a treasure-trove of history for researchers, it also serves as a popular attraction with the lay public by displaying hundreds of unusual medical specimens.

A private medical society established in 1787, the College began a small "cabinet of pathological specimens" in 1849 for the benefit of its members. In 1856 that small collection received a major boost in the form of the specimen collection of retiring physician Dr. Thomas Dent Mütter. The collection contained hundreds of pathological models, examples of diseased tissues preserved in jars, and bones, including the skeleton of a woman whose rib cage had been compressed by the wearing of tightly-laced corsets.

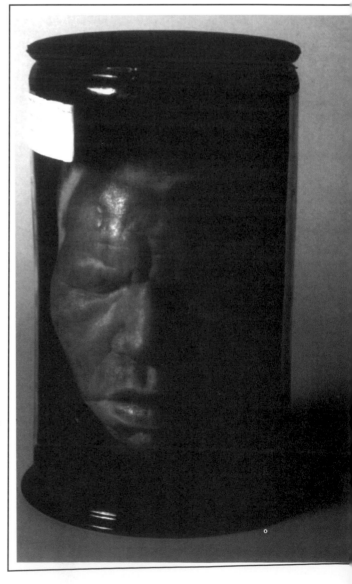

One of the museum's
pathological models of diseased tissue

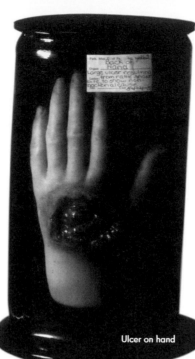
Ulcer on hand

Today, the museum has more than 900 fluid-preserved medical specimens. Included is a colon the size of a cow's that was removed at autopsy from a severely constipated man in 1892.

For the next several decades, the College, in keeping with Dr. Mütter's intent to promote medical education, set out to acquire hundreds of additional specimens as well as obsolete medical instruments. In 1874, for example, the museum acquired the skull collection of an anatomist from Vienna as well as the connected livers of Siamese twins.

Today, the museum has more than 900 fluid-preserved medical specimens. Included is a colon the size of a cow's that was removed at autopsy from a severely constipated man in 1892. Over the years, he had consulted with Philadelphia doctors but they were unable to help him given the limita-

tions of abdominal surgery at the time. He ended up displaying his swollen abdomen at a dime museum, where he was billed as the "Windbag Man" or "Balloon Man." He died at age 29 while on a commode seeking relief.

While there's a tragic story behind every specimen here, there's also a medical lesson. The museum is an invaluable research tool because it represents the extent of physicians' knowledge during the 19th and early 20th centuries. However, the educational aspects of the museum are often overlooked by a queasy public overcome by the grim nature of the medical specimens on display.

The Windbag Man's colon

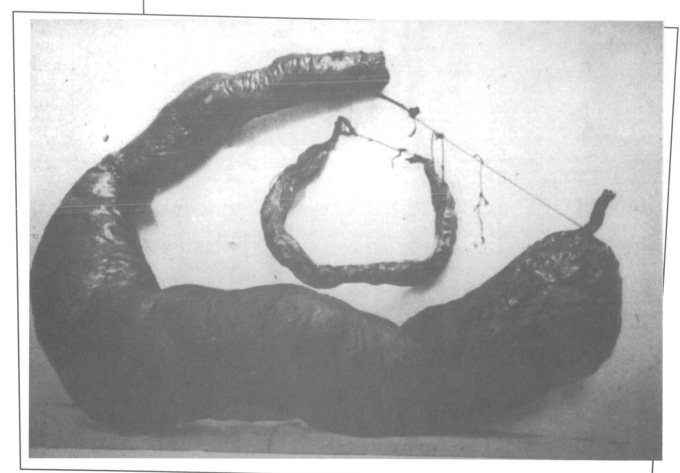

In recent years, the College has mounted more mainstream health exhibits in order to fulfill its goal of keeping the public aware of medical science topics. They've opened a new College Gallery with changing health exhibits, as well as the C. Everett Koop Community Health Information center, a resource library for consumer health information. The College staff advises visitors to check in at these two stops before or after a visit to the Mütter. The College also maintains a medical library with extensive modern and historical holdings, and an 18th century-style medicinal herb garden.

Floating Medical History

Suspended in preserving fluids are some unusual pathological specimens as well as ones that are historically significant. Most of these items were donated by physicians who were involved with the College and had access to them.

For example, College members performed the autopsy on the famous Siamese twins Chang and Eng in 1874. The College was permitted to keep the connected livers of the twins, and had a plaster cast made of their torsos showing the skin and cartilage connection between their bodies.

Also preserved in a jar is the cancerous tumor removed from

College members performed the autopsy on the famous Siamese twins Chang and Eng in 1874. The College was permitted to keep the connected livers of the twins, and had a plaster cast made of their torsos showing the skin and cartilage connection between their bodies.

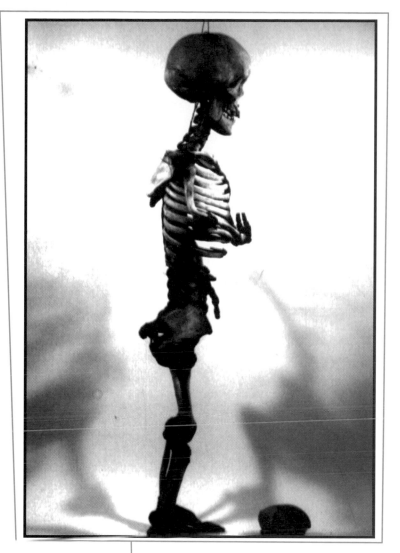

Dwarf with her baby's smashed skull

Bones and More Bones

The museum has more than 1,400 bones and assorted skeletons which were also accumulated for medical teaching and research. There are 139 skulls, for example, in the collection of Professor Joseph Hyrtl of Vienna, who studied differences in bone structures among ethnic groups in central and eastern Europe. The museum bought the collection in 1874.

There are also skeletons of a dwarf and a giant. The giant skeleton belonged to a Kentucky man who was 7 feet 6 inches tall. It was acquired in 1877. In 1857, the museum received the skeleton of a woman who was 3 feet 6 inches tall. In a desperate attempt to save her life during childbirth, doctors had been forced to break up the smashed skull of her baby, whose head could not fit through her pelvis. They were unsuccessful, and they had to remove the infant by Caesarean section. The woman died three days later of peritonitis. The smashed baby skull is exhibited along with her skeleton.

President Grover Cleveland's jaw in 1893. The operation was performed in secret aboard a yacht. The doctor who donated it preserved both the tumor and the secret for more than a decade after Cleveland's death, then published an account of the operation and gave the specimen to the museum.

The museum also displays a specimen that was removed from John Wilkes Booth during his autopsy in 1865, and the nation's Supreme Court is represented by bladder stones removed from Chief Justice John Marshall in 1831.

Specimen removed during the autopsy of John Wilkes Booth

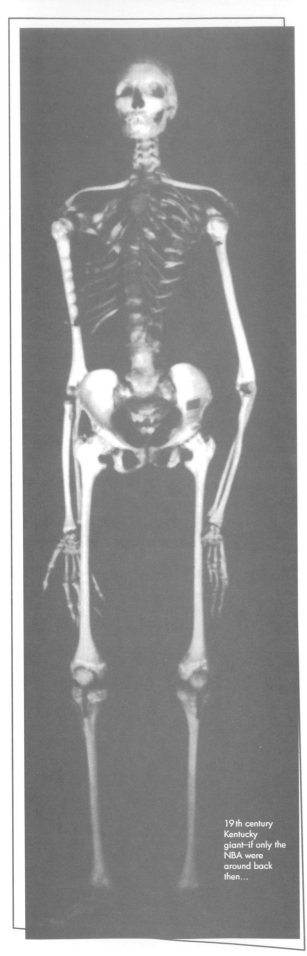

19th century Kentucky giant–if only the NBA were around back then...

Other Museum Highlights

Also of interest is the preserved body of a woman known as the "Soap Lady." Her body decomposed in 1874 into a grayish white fatty wax similar in chemical composition to soap. This condition was discovered when her body was being relocated from a Philadelphia graveyard in 1874.

An abnormal fetal development section offers preserved specimens of malformed fetuses. There are also dozens of wax models once used to show diseases affecting the skin and eyes, including syphilis, smallpox and ulcers. Such models are still used as teaching devices in Europe.

The collection of Chevalier Jackson, a doctor practicing during the first half of the 20th century, consists of items he removed from patients' food and air passages with his own specially-designed instruments. They are exhibited at the museum in drawers. Included are dentures, safety pins, toy jacks, a "Perfect Attendance" pin, toy animals, board game markers and pieces of food. The collection was presented to the museum in 1924.

That's a lot to swallow, just like many of the museum's specimen displays.

An abnormal fetal development section offers preserved specimens of malformed fetuses.

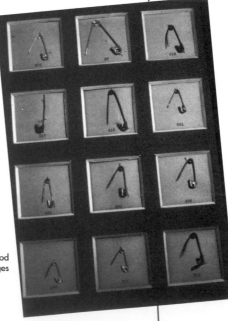

Objects removed from food and air passages

The Museum of Menstruation

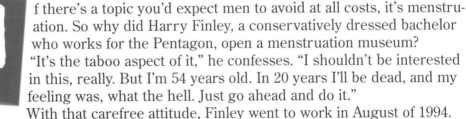

PO Box 2398
Landover Hills Branch
Hyattsville, Maryland 20784-2398

301-459-4450

www.mum.org.

By appointment
on weekends.

Free.

In New Carrollton,
about 7 miles northeast
of Washington D.C. Take
exit 20B off Highway 95.

If there's a topic you'd expect men to avoid at all costs, it's menstruation. So why did Harry Finley, a conservatively dressed bachelor who works for the Pentagon, open a menstruation museum?

"It's the taboo aspect of it," he confesses. "I shouldn't be interested in this, really. But I'm 54 years old. In 20 years I'll be dead, and my feeling was, what the hell. Just go ahead and do it."

With that carefree attitude, Finley went to work in August of 1994. He turned the wood-paneled basement of his ranch style home in a sleepy Maryland suburb into a showcase of the female period and related topics. The Museum of Menstruation has a quaint acronym in MOM, but its exhibits are decidedly not down-home or all-American.

Suspended from the ceiling by fishing line are several midriff mannequins sporting historical menstrual pads. Wall displays include magazine advertisements for menstrual hygiene products from around the world—some more than 100 years old. You can also view

Harry Finley, curator and menstruation expert

contemporary feminine hygiene products such as a New Age Velcro menstrual belt and an earthenware pad-soaking bowl. Foreign samples are displayed too, including barbaric-looking tampons produced in Russia and some more sophisticated European varieties.

Finley, a graphic designer for the Defense Department, used his visual skills to create a display of diagrams and text explaining the physical aspects of menstruation. He researched the subject in a gynecology textbook. The display includes a cup filled with red putty, illustrating the amount of blood a woman loses during the monthly process.

An Important Topic, but a Whole Museum?

The topic of menstruation has attracted scholarly interest, and museums have mounted exhibits exploring the cultural and aesthetic aspects of the female period. What makes critics uncomfortable with Finley's museum is that it's run by a man.

Sassy magazine, for example, coldly dismissed the menstruation institution by sniffing, "Stick to jock-itch products, buddy." An outraged woman from Wyoming suggested that, in her humble opinion, Finley should be burned at the stake. Finley's Pentagon supervisors, and even his own family, have kept their distance from his basement institution.

"Only a man could do this," Finley says in his defense. "Women are so close to this, literally. And our society holds such low regard for it, that probably 99 percent of women would rather just forget about it. For me, I have no participation in this at all. It's just a curiosity."

And a fascination he's pursued to the point of obsession. Finley offers guided tours of the museum by appointment on the weekend, and answers research questions from around the world. He also publishes a free newsletter called "Catamenia" (Greek for menses), a publication that explores current information on the menstruation front, including reviews and news of the latest products.

Mixed Response

Finley's museum has received serious attention from some researchers, including college professors and representatives from the Smithsonian.

But when Finley contacted companies that make menstrual products and asked if they wanted to donate items to the museum, the response was a bit chilly.

"They said no, but it was not only no, but hell no," Finley laughs. "I think they were shocked that anyone would have such an idea."

The concept came to Finley when he worked as an art director for a magazine pub-

An outraged woman from Wyoming suggested that, in her humble opinion, Finley should be burned at the stake.

"Only a man could do this," Finley says in his defense.

The museum's newsletter, with the latest menstruation news

19

"It has women's enthusiastic approval!"

KOTEX

The IMPROVED KOTEX

combining correct appearance and hygienic comfort

HOW many times you hear women say — indeed, how many times you, yourself, say: "What did we ever do without Kotex?"

This famous sanitary convenience is now presented with truly amazing perfections. And already women are expressing delighted approval.

"It is cut so that you can wear it under the sheerest, most clinging frocks," they tell one another. "The corners are rounded, the pad fits snugly — it doesn't reveal any awkward bulkiness. You can have complete peace of mind now."

The downy filler is even softer than before. The gauze is finer and smoother. Chafing and binding no longer cause annoyance and discomfort.

Positively Deodorizes While Worn

Kotex is now deodorized by a patented process (U. S. Patent No. 1,670,587), the only sanitary pad using a Government-patented treatment to assure absolutely safe deodorization. Ten layers of filler in each pad are treated by a perfect neutralizer to end all your fear of offending in this way again.

Women like the fact that they can adjust Kotex filler—add or remove layers as needed. And they like all the other special advantages, none of which has been altered: disposability is instant; protective area is just as large; absorption quick and thorough.

Buy a box today and you will realize why doctors and nurses endorse it so heartily—45c for a box of twelve. On sale at all drug, dry goods and department stores; supplied, also, in rest-rooms, by West Disinfecting Co. Kotex Company, 180 N. Michigan Avenue, Chicago, Illinois.

Lee Miller, the *Life* magazine photographer and lover of the artist Man Ray, posed here as the first real person to appear in a menstruation hygiene ad. Her photo was taken by the great Edward Steichen.

lished in Germany by the U.S. government for American soldiers stationed overseas. Looking for ideas for layouts, Finley searched hundreds of magazines and began collecting a series of ads, including many for menstrual products. By the time he returned home, he had hundreds of ads that revealed differences in the ways countries treat the subject of menstruation. On the whole, European nations were much more open about it, he says.

Examples of these ads are plastered on museum walls for comparison. One of the earliest examples of an American magazine advertisement for Kotex shows a smiling woman enjoying a vacation setting because the product offers "absorbency that doesn't fail." The woman is fully dressed. In European ads, women are nearly naked as they cheerfully explain the proper use of menstrual products.

Museum Highlights

In the central part of the museum, suspended mannequins model assorted, historic menstrual pads. Finley says he uses only the midsection of the mannequins, from the knees to the lower torso, "because that's all I need."

His favorite menstrual device is a sanitary apron. Finley saw an ad for one in a 1914 Sears, Roebuck catalog and asked a costume designer to make a copy. The replica is now worn by one of the mannequins. Like the original, it's made of rubber. Finley says it was designed to be worn under a dress to prevent blood from soaking through clothes.

Next to this exhibit is a menstrual traveling kit from the same era. It has a little pouch to place washable pads and a belt to wear with them. It sold for 75 cents.

Tracing the History of Menstrual Products

The museum displays a timeline that shows the development of menstrual products. It's a subject that Finley has become quite knowledgeable about since he opened the museum. He explains, for example, how Kotex sanitary napkins were invented when nurses during World War II used absorbent surgical bandages to control their menstrual bleeding. These bandages were made from wood pulp and were not only absorbent but also cheap enough to throw away after use.

The exhibit points out that Johnson & Johnson developed a disposable menstrual pad in the late 19th century

Finley says he uses only the midsection of the mannequins, from the knees to the lower torso, "because that's all I need."

Right: "Sanitary apron" sold in a 1914 Sears, Roebuck catalog

but that it didn't catch on because magazines wouldn't accept advertising for it.

The first successful German disposable pad was called Camilia, Finley says. Because makers of the product believed women would be too embarrassed to ask for it at the sales counter, they inserted slips of paper in each box that read: "Give me a box of Camilia." Women could then discreetly slip these to a salesperson when they needed more supplies.

Tampax tampons came along in the 1930s, while the first commercially available menstrual cup hit the market in 1969. Stayfree, the first stick-in pads, were introduced a year later.

The museum stays current with information about new menstrual products, offering details about non-disposable products that have

Exhibits highlight cultural attitudes about menstruation

emerged in these ecologically sensitive times. The exhibits include information about two new menstrual cups that are designed to last for up to 10 years.

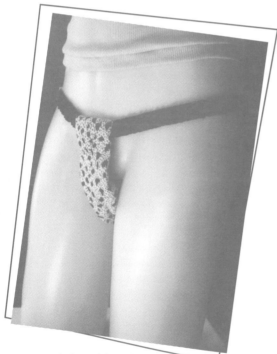

The leopard skin look

The Museum of Menstruation
Eight miles east of the U.S. Capitol
Catamenia
The newsletter of the museum
Harry Finley
Founder and director
Mailing address:
P.O. Box 2398
Landover Hills Branch
Hyattsville, Maryland 20784-2398 U.S.A
Ph: (301) 459-4450 FAX: (301) 577-2913

The Museum of Questionable Medical Devices

201 South East Main Street
Minneapolis, Minnesota 55414

612-379-4046

5 P.M. to 9 P.M. Tuesday through Thursday, 5 P.M. to 10 P.M. Friday, and Noon to 5 P.M. Saturday. Closed Sunday and Monday.

Free.

From State Highway 47, take Hennepin Avenue west to South East Main Street. The museum is located two blocks south of the north end of the Hennepin Suspension Bridge.

I f you're ill, Robert McCoy just might have a machine designed to make you better. Unfortunately, it probably won't work.

McCoy's collection of more than 400 medical contraptions documents a century of bogus science. Employing the powers of electricity, radio waves, magnetics, vibrations and other magical means, these machines were sold to desperate patients looking for cures for everything from cancer to impotence.

McCoy opened the museum in 1984. Before that, he worked as a printer, steel salesman, Humanist minister, soap seller and operator of a family planning clinic. In his younger days, he posed for characters drawn by his father for the comic strip, "The Phantom."

McCoy says he opened The Museum of Questionable Medical Devices as an antidote to medical quackery, which he says thrives even today. When asked to name the period he considers to be the heyday of phony medicine, he doesn't hesitate.

"The 1990s," he answers emphatically. "Because of the advent of TV, infomercials and catalogs, there is more stuff going on now than ever before."

In the 1970s, McCoy points out, 4 million women spent $9.95 on a foot-operated breast enlarger. It featured a rubber pedal and a cylinder from which plastic tubes sprouted, all connected to a cup. It came in three sizes—large, larger, and even larger still.

The Ellis Micro-Dynameter was falsely promoted as a way to diagnose and cure a wide array of diseases

Curator Robert McCoy demonstrates the Crosley Xervac, which was purported to stimulate hair growth

Psychograph machines were built to perform phrenology readings by way of a metal-domed device placed on a user's head.

Many fraudulent devices sold today are merely copies of phony cures sold long ago.

In the early part of the century, for example, the public was encouraged to buy something called Boyd's Battery, a device worn around the neck that could ward off the damaging effects of the earth's magnetic rays. A modern catalog, McCoy notes, offers a product called the Bio-Electric Shield, a necklace that makes the same claims as Boyd's Battery.

Science of the Forehead

The Psychograph machines of the 1930s incorporate all the elements of the classic medical fraud. They were rooted in science, manufacturer's claimed. Only in this case, it was the science of phrenology, which theorized that character traits were revealed by the bumps on a person's forehead. Dozens of books were written about this "science," and it proved popular in the early part of the 20th century.

Psychograph machines were built to perform phrenology readings by way of a metal-domed device placed on a user's head. The dome looked like an antique hair dryer and featured protruding wires, screws and bolts. The whole contraption was hooked up to a wood cabinet that spat out a printed reading rating the person's cranial bumps for dozens of character traits. Suavity, agreeability and even something called "sex amity" were measured and rated on a scale of one to five.

In the 1930s, Frank P. White, proving that he should have had his own head examined, took out $38,000 of his life savings from a growing local sandpaper company called 3M. He invested the money instead in a Minnesota company that built Psychographs, an operation doomed to fail by the end of the decade when phrenology was debunked.

In the 1960s, McCoy met Frank White's son, John, whose inheritance from his father was not shares of 3M but dozens of Psychographs. Together they restored some of the machines. McCoy bought them with the intention of selling them, but no one made an offer.

PSYCOGRAPH
KNOW THYSELF!

Measures thirty-two mental faculties and prints record, rating each faculty from 1 to 5, with an explanation of each development. It will bring out your strong and weak characteristics. It will help parents understand their children. Vocational chart given with each measurement. No one sees your reading but you.

SEE YOURSELF AS OTHERS SEE YOU!

Then McCoy, a W.C. Fields look-alike, turned huckster himself. When an upscale Minneapolis shopping center opened in 1984, he set up a restored Psychograph and offered "readings" for $1.00 to amused passersby.

"People liked the contentious readings better than the nice ones," McCoy laughs. A banker, for example, was pleased that he scored high on greed.

If customers weren't satisfied with their forehead ratings, McCoy, in his best W.C. Fields drawl, offered to correct the problem by saying, "I have a mallet handy."

Left: The psychograph is the classic quack device

Let The PSYCOGRAPH READ YOUR CHARACTER! FREE!

Antique Phrenology Machine
You Ought To Have
Your Head Exa...

THE MUSEUM OF QUESTIONABLE MEDICAL DEVICES

YOU OUGHT TO HAVE YOUR HEAD EXAMINED

MINNEAPOLIS MINNESOTA

One day a producer from the "Today Show" made a request. "She said, 'Is this thing portable and can you bring it over to St. Paul tomorrow and put it on Willard Scott's head?'" McCoy recalls. McCoy, of course, happily obliged.

The exposure brought requests for McCoy to make other appearances, including one on the "David Letterman Show." Since he was always being asked to display more quack devices, he hit the road in a beat-up van and scrounged for them at garage sales. Other machines were leant to him by agencies such as the Food and Drug Administration and the American Medical Association—organizations that share McCoy's interest in exposing medical quackery. Many of the fraudulent machines were being kept in storage until McCoy opened the museum.

"Is this thing portable and can you bring it over to St. Paul tomorrow and put it on Willard Scott's head?"

The makers of the Nemectron claimed that their device rejuvenated glands, cured acne and "normalized" underdeveloped and overdeveloped breasts

Dangerous Cures

Most of the devices at the museum are harmless, but some are downright dangerous. Quacks always proclaim to heal using powers that are somewhat known to the general public but not fully understood. That's why at the turn of the century, hundreds of cures were offered that used electricity, radio waves and magnetism. The more wires and tubes a machine had the better. Makers of these machines claimed that they cured a multitude of ailments, but most often they focused upon cancer, arthritis and aging.

"These are three things that you can't do too much about," McCoy points out. Sometimes the bogus cures worked in spite of their fraudulent claims.

"A lot of people would try these things and get better," McCoy says. "Mother Nature is a wonderful healer."

Museum Highlights

The G-H-R Electric Thermitis Dilator is not for the squeamish. This device is also known as the prostate warmer. One end plugs into a 25-watt lamp bulb. The other end, a metal prod resembling an elongated tear drop, is inserted into a man's rectum. Promotional literature claimed it would increase a man's sex drive by stimulating the prostate gland.

The Foot Operated Breast Pump Enlarger is a suction tube that was supposed to increase breast size. Manufacturers assured users that any bruising that occurred during use was only temporary.

McCoy likes to have fun with couples who approach this device. Inevitably, the man suggests that the woman try it out. "I'll come up and say, 'She'll

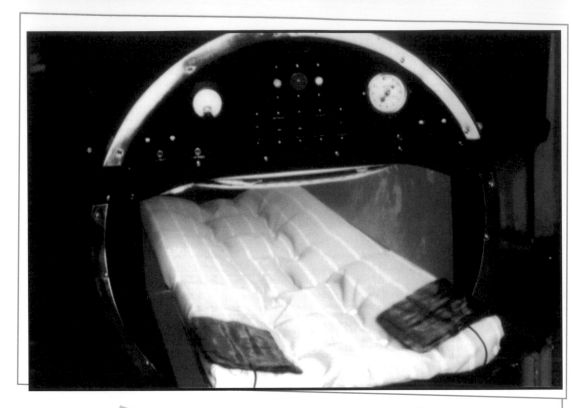

In the 1930s, Dr. M.E. Montrude Jr. claimed that his MacGregor Rejuvenator could reverse the aging process

"She'll try that if you come and try this prostate warmer."

try that if you come and try this prostate warmer,'" McCoy laughs.

The Auto Sweep Resonator looks like a cigar box and contains a copper-lined hollow well. The machine could supposedly determine the health of any person whose photograph was placed in the well. As if this wasn't amazing enough, makers of the magical device also claimed that it could project healing rays to the afflicted person's brain, no matter where in the world the patient was. Other machines in McCoy's collection also were said to have long-distance healing powers. Producers of the Coetherator, for example, assured farmers that if they wanted healthy crops, they should cover a photograph of their field with insecticide and put it in the machine. The Coetherator would then emit pest-killing rays that reached up to 70 miles away.

The Spectro-Chrome

This device had six colored lenses and a 1,000-watt bulb. Each color was said to cure a different disease—for example, a red light for heart problems and a yellow light to help build up bones. Patients were instructed to

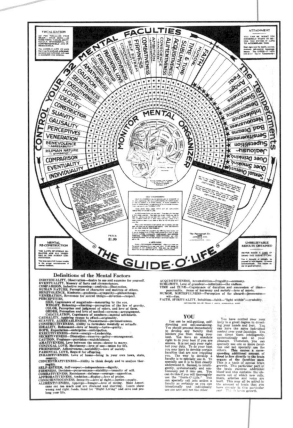

sit naked and in the dark in front of the appropriately colored light, facing north, during certain moon phases.

The maker of the Spectro-Chrome, Dinshah Ghadiali, sold 10,000 of the machines at $150 each.

In 1931, Ghadiali was brought to court on charges of violating the Medical Practices Act. In his defense, Ghadiali presented 65 witnesses he said had been healed by his device. One of them was a woman supposedly cured of epilepsy. As she was testifying, she had a seizure on the stand and had to be attended by doctors in the courtroom. Ghadiali was convicted.

The Spectro-Chrome

King of the Quacks

Albert Abrams was a San Francisco charlatan in the 1920s who maintained a thriving mail-order healing practice. He solicited samples of bodily fluids from patients. Using an electrical "Radionics" machine, he claimed that he could diagnose their ailments by analyzing the sample. The museum has about a dozen of these machines on display.

Abrams' device was a little round disk connected to a water pipe and a "hodge-podge of machines," McCoy says. Abrams diagnosed many patients as having syphilis and offered a cure by mail. Out of embarrassment, many patients avoided going to the doctor and instead sent away for Abrams' $300 cure.

Using the same machine, McCoy will offer visitors the same diagnosis and cure—but he'll do it all for free.

Barney Smith Toilet Seat Art Museum

239 Abiso Avenue
San Antonio, Texas 78209

210-824-7791

Museum visits by
appointment or drop-by.

Free.

From airport take Loop 410
to Broadway, turn south
toward downtown and go
approximately 2 miles to
Alamo Heights. Staying in
the right lane, go to Abiso
Street and make a right.
Proceed two blocks to 239
Abiso. The museum is
located behind the house.

One day friends brought Barney Smith a piece of charred metal that had washed up on a Florida beach. They told him it was wreckage from the ill-fated space shuttle Challenger, which exploded shortly after takeoff in 1986.

Smith took the honeycombed artifact to the Johnson Space Center in Houston, where he was told it was probably a piece of Challenger insulation tile. NASA didn't want it, but Smith did.

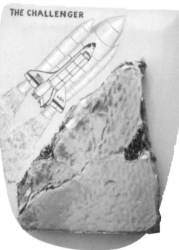

He went home and glued the shuttle debris onto a toilet lid. On the same lid he painted a portrait of the Challenger roaring into space with its booster rockets flaring. In plain lettering across the top arc of the lid, Smith added the words: "The Challenger."

This wasn't odd behavior for Smith. He practices one of the most unusual folk mediums: artworks mounted on toilet seats. If he worked with canvas or more traditional materials, Smith's creations would hardly draw attention. His "representation" of the 1996 Super Bowl, for example, merely consists of a painted-on National Football League emblem, a Super Bowl ticket stub and an inscription that reads: "1996 Super Bowl."

It's the mounting of these artifacts upon a standard-issue, white toilet lid that has proven to be Smith's genius. He has created 375 artworks mounted on toilet seats or lids and no one's calling it bathroom humor. Smith has been accorded respect and media attention. Students on field trips show up at his door and he has had exhibits in local museums, churches and at festivals.

It Began with "My Little Spike"

It came naturally to Smith to elevate the humble commode lid to the level of art. He grew up in a family of plumbers in Tennessee and went on to become a master plumber himself, teaching the trade at a local high school. But he also had a flair for arts and crafts, and taught that subject at a Texas orphanage.

After a successful day of deer hunting in 1970, Smith watched his dad mount a buck's horns on a shield. His creative instincts, and his knowledge of bathroom equipment, took over as he decided what to do with his own set of deer antlers.

"I said, 'I'm going to cut off the horns and mount my little spike on a toilet seat lid.' That's how I started. Putting deer antlers on toilet set lids," Smith recalls.

With a little imagination he branched out to animal hides. Then his vision widened to include other themes. He's used toilet lids to chronicle his trips with his wife, mounting souvenirs such as hotel keys, foreign money and maps.

Almost all of his works are mounted on toilet lids, not seats. Making art out of toilet seats, or "rings," as Smith calls them, just doesn't sit well with him. "I almost never use the ring," he says. "I never expect to put anything in the hole and hang it on the wall. It's too much of a toilet seat. The lids look more like plaques."

Smith gets his supplies from local plumbing wholesalers, who save slightly damaged goods for him. He uses most brands, but insists that, "the Church seat has been good to me."

Barney Smith at work

Museum Highlights

One of Smith's latest works is an owl mounted on a cactus limb. Others are of a more serious nature. There are lids that feature ash from Mt. St. Helens, barbed wire from the Auschwitz concentration camp, and a piece of the Berlin Wall.

One lid is decorated with 20 pairs of claws from bears killed in the Smoky Mountains. Rangers would shoot animals that wandered into camping grounds and give them to Smith, who was working as a crafts instructor at the Church of God orphanage in Severfille, Tennessee. Smith butchered the bears and barbecued the meat for the kids. He kept the claws for his future art work.

"Training," a tribute to guide dogs, features a painting of a guide dog as the centerpiece with dog tags and dog biscuits glued around the edges of the lid.

"They Shall Study War No More" consists of hand grenades, shells and bullets mounted on a lid with the title painted across the top arc.

"Cosmetology" has clumps of hair stuck into 22-caliber shell casings and an assortment of hair care products, including clippers, rollers, combs, brushes, barrettes and pins.

"M.D. Cardiology" uses patches Smith's wife wore when she took a heart stress test. A heart is painted in the lid's center and a coat hanger is shaped to represent the spike lines from a heart monitor.

"Lost a Key?" If the answer to that question is yes, you might want to look for it on this piece of toilet seat art. It features a sketch of a giant key and a wire key ring that winds around the lid and holds dozens of assorted keys. Also

"Cosmetology" has clumps of hair stuck into 22-caliber shell casings and an assortment of hair care products, including clippers, rollers, combs, brushes, barrettes and pins.

attached are motel keys held by giant diaper-pin rings, and a set of house keys dangling from a small black leather holder.

"Sight & Sound" could also be titled "Lost Any Glasses?" It consists of 20 assorted pair of eyeglasses arranged in two rows, not entirely straight, and several pairs of hearing aids glued down along the lid's tip.

"Ride 'em Cowboy" is a tribute to rodeo riders. It features stirrups

arranged on a wooden rail fence which also holds a small holster. Above this is a picture of a cowboy riding a bucking horse.

Most of Smith's works are up in his garage. If he's home, and you call at a decent hour, he'll flip open the door and show you around.

The artist and his lids

The National Atomic Museum

Kirtland Air Force Base
PO Box 5800
Albuquerque, New Mexico 87185-1490

505-284-3243
Fax: 505-284-3244

www.sandia.gov.AtomMus/AtomMus.htm

9 A.M. to 5 P.M.
Monday through Sunday.

Free.

From downtown Albequerque, go west on Interstate 40. Take the Wyoming Boulevard exit South and travel about three miles to Kirtland Air Force Base. The museum entrance is one mile south of the Wyoming Boulevard gate.

O n July 16, 1945, America's top scientists anxiously awaited the results of a top-secret project they had been frantically working on for the previous four years. The Manhattan Project's goal that day was to explode the world's first atomic bomb at Alamogordo, New Mexico. The research team, led by Robert Oppenheimer, wasn't sure what was going to happen at the Trinity test site. Members placed bets on everything from a total dud to a chain reaction that would result in the world's complete destruction.

Minuteman, Titan and Redstone missles stand guard outside of the National Atomic Museum

The weapon they detonated that day proved to be highly destructive, and the test was deemed a success. Three weeks later the bomber Enola Gay dropped a four-ton atomic bomb over the Japanese city of Hiroshima. A second A-bomb was exploded three days after that at Nagasaki. The Japanese surrendered the next day, bringing the war to a close but opening up the age of atomic weaponry.

34

Fat Man and Little Boy

At the National Atomic Museum, visitors are encouraged to step forward and examine dozens of nuclear weapons...

Thousands of nuclear weapons have been produced since Trinity, with modern bombs becoming more sophisticated and powerful. For years, Americans were taught to duck and cover when warned of an incoming nuclear weapon. At the National Atomic Museum, visitors are encouraged to step forward and examine dozens of nuclear weapons, ranging from tactical and strategic thermonuclear bombs to fleet ballistic missiles, anti-submarine weapons, and nuclear warheads and artillery rounds.

While there are some gaps, the devices displayed here represent almost every type of nuclear weapon ever stocked in the U.S. arsenal, states museum historian Jim Wadell. In addition, the museum features several examples of "delivery systems"—bombers designed to carry and, if necessary, drop the atomic weapons.

Because it's located on a military base, the museum gets its share of service people stopping by. World War II veterans also have a strong interest, but Wadell says the museum appeals to the broader public as well. "Not many people have ever seen a nuclear weapon," he points out. "They want to know what they look like. Are they green, gray or silver? I think it's curiosity that drives many people to visit."

The museum opened in 1969 as part of the U.S. Defense Department, and was later transferred to the Department of Energy. In 1995, the museum became part of Sandia National Laboratories, a division of Lockheed Martin Corporation.

Under Sandia's direction the museum is undergoing a period of growth and renovation. A new building is being constructed and additional exhibits are planned.

Thousands of photographs in the museum's archives that document the atomic age are being cataloged. Wadell hopes to make them available to the public through a computer database. More weapons will be acquired for display, and future exhibits will explore in more detail the peacetime role of atomic energy and nuclear medicine.

"We try to offer a balance between the military application of atomic energy and the peaceful use. I think over time the peaceful side will be seeing more emphasis," explains Wadell.

Atomic Arsenal Through Time

The museum's opening exhibit tells the story of the Manhattan Project through photographs, text, newspaper clippings and artifacts.

Highlights are Fat Man and Little Boy, disarmed examples of the original A-bombs. Other artifacts include a Manhattan Project ID card and a piece of trinitite—a section of the desert floor that was fused into a hard-green substance by the intense heat of the first atomic explosion at the Trinity test site.

A documentary on the Manhattan Project called "Ten Seconds that Shook the World" is shown four times daily.

Other nuclear weapons on display include missiles that are three-stories tall and an example of the smallest nuclear weapon, the Davy Crockett, an eight-inch projectile that could be shot at a target with a bazooka from seven miles away.

Also included are examples of "city-busting" weapons developed during the height of the Cold War with Russia. They were designed to

Dented B28 thermonuclear bomb recovered from Palomares, Spain mishap

B52B plane and B17 thermonuclear bomb

B61 thermonuclear laydown bomb, with ribbon parachute deployed

force of an atomic blast by using a map showing Albuquerque as ground zero for a nuclear explosion. The "kill zone," Salazar says, would be eight miles out, but devastation and radiation hazards would continue for up to 25 miles from the bomb center.

"That sounds horrible, but these are the facts. That's part of the deterrent factor of these weapons," Salazar states.

A Nuclear Oops

The museum showcases two nuclear bombs that were recovered after a mid-air collision between a B-52 and a KC-135 tanker during refueling over Palomares, Spain in 1966. Four nuclear weapons involved in the crash never reached critical mass and exploded their nuclear components. However, radiation from the bombs leaked out, prompting a massive $50 million cleanup involving 4,000 military personnel. After their nuclear components were removed, two of the dented bombs were placed on display at the museum, which offers a detailed presentation on the accident.

Contamination Concerns

The museum regularly receives a list of nuclear weapons that are being decommissioned by U.S. military forces. Museum staff members then decide if they want to add any to their exhibit arsenal. If they do, the weapons are carefully checked by health officials to ensure that no radioactive elements remain.

A sign at the entrance to the museum assures visitors that there is no danger from contamination within the museum. Still, some people are reluctant to visit for just this very reason, Salazar points out.

"Everything's been checked out," he says with confidence. "After all, *we're* all working here."

"It was the kind of thing where we said if you wipe out New York, you can kiss St. Petersburg good-bye."

destroy massive regions of each country.

"It was the kind of thing where we said if you wipe out New York, you can kiss St. Petersburg good-bye," Wadell says.

Nuclear bombers displayed outside the museum include the B-29, the B-52 and the F-105. There are also nuclear missiles and rockets such as the Minuteman, Polaris and the Honest John, as well as a unique Army atomic cannon.

One challenge facing exhibits director Tom Salazar is how to convey the destructive power of atomic weapons. The power or yield of these weapons is measured in relation to the equivalent power of the explosive TNT. Because atomic weapons are so powerful, this measurement is expressed in kilotons and even megatons of TNT.

"How do you explain that?" Salazar asks. "That's what I'm working on." He plans to illustrate the awesome

The Shoe Museum

Pennsylvania College of Podiatric Medicine
8th and Race Streets
Philadelphia, Pennsylvania 19107

  215-625-5243

  By appointment only.

  Free.

  From the airport, take Interstate 95 north to the Callowhill Street exit. Take Callowhill five blocks to 8th Street and turn left. The College is located two blocks south on the right hand side.

A ll the average person demands of shoes is a certain degree of comfort and style. At The Shoe Museum, more than 800 pairs of shoes, ranging from mukluks to satin pumps, serve a much higher purpose. Showcased in glass display cases, this collection reveals the way social history can be traced by what's worn on the feet.

On another level, a stroll through the long corridors of the museum offers the chance to ogle shoes that once shod the famous. There are shoes previously worn by sports greats, politicians and stars of theater and film.

The museum opened in 1976 as part of Philadelphia's Bicentennial festivities. The U.S. Park Service, fearing that visitors would overwhelm Independence Park, the heart of the city's historic district, asked neighboring institutions to mount exhibits of their own to draw away some of the crowds.

The Pennsylvania College of Podiatric Medicine fell within this boundary; it's located, appropriately enough, between Arch and Race streets. The college delighted Bicentennial celebrants by displaying shoes from its own collection and many others donated especially for the event. Contributions included pairs from several former First Ladies and sports figures such as

Shoe worn by person suffering from gigantism next to an average-sized woman's high heel

tennis great Billie Jean King and basketball legend Julius Erving.

Dr. J's high-tops

The museum's opening exhibition featured the historical shoe collection of Dr. H. Augustus Wilson. It's now on permanent loan from the Mütter Museum. Wilson was a Philadelphia orthopedist who lived from 1853–1919. He traveled widely, collecting shoes of various shapes and sizes from more than 30 countries. The Wilson collection includes 200-year-old Dutch Sabots, shoes that symbolize a form of protest. The Sabot shoes were used by peasants to crush crops in a protest of harsh working conditions, giving rise to the term "sabotage." The Wilson collection also includes antique South African clogs and a pair of Spanish leather sandals worn by the Archbishop of Toledo in 1492.

Colonial Americans, for example, believed in the healing power of shoes. They were convinced that stomachaches could be relieved by placing heavy boots on the abdomen.

Superstition and Shoes

In addition to showing how shoes relate to fashion and customs, the museum examines the role of footwear in superstitions and folk traditions. Colonial Americans, for example, believed in the healing power of

shoes. They were convinced that stomachaches could be relieved by placing heavy boots on the abdomen. And, according to Dutch custom, the relatives of a person struck by lightning immediately buried all of the victim's shoes to prevent the spread of supernatural forces.

Athlete's Feet

The museum has several pairs of shoes that provided firm footing for athletes on their way to greatness. Included are Billie Jean King's powder blue Adidas tennis shoes which she wore while winning the 1975 women's singles championship at Wimbledon. Also featured are the 18-eyelet white boxing boots worn by Joe Frazier the night he defeated Muhammad Ali in 1971 in Madison Square Garden, and the skates that helped Philadelphia Flyers' goalie Bernie Parent glide with his team to the Stanley Cup championship in 1975.

The most popular athletic shoes are basketball high-tops worn by local great Julius Erving. Williams says that many visitors, especially those from Philadelphia, pause during their tour to have their picture taken with them.

Sultan's sandal

Political Feet

The museum houses an assortment of shoes worn by First Ladies. These include dainty, black silk pumps that slipped on the feet of Lady Bird Johnson, and green opera shoes with rhinestones worn by Nancy Reagan. Silver, closed-toe sandals worn by Betty Ford reveal her practical side.

"She was a dancer. They look worn. She obviously knew how to be comfortable and still look nice," Williams observes.

Shaping Shoes

The museum exhibits not only shoes but also lasts—the molds from which they are built. Lasts of centuries past were crude models made of stone and, later, from woods such as rock maple. For a long time lasts were only made as "straights," not differentiating between a right and a left shoe. Right and left lasts were invented in Philadelphia in 1822 but not used widely until the Civil War.

Lasts also determine shoe styles. Shoe fashions changed slowly until World War I, but novelty shoes introduced in the 1920s created a booming market for last makers. By 1944, 27 factories employing about 850 workers made more than 2 million pairs of lasts.

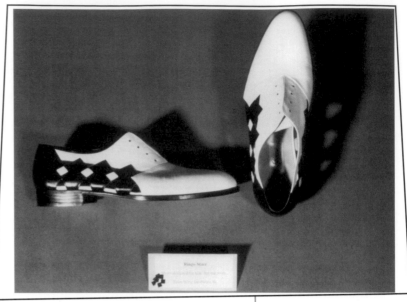

A sporty pair from Ringo Starr's collection

The Long and the Short of It

Shoes in the collection range from colossal sizes down to tiny replicas used by traveling salesmen to promote their products.

There is a pair of 18D Oxfords worn by Ringling Brothers circus tall man Jack Earl in the 1930s, and a pair of towering, 6 ½-inch high heels from a more recent time.

There are examples of European chopines, which were wooden step-in shoes designed to protect indoor footwear from outdoor perils such as mud and other road debris. Stylish women in Renaissance Venice wore such high chopines—in some cases

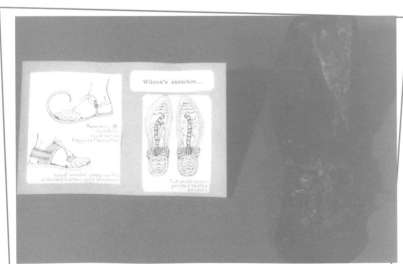

Eygptian burial sandal

The museum houses an assortment of shoes worn by First Ladies. These include dainty, black silk pumps that slipped on the feet of Lady Bird Johnson, and green opera shoes with rhinestones worn by Nancy Reagan.

Chinese lotus slipper

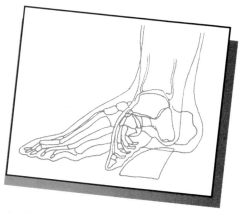

This drawing shows the twisted and deformed bone structure of a bound foot as compared to a normal one.

more than 2 feet off the ground—that in order to stay upright while wearing them they had to be supported by servants on each side. The museum points out that men at the time applauded this fashion because it supported the perception that women were frail and dependent.

On the flip side, the museum features an exhibit on the ancient Chinese practice of foot binding, a tortuous custom that flourished from the 10th century until the early 1900s. Stiff bandaging was applied to the feet of girls starting at age six to stunt their growth. The aim was to achieve the ideal, "Golden Lotus" length of three inches. Tiny feet were considered to be erotic and an attribute for girls wishing to marry well.

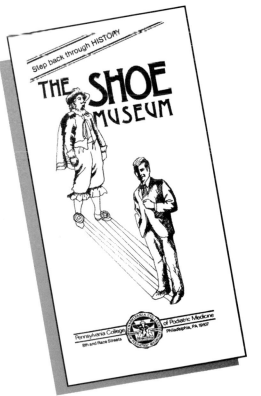

Step back through HISTORY

THE SHOE MUSEUM

Pennsylvania College of Podiatric Medicine
8th and Race Streets
Philadelphia, PA 19107

Hamburger Hall of Fame

126 North Main Street
PO Box 173
Seymour, Wisconsin 54165

414-833-9522

Open from Memorial Day to Labor Day. 10 A.M. to 4 P.M. Monday through Saturday, Noon to 4 P.M. Sundays.

Free.

Seymour is located about 10 miles west of Green Bay, at the intersection of Highways 54 and 55.

The way they tell it here, Charlie Nagreen first showed up at the Seymour-Outagamie County fair in 1885. The 15-year-old arrived with an ox-drawn wagon and plans to open a food stand. Trouble was, no one at the fair was interested in his main offering—fried meatballs. Not because they weren't tasty, but because they were hard to eat while strolling the grounds.

Forced to innovate or watch his business fail, Nagreen flattened the meatballs and made them the basis for a portable fried meat sandwich he called the "hamburger." A legend was born. Nagreen became known as

"Hamburger Charlie" and returned every summer for the next 65 years, setting up his food stand first in Seymour and then moving to other stops along Wisconsin's fair circuit. His burgers never changed, but his mode of transportation did. He went from oxen to horses to train and finally, Dodge truck.

Then they rolled out 5,520 pounds of lean hamburger beef and cooked a patty large enough to land Seymour in the 1991 Guinness Book of World Records.

So the story goes, at any rate. Several other cities and individuals lay claim to the invention of the hamburger. But perhaps none has pursued the matter with as much zest as the folks of Seymour.

In 1989 there was a national centennial celebration for the hamburger. The year was picked because the Oxford English Dictionary traces the first reference to the hamburger to 1889. Seymour residents joined in the hamburger celebration, although they contested the date of the event, believing that their own Hamburger Charlie had invented the beef patty sandwich four years earlier at their fair in 1885. Historical disputes aside, the centennial event put the hamburger in the spotlight, and Seymour leaders saw an opportunity.

Big Boy serves one up

As Seymour resident Tom Duffey puts it, "That was the beginning of our hamburger awareness."

They marched in a hamburger-theme parade that summer in 1989. Then they rolled out 5,520 pounds of lean hamburger beef and cooked a patty large enough to land Seymour in the 1991 Guinness Book of World Records. Before the grease had hardened on the giant frying pan, the town cooked up a plan to open the Hamburger Hall of Fame, now housed in a modest building.

Town leaders are so happy with what it's done for civic pride and tourism that they're already planning a four-story, hamburger-shaped shrine to the beef patty that will cost $15 million to build. The Hall's first two inductees are Hamburger Charlie, of course, and the White Castle hamburger chain, makers of the two-bite burger masterpieces called "sliders."

The exhibit area is crammed with thousands of items that reveal just how deeply the hamburger is ingrained in American culture. There are hamburger telephones, Frisbees, candles and salt and pepper shakers. There's even a hamburger-shaped compact case with blusher and lip gloss put out in the 1970s by Avon.

Hamburger vendors known more widely than Hamburger Charlie are given their due as well. Posters, props (a Big Boy statue), menus and souvenir toys made by major hamburger chains are displayed throughout.

Tossin' the Bun

Probably the best time to visit is the first Saturday in August, when the town puts on its annual burger festival. Among the events are the bun toss and the ketchup slide. The competitions are exactly as you would imagine. If you want to practice at home, beware that the bun used in the tossing event is "specially formulated," says Seymour's Tom Duffey. "It's harder than your average bun, and a little more aerodynamic. There's been a lot of study on the curvature of the top of the bun to get it to go the greatest distance."

Uh-huh. It's all tongue-in-cheek, you see. Which is the best way to describe this town's approach to its hamburger fame.

Hamburger Charlie on the Fair Circuit

The following is a portion of a letter written by Emil Wurm in 1989. Wurm worked for Hamburger Charlie from 1917–23. They traveled each summer with Charlie's burger stand along Wisconsin's fair circuit.

"When business was a bit slow, Charlie would get out his guitar and mouth organ and play a few tunes. This usually drew a crowd and then he would chant something like, 'Hey, you skinny rascals, don't you ever eat?' or 'We have seats to sit down so you can rest your old grandmother.'

"Charlie usually fried the hamburgers and onions and hot dogs, but he usually got sick after part of the day at the big pan, so I usually relieved him. We always chanted one of the spiels to attract people walking down the midway.

The exhibit area is crammed with thousands of items that reveal just how deeply the hamburger is ingrained in American culture. There are hamburger telephones, Frisbees, candles and salt and pepper shakers.

A chef seasons the world's largest burger

Seymour, Wisconsin
"The Home of the Hamburger"

The burger fed 1,300 people. Or was it 12,000? It depends now on whom in town you ask.

"The hours were long and tiresome, but the pay was good. Eight dollars a week and meals, and a blanket and pile of hay in the horse barn.

"I worked for Charlie for six summers and he always claimed to have been the first to call ground beef and a bun a hamburger. He claimed to have started coming to the Seymour Fair when he was 15 years old in 1885. Few of us here are in a position to contest this claim."

A Record Well Done

When you create the world's largest hamburger, it's not by accident. Seymour planned it out carefully in 1989. They were ready with 5,520 pounds of lean ground beef, stored in 60-pound tubes. They constructed a steel pan supported by cement blocks and measuring 24 feet by 24 feet.

"Then a crew of highly-trained chefs got out there and slammed the meat down into the pan under the most sanitary conditions. They simply got in and got

down on their hands and knees," laughs Duffey.

It took 12 propane torches and a giant crane that lowered a massive steel lid over the makeshift pan to heat up the meat to the required temperature. Cooking time for the four-inch thick patty was more than two hours. A chef swinging over the pan on an industrial hoist seasoned the whopper with salt. When it was done, the burger fed 1,300 people. Or was it 12,000? It depends now on whom in town you ask.

One thing's for sure. Seymour is ready for any challenge.

"We're waiting for someone to beat it. We would come right back," Duffey promises.

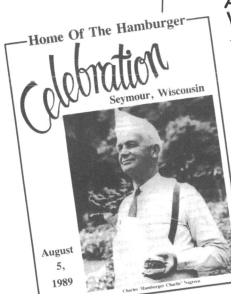

Home Of The Hamburger

Celebration

Seymour, Wisconsin

August 5, 1989

Charles 'Hamburger Charlie' Nagreen

Kansas Barbed Wire Museum

120 West 1st Street
La Crosse, Kansas 67548

913-222-9900

10 A.M. to 4:30 P.M.
Monday to Saturday,
1 P.M. to 4:30 P.M. Sunday.

Free.

La Crosse is located
at the intersection
of US 183 and K-4.
The museum is on
the southern edge
of town, at the
intersection of 1st
and Main Streets.

The Homestead Act of 1862 offered willing pioneers the chance to claim their own land. It took twisted strands of fence wire to deliver on that promise.

To homesteaders, a land stake meant little if they couldn't farm it successfully. It was a tough go even under favorable conditions, but nearly impossible for many who encountered a harsh climate and unyielding soil.

Then there were the ranchers.

"In those days, in this part of the country, cattle ranchers would brand their cattle and let them roam free through the country. A lot of the farmers had cultivated grounds and they didn't like the animals tromping through their crops," says Bradley Penka, director of the Kansas Barbed Wire Museum.

The solution was barbed wire fencing. Not only could it withstand the rigors of the extreme weather, but its prickly points repelled stampeding herds.

Barbed wire production exploded in the U.S. as homesteaders headed west. More than 80 million pounds of it were sold by 1880. Barbed wire was on the front lines of the range wars, as nasty battles erupted over land rights. Disputed claims were settled by night raiders who cut miles of barbed wire. A farmer who put up barbed wire fencing against a rancher's wishes might find a coffin placed on his porch, a blunt suggestion to take down the fencing or else. Ranchers began stringing up their own barbed wire, using it to grab wide swaths of territory, sometimes beyond their legal rights.

While the range wars eventually faded away, a legal battle over patent rights to barbed wire, begun in 1874, raged on, all the way to the U.S. Supreme

The Dodge Star Rowell wire—
one of hundreds of barb styles on display

Court. Finally, in 1892, John Glidden, a De Kalb, Illinois farmer who had developed a barbed wire to protect his wife's vegetable garden, emerged as the winner.

By that time, however, hundreds of different kinds of barbed wire had been created. As many as 750 new patents were eventually issued. Some wire was produced in factories by machine, while other types—often referred to as "moonshine wire"— were handmade by individual farmers.

CAREY'S MACHINE "PATENT "WRAP AROUND"

The Kansas Barbed Wire Museum opened in 1971 to document and showcase varying forms of what pioneers called "devil's rope."

Devil's Rope

T.V. ALLIS "BUCKTHORN" PAT. JULY 26, 1881

The Kansas Barbed Wire Museum opened in 1971 to document and showcase varying forms of what pioneers called "devil's rope." Strips of wire measuring the standard collector's length of 18 inches are carefully mounted in row after row and displayed on tall boards. In all, hundreds of strands of barbed wire are exhibited, almost all dating from the last decade of the 19th century.

While significant as historic artifacts, antique strands of barbed wire have also inspired a thriving market among collectors. On the first weekend in May each year the museum holds a "Swap and Sell" market where collectors come to buy or simply admire the wires of others. The market was the first of its kind when organized in 1976, but now others are held around the country. Meanwhile, barbed wire collectors in several states have established associations and clubs devoted to their interest.

The trend has made a best-seller out of Jack Glover's self-published work, *The Bobbed Wire Bible*. First released in 1966, it's now in its 11th printing.

Glover, who runs a cowboy museum

SAW TOOTH RIBBON WIRE

in San Antonio, says he has documented more than 1,000 different types of barbed wire.

"Some sell for a thousand dollars a cut, depending on how scarce it is," he points out. He travels to many barbed wire shows around the country and has observed some fierce competition among collectors for prized strands.

"You know how it is. Someone says, 'old so and so's got that and I've got to have it too.' Some people are so up in the air about having the best," Glover says. His own favorite is called "The Buckthorn."

"It's the most common, but I don't like the showy stuff. It has a twisted ribbon with the barb sticking out of the side of it."

Museum Highlights

The artifacts on display in the museum show traditional forms of barbs, but many feature more decorative flourishes. There are barbs shaped like spirals, leaves, spurs, stars and buckles. Some of the more valuable types are those that contain stars.

In addition to wire used for agriculture, the museum features examples of barbed fencing used for U.S. military campaigns. There is wire that

HARBROUGH'S "TORN" RIBBON WIRE

was employed in several wars, including World Wars I and II, Korea, Vietnam and the Persian Gulf conflict. In addition, examples of wire produced in other countries are displayed. There is a strand that once lined the top of the Berlin Wall.

MALLABLE STEEL TRIANGLE LINE WITH LANCE TYPE BARBS

"You know how it is. Someone says, 'old so and so's got that and I've got to have it too'."

Tools used in the making of barbed wire are similar to pliers but are especially made for the trade. The museum exhibits several of these, as well as hammers and staples also used in barbed wire production. Some of the tools are conventional ones that were once sold by hardware stores. Others reveal the ingenuity of the pioneer farmer.

Exterior view of the museum

"A lot of the time farmers didn't have any money. If they needed something they just went out to the shed and scooped up whatever they could find from the junk pile and made whatever they thought they would need," Penka explains.

sledged by hand and then shaped into pillars. These posts weighed up to 400 pounds and stood as high as six feet. It would take a team of horses to haul up to six of them at once. These posts were widely used up until the 1920s. Many are still standing. The museum, at 202 West 1st Street, is located in a stone house built in 1883 that was restored to house the museum. The museum contains many photographs and artifacts that tell the story of the region's legendary post rock.

Crow's Nest

One of the most unusual exhibits in the museum is a crow's nest, a tangled swirl of wire built over many years by ravens that would scoop up pieces of scattered wire in the fields. The wire formed the foundation to a nest, which was then lined with straw to make it more comfortable.

Post Rock

As a bonus, while in La Crosse visitors should pay a visit to the Post Rock Museum, which celebrates the stone pillars used to anchor the wire fencing. Because there were so few trees in the area, rock was excavated,

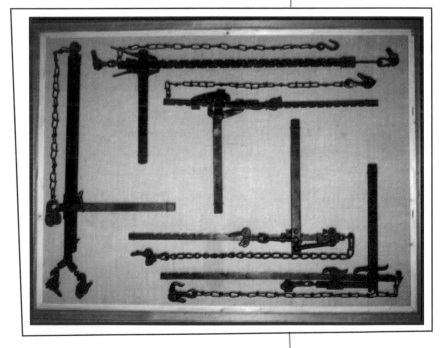
Wire stretcher display

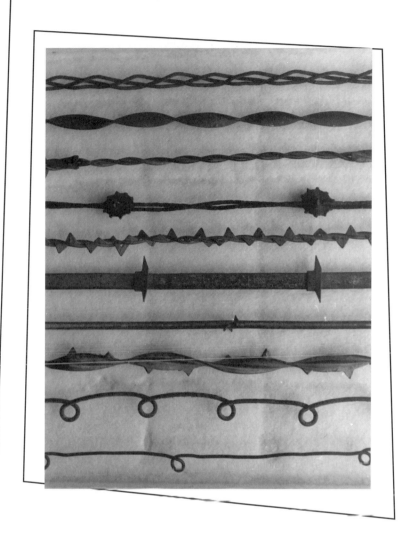

New Orleans Historic Voodoo Museum

HOW TO USE YOUR VOODOO DOLL *for serious practitioners* by C.M. Gandolfo 3.95

724 Rue Dumaine
New Orleans, Louisiana 70116

504-522-5223
Fax: 504-523-8591

http://www.voodoomuseum.com

10 A.M. to dusk every day.

$5.25 adults,
$4.20 students and seniors,
$2.10 grade school,
free for under 5.

From Interstate 10, take the Vieux Carre exit into the French Quarter. The museum is on Rue Dumaine, between Bourbon and Royal Streets.

I n 1794, a future pope was born in New Orleans. She would never go on to live in the Vatican. Marie Laveau, you see, was a practitioner of voodoo.

As she matured into a woman, Laveau's voodoo skills became legendary. Confident of her great powers in the 1830s, she declared herself the "Popess of Voodoo." No one questioned her authority. She was respected and feared, even by the local Catholic community.

She was allowed to practice regular voodoo rituals behind St. Louis Cathedral every Sunday following mass, a service which she also regularly attended.

Outside New Orleans, the name Queen Laveau doesn't have quite the same recognition as say, Pope John Paul II. That's not surprising, according to New Orleans native Charles Gandolfo. Voodoo is one of the least understood of world religions. What little people know comes from movies, where voodoo is usually portrayed as a sinister cult with ritual sacrifices, deadly hexes and assorted witchcraft.

"People look at it as evil because they don't understand what's going on," explains Gandolfo. He opened the Voodoo Museum in 1972 to elevate public knowledge beyond a vague awareness of the voodoo doll.

Portrait of Voodoo Queen Marie Laveau

Of course, there are voodoo dolls at the museum. A display case holds dolls from around the world. From the exhibit you'll learn that the smartly attired dolls most often were used in healing rituals, as opposed to having pins stuck into them in order to put the whammy on some unfortunate victim.

Aside from these dolls, there are dozens of artifacts displayed at the museum that are used in voodoo ceremonies and rituals. Exhibits range from musical instruments to altars offering worldly gifts such as rum and fruit to the spirit gods.

Visitors can embark on guided tours of the museum and nearby sites that illuminate New Orleans' rich voodoo history. The tours include visits to cemeteries, a haunted house, a voodoo pharmacy and a voodoo temple.

If all this instruction makes you a believer, the gift shop offers a full line of voodoo remedies, including the house special, "Love Potion #9." If your love life is set, other powders promise help with career, wealth, health and even fertility.

A Hybrid Religion

Voodoo dates back 7,000 years to Africa. Followers believe in a supreme god, but also pay tribute to spirits who rule over different aspects of life. To make offerings, voodoo practitioners create altars piled high with earthly goods favored by these spirits. Each spirit is known to prefer specific colors, foods, drinks

The gift shop offers a full line of voodoo remedies, including the house special, "Love Potion #9."

and other worldly pleasures. Gifts are intended to persuade spirits to look favorably upon the worshipper.

Voodoo evolved as it spread to other regions of the world. Voodoo practiced today in New Orleans is a hybrid religion that incorporates aspects of several cultures and religions, including Catholicism.

Gandolfo was raised hearing stories of voodoo and how it affected earlier generations of his family. Ancestors, he was told, were saved by a voodoo priestess during slave uprisings in Haiti in the early 19th

century. The priestess hid the family and then saw that they were safely stowed away on a boat to New Orleans.

In 1932, a great grandfather was cured of lockjaw by a voodoo priestess named Mama Midnight, who prescribed her trademark Roach Potion Tea.

"Voodoo fascinates a lot of people, including myself," Gandolfo admits.

He has studied the religion and learned recipes for many of its ritual potions, called "Gris-Gris." He's also collected many voodoo artifacts which form the basis of the museum's collection.

Museum Highlights

The museum's interior consists of two main exhibit rooms. On hot days the atmosphere can be stuffy, so it's best to visit in the morning or late afternoon. There's not much in the way of explanatory texts, so taking one of the many tours offered at the museum may be the best way to experience it.

You enter the museum's exhibit area by passing under an alligator's head and a broom—two religious tokens, or "Ju-Jus." The alligator head is designed to scare away evil spirits, while the broom is there to sweep out sickness and sweep in business. As you pass the threshold, a museum staff member may sprinkle you with good luck herbs.

The Occult Room features a voodoo altar dedicated to the spirit Exu. He is the youngest of the spirits, a mischievous entity who creates confusion if not honored. An examination of Exu's altar reveals that his tastes lean toward rum, cigars, candy and money.

The rest of the room contains ceremonial masks, carved statues, Haitian prayer mats, a display of musical instruments used in rituals, and photographs of voodoo ceremonies. The room even features a miniature Cajun cemetery with whitewashed tombstones and ancient skulls and bones.

A live python named Zombie slithers about in a glass cage against one wall—that is, when he's not catching a nap or sleeping away a hot afternoon. Snakes play an integral part in voodoo ceremonies and Zombie's display illustrates the reptile's significance as a symbol of wisdom.

"Everything in the museum means something. It's not just there for some spooky effect," points out Brandi Kelley, the museum's director.

Left: Alligator heads are thought to scare away evil spirits

In 1932, a great grandfather was cured of lockjaw by a voodoo priestess named Mama Midnight, who prescribed her trademark Roach Potion Tea.

Sweep out sickness, sweep in business

Voodoo altar

A second room contains more altars, including a series of memorial tributes. In an adjoining hallway you encounter a replica of Marie Laveau's wishing stump. The actual wishing stump she used is also displayed at the museum but it's so brittle that it can't be used by the public. As you pass the replica stump, you may receive a blessing if you enclose a wish written on parchment, along with a coin.

Drop in for a Spell

The museum's gift shop specializes in custom gris-gris

bags. You can relate your problems to a practitioner, who will mix up a potion of herbs to ease your troubles. The mixture will be placed in a red flannel bag, anointed with oil and sealed with black yarn.

You can also buy a voodoo doll in the shop, which may be a tempting purchase if there's someone you want to lay a curse upon. However, as Gandalfo points out, that's not how these dolls are mostly used in voodoo rituals.

In fact, one of the richest traditions involving these dolls is to promote marital bliss. They are used before a wedding ceremony to bring a man and a woman spiritually closer before their physical union. Two dolls, a male and a female, are placed at opposite ends of an altar. For nine straight days the dolls are slowly nudged together until they are side-by-side on the wedding day.

"Dolls have been used in many traditions all over the world as a way to affect reality. It's an ancient practice," Kelley explains. "Dolls were used for good purposes. You would try to effect some kind of change in your own life or someone else's by focusing on that doll and thinking of that person."

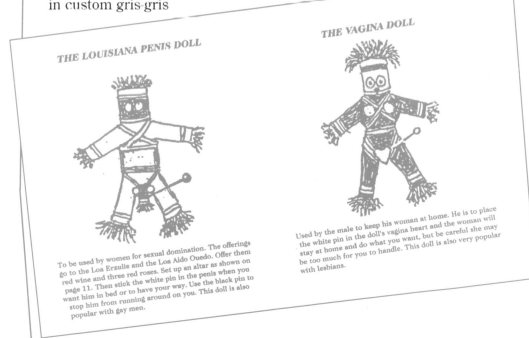

THE LOUISIANA PENIS DOLL

To be used by women for sexual domination. The offerings go to the Loa Erzulie and the Loa Aido Ouedo. Offer them red wine and three red roses. Set up an altar as shown on page 11. Then stick the white pin in the penis when you want him in bed or to have your way. Use the black pin to stop him from running around on you. This doll is also popular with gay men.

THE VAGINA DOLL

Used by the male to keep his woman at home. He is to place the white pin in the doll's vagina heart and the woman will stay at home and do what you want, but be careful she may be too much for you to handle. This doll is also very popular with lesbians.

The Menczer Museum of Medicine and Dentistry

230 Scarborough Street
Hartford, Connecticut 06105

860-236-5613

10 A.M. to 4 P.M.
Monday through Friday.

$2 adults, free for
children with adults.

From Interstate 84
take exit 46 to West
Boulevard. Turn right
onto South Whitney
Street and travel one
and one half miles to
Scarborough Street.
The museum is located
in a red-brick build-
ing on the right and
has free parking.

The Hartford Medical Society was founded in 1846 as an educational resource and support group for local doctors. Probably the best step the society took to promote the field of medicine was to open this museum in 1974. The collection showcases medical devices dating from the Revolutionary War to the mid-20th century. Visitors examining the earlier, barbaric instruments can only come away with a solid appreciation for modern medicine.

The introduction to the museum's catalog provides a relevant historical overview: "Early surgical operations were, virtually, only those to set or amputate limbs, 'let blood or cut for stone.' Such operations were allowed by the patient only because of unbearable and excruciating pain."

The artifacts in the Menczer Museum of Medicine and Dentistry were donated through the years by local doctors and collectors. As people dropped by to use the medical society's extensive library, they became fascinated with the historic items that were on hand but not formally displayed. Noticing the attention that the artifacts generated, the society's staff decided to open a museum. The exhibits highlight the development of early American medicine and reveal some of the quackery that was often practiced during the same time. The library's collection remains strong, offering a vast collection of

Dental office, circa 1919

54

Right: 18th century dental surgical tools

books pertaining to the history of medicine.

Museum Highlights

Two major exhibits include a complete dental office from 1919 and a doctor's office from 1923. The dental exhibit includes tools used in scaling teeth, medical cabinets, a reclining dental chair and fearsome power drilling equipment. There's also a display on how to make dentures.

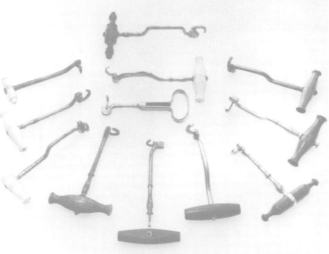

Surgical instruments, circa 1840

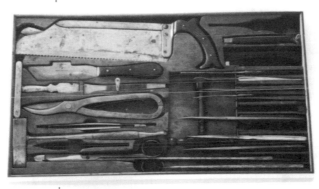

In the doctor's office there is a 200-year-old Chinese acupuncture set for starters. Also displayed is a most unusual piece of furniture—a large red leather Victorian chair that folds out into an examining table at the push of a lever. It's made of oak and includes brass stirrups.

The Menczer collection could also be referred to as a museum of pain. One exhibit notes that before the development of dentistry, when colonial Americans needed a bothersome tooth removed, they often sought the aid of the local blacksmith.

There are also several complete surgical kits from the 18th and 19th centuries, which are exhibited in mahogany showcases built by the museum's co-curator, Dr. Leonard Menczer. He was a local dentist who died in 1994.

Before the development of dentistry, when colonial Americans needed a bothersome tooth removed, they often sought the aid of the local blacksmith.

At first glance, many of these surgical kits look like the contents of a carpenter's tool box. They include serrated saws, vices, knives, pliers and mallets. You may cringe when you realize that these were medical instruments most often used for bloodletting, amputation and teeth-pulling. However, visitors tend to appreciate their artistry and overlook the sinister implications of what these meant to patients who had the misfortune to fall ill when they were in use.

"They look more like carving sets. They don't look that gruesome at all," insists Diane Neumann, the museum's director.

Then there's the frontier delivery set, which includes a foreboding pair of forceps, a small saw, probes and clamps. "That exhibit looks a lot scarier to the women than the men," Neumann says.

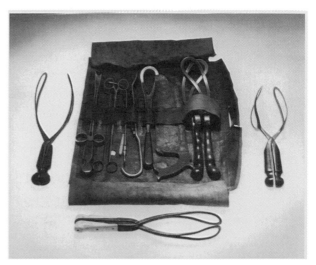

Right: Assorted obstetrical instruments from 1855, with requisite amputation saw

of ills, including consumption, palsy, stones, venereal disease, cancer, blindness and worms. The museum displays two of these much-hyped electrical cures, the Improved Patent Magneto Electric Machine made in London in 1862, and the Fleming Battery from Philadelphia in 1885.

Thank You, Dr. Wells.

Local dentist Horace Wells is credited with being a pioneer in the use of anesthesia during surgery. The museum pays tribute to him with exhibits that trace the development of surgical anesthesia.

Wells thought of the idea while watching a sideshow in 1844. He observed a man suffer an accidental injury who didn't appear to feel any pain. It turned out the victim had been sniffing nitrous oxide, otherwise known as laughing gas.

On December 11, 1844, Wells

One of the exhibits stares back at each visitor. It's a tray of glass eyeballs once used as prosthetic devices.

Some of the artifacts that can be appreciated for their beauty include ivory-handled scalpels, brass mortar and pestle sets, and dental instruments with mother-of-pearl shafts.

One of the exhibits stares back at each visitor. It's a tray of glass eyeballs once used as prosthetic devices.

Bright Cures

Electricity was first prescribed as a medical treatment in Germany in 1743. Through the years it was touted as a miracle cure for a variety

A 19th century physician's saddle bag

The Improved Patent Magneto Electric Machine was a hand operated electrical generator, believed by many to cure a variety of ills

Wells couldn't duplicate his experiment before a panel of Boston doctors and was discredited. He committed suicide four years later.

sniffed the gas through a hose connected to a leather bag. Then he had another local dentist remove one of his molars. Wells, thankfully, noticed that during the operation he didn't feel any pain.

Unfortunately, his story does not have a happy ending. Wells couldn't duplicate his experiment before a panel of Boston doctors and was discredited. He committed suicide four years later.

THE MENCZER MUSEUM OF MEDICINE AND DENTISTRY

THE HARTFORD MEDICAL & DENTAL SOCIETIES

Toothkey

Bullet Forceps

THE HARTFORD MEDICAL SOCIETY
230 Scarborough Street
Hartford, Connecticut 06105

860-236-5613

Nikola Tesla Museum of Science and Industry

2220 East Bijou Street
PO Box 5636
Colorado Springs, Colorado 80931

719-475-0918
Fax: 719-475-0582

10 A.M. to 4 P.M. Monday through Friday, 11 A.M. to 4 A.M. Saturday. Closed holiday weekends.

Walk-through of museum is free. $5 adults, $3 children age 12 and under for laboratory demonstrations.

From Interstate 25, take Uintah Street west to Union Boulevard. Go south on Union to Bijou Street. Make a left on Bijou and travel three blocks east. The museum is on the north side of the street.

When most Americans think of invention and electricity, Thomas Edison is the first name that comes to mind. Often overlooked is another great American inventor and an Edison rival named Nikola Tesla. He made vital contributions to the development of electrical power and to many other technological advances that we now take for granted.

Perhaps because he was as enigmatic as he was brilliant, Tesla is not a revered figure today in America. He was born to Serbian parents in 1856 in what was then part of Austria-Hungary. The son of a clergyman, Tesla might have been forced into religious training had he not shown early skills in mathematics and science. He ultimately persuaded his father to let him enroll in a polytechnic college in Austria.

After watching a demonstration of a dynamo motor in class, Tesla went home and devised a method for it to run more efficiently. He went on to work in Europe as an engineer, then traveled to New York City in 1884 to promote his new alternating-current motor. He arrived in America with a few pennies and some poems in his pocket.

Tesla worked with Edison for a year but then left to work on his own

2 mega volt coil

inventions. Several of his patents for motors that ran on alternating current were bought by George Westinghouse.

Tesla was one of the prime scientific figures of the late 19th and early 20th centuries, a period rich with invention and technological advancements. Tesla, who became a U.S. citizen in 1889, patented more than 700 inventions related to electricity, motors, radio, television, robotics and computers.

Tesla demonstrated wireless communications two years before Marconi's first experiments with radio. He laid the groundwork for the modern electrical power grid when he created the first power machinery at Niagara Falls. It delivered power to residents of Buffalo,

New York, in 1896. Tesla also carried out early experiments with "shadow graphs," the forerunner to X-rays.

Although known for staging dramatic public demonstrations of electricity and other modern marvels during the prime of his career, Tesla became reclusive in later years. He died in a New York City hotel room in 1943 just as he was preparing to demonstrate his "death ray," a device that he said could destroy enemy forces 250 miles away.

In Europe, a Hero

After Tesla died, his papers were donated to the Nikola Tesla Museum in Belgrade, Yugoslavia, a part of the world where he is revered as a national hero.

At the Tesla Museum in Colorado Springs, a more modest tribute is maintained by the International Tesla Society. The society was created in 1984 to generate public awareness of Tesla's inventions and scientific contributions. In its promotional material, the society calls Tesla the "Galileo of the 20th century," and suggests he should be offered thanks "every time you turn on a light switch."

The society encourages the exploration of "alternative forms of energy and medical advancements."

"Tesla was beyond the mainstream and we feel that we are too," says J.W. McGinnis, president of the society. "We focus on the political issues around science. We provide information and let people reach their own conclusions."

For example, they don't support the prevailing notion in the scientific community that harmful chemicals from propellant sprays are the cause of ozone depletion. Rather, McGinnis claims, what's tearing up the ozone layer is the steady parade of rockets being sent into outer space.

Giant Tesla coil

"Every time they launch a space vehicle they are dropping tons of chlorides into the upper atmosphere," McGinnis points out.

The society holds annual conventions where many alternative scientific theories are demonstrated and discussed. Recent seminar topics ranged from the health benefits of colloidal silver to Tesla's contribution to the development of microwave technology. The society also publishes a quarterly magazine called *ExtraOrdinary Science* and a members-only publication called *After Hours*.

The Adam's free energy motor

Significant Site

The museum is located eight blocks from the site where Tesla maintained a laboratory during the summer and fall of 1899. The region was known for thunder and lightning storms during these seasons, and Tesla wanted to conduct experiments related to the study of wireless electric energy transmission.

During his research here, Tesla proved that the earth was an electrical conductor. He also produced artificial lightning in million-volt flashes that reached 135 feet into the air. It's a demonstration that's never been duplicated.

Tesla... produced artificial lightning in million-volt flashes that reached 135 feet into the air. It's a demonstration that's never been duplicated.

His Life and Inventions

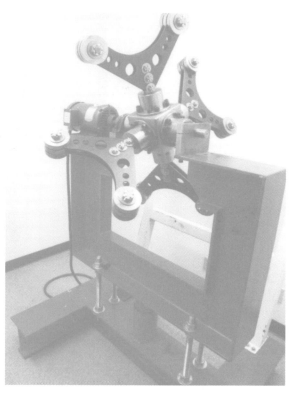

From Labor Day until Memorial Day, the museum offers guided tours beginning at 2 p.m. every Saturday. Visitors can learn about Tesla's life through text and photo displays, and also by viewing a 40-minute film.

Of most interest are the demonstrations of his electric inventions, including the Tesla Coil, an electrical generator. The model here was built for the set of a Frankenstein movie. It emits up to one million volts of electrical energy and sends out sparks and lightning bolts that reach seven feet into the air.

During laboratory presentations, visitors can see such working devices as the "lightning in a jar," and various generators and pumps that Tesla designed.

These presentations are very reminiscent of the way that Tesla and other inventors and scientists of his day introduced breakthrough technologies to a wary public. For example, Tesla once lit lamps in his lab by flowing current through his body in order to ease public fears that electricity was dangerous. In 1898, he demonstrated a remote-controlled boat before a crowd at Madison Square Garden in New York City.

Tesla was very interested in wireless communication. He may have lost credibility with some scientists, however, when he claimed in 1892 to have received signals from other planets.

Long before CNN, financier J.P. Morgan backed Tesla's project to establish a worldwide communications system based on a 200-foot transmission tower that was to be built on Long Island. In 1905, however, Morgan withdrew his backing and the project fell through. Nine years later, a mysterious dynamite blast destroyed the tower.

In his later years, Tesla made fewer public demonstrations but wrote considerably. He also amused the public by making predictions and even wrote an annual science report for *Time* magazine. Much of his writing and the work of other forward-thinking scientists can be found in the comprehensive collection in the museum's bookstore.

Tesla was very interested in wireless communication. He may have lost credibility with some scientists, however, when he claimed in 1892 to have received signals from other planets.

A double bucking scalar wave generator

INTERNATIONAL TESLA SOCIETY
COLORADO SPRINGS, CO

Grandpa Moses' Traveling Museum

Various locations throughout Chicago, Illinois.

708-848-0982

By appointment.

Free.

Call for directions.

When John Urbaszewski suddenly became a folk artist late in life, he did so to escape boredom. He reached retirement age in 1975 and stepped down from his job in the Illinois property department, where he had been assigned to track down lost government equipment. He wasn't much for being idle, so he offered to help out at his son's mortuary, mostly answering phones. Business was far from brisk.

"I was sitting around waiting, with nothing to do. I read so much I would fall asleep and then I'd feel like I wasted my whole day. I'd feel guilty about it," he remembers.

The waste of anything, whether it be a day or merely something tossed in the trash, bothers Urbaszewski immensely. He began gathering up discarded items around the chapel and crafting them into unique bird cages. He started with simple shapes, but his creations soon grew more elaborate. He moved on to buildings, including churches and tourist landmarks such as the Taj Mahal, the Grand Hotel on Mackinaw Island, Rome's Spanish Steps and the Leaning Tower of Pisa.

He hasn't visited many of these attractions. Instead, he often works from photos or postcards that depict them. Even though images he studies are in black-and-white, he sometimes creates in dazzling hues of pink, green, blue and gold, because this is how these places exist in his imagination.

John Urbaszewski, a.k.a. Grandpa Moses

Grandpa Moses and Cathedral

For tools he uses scissors, glue, paints, hammers, saws and other hand tools. Mostly he puts his imagination in gear and a pile of junk is transformed into a fanciful, scaled-down architectural wonder.

In his world, a plastic cream container becomes a dollhouse lampshade, and the sliced-off top of an empty bleach bottle mutates into the Liberty Bell. He usually finds his raw materials around the house, but other times he ventures out to scavenge. "I'll walk along, daydreaming. Anything you pick up and look at it . . . you never know," he says. "We're so wasteful in this country, it's unbelievable. All the stuff I use, it doesn't cost me a penny."

"Take the cardboard from a package of 24 beers. I make beautiful churches out of that."

From Churches to Merry-Go-Rounds

To appreciate Urbaszewski's works, viewers also must use their imaginations. How else can you see a drink stirrer and believe that it's a church spire? From a distance, you see a church dome. Come closer, and you realize he's capped the church with an old plastic fruitcake cover.

"Take the cardboard from a package of 24 beers. I make beautiful churches out of that," he says proudly. Old Christmas cards are used to create stained glass windows, and old twine spools serve as conical domes. Corrugated cardboard, when painted, can be made to look like ornate roof tile. Urbaszewski is fond of taking small pine cones and placing them around his sculpture to simulate trees.

He says he doesn't create anything to exact scale—his works are proportional to the vision he sees in his mind. His sculptures are never finished. He's always adding to them. Many props break off, but what can he do? His artworks are not in display cases but are usually exhibited out in the open for people to inspect, probe and, at Urbaszewski's friendly urging, to play with.

The Taj Mahal

Many of his designs are readily familiar and include the Golden Gate Bridge, London Bridge (with a small figure of Donald Duck crossing it), Soldier Field in Chicago, Notre Dame in Paris and even a Long John Silver's restaurant. In his Notre Dame sculpture, the ends of old curtain rods are used as ornate flower pots outside the cathedral.

Sometimes, what he discovers determines what he makes.

"I was walking down the street and I found an umbrella. I said, 'Jeez, I have a round table at home. I think I'll make a merry-go-round,'" he laughs. "Anything lying around that's garbage, I utilize it and it turns into something that people are enthused about."

For the merry-go-round, Urbaszewski carved horses out of scrap wood, and dressed them with saddles made from old leather wallets. The miniature ride revolves like the real thing. In fact, many of his other works feature moving, spinning parts. Among his carnival sculptures is a Ferris wheel that has tiny plastic medicine dose cups for the passenger buckets.

Schlepperman

Urbaszewski's works have been showcased at art galleries and museums, including Chicago's Children's Museum and the Chicago Athenaeum, a center for architecture, art and urban studies. Although he's been featured in group shows of folk artists, he resists that classification. Instead, he refers to himself merely as a "Schlepperman," because he's always hauling things about.

He promotes himself as a traveling museum, displaying an ad for his services on another found object, a discarded counter menu board that still bears its Pepsi logo. Plain white letters

"I was walking down the street and I found an umbrella. I said, 'Jeez, I have a round table at home. I think I'll make a merry-go-round.'"

He refers to himself merely as a "Schlepperman," because he's always hauling things about.

The Chicago river skyline, complete with working bridges

Grandpa Moses' workshop

He's also created a scale model of a mile-high building that he thinks is a great solution to revitalize urban living and save ground space. "You've got to go vertical."

announce that his traveling museum is available for parades, conventions and other special events.

He enjoys visiting schools because he has an important message for children. He thinks kids watch too much television and too often don't explore their own creativity. To inspire his young audiences, he'll show them familiar items such as plastic dessert boats from McDonald's, and then demonstrate how to easily turn them into replica pleasure crafts that float along his imaginary rivers.

"We used to make our own toys," recalls Urbaszewski, who was one of 15 children. "These kids are smarter than I am. They are born with a talent. They can make something themselves."

One of his largest works is a view along the Chicago River skyline from Wacker Drive. It's 25 feet long and includes many landmark buildings and bridges. He's rigged a system so that his replica boats float along a mirror and trigger magnets to raise and lower bridges as they pass. "It's an attractive, workable thing," he points out. "There's nothing I bought in any of that stuff."

Urbaszewski is something of a visionary when he creates. For example, in his model of Soldier Field, he includes his own design for railings on the roof that would open and close and shave more than $300 million off the estimated costs of building a new stadium.

He's also created a scale model of a mile-high building that he thinks is a great solution to revitalize urban living and save ground space. "You've got to go vertical," he

asserts. "You can't be going horizontal. The people who live in the suburbs, they waste two or three hours a day of traveling time."

Urbaszewski's mile-high building features colorful buttresses of pink, green and blue. He expects that each one would house hundreds of tenants and be owned by a different casino. Urbaszewski has written to the governor and the Epcot Center to see if there's interest in building a real tower, but so far no one has accepted his challenge.

Grandpa Moses poses with one of his many fans

The Disney Castle

The Children's Garbage Museum of Southwest Connecticut

1410 Honeyspot Road Extension
Stratford, Connecticut 06497

800-455-9571
Fax: 203-377-1930

Open for school group tours during the week. Family Days with open admission on the first Saturday of every other month from 10 A.M. to 2 P.M.

Free for school groups. Family Day: $5 per family, or $2 per person.

Take Interstate 95 to exit 30 and go south to Lordship Avenue. Travel west on Lordship Avenue to Honeyspot Road Extension and make another right. The museum is the last building on the right.

I n the late 1980s a garbage crisis struck many areas of the country. Landfills overflowing with the trash of generations of wasteful Americans were forced to close and begin turning away garbage trucks. Trash became a hot political topic. Suddenly, recycling was no longer just a trendy environmental gesture but an absolute necessity.

Like many states, Connecticut was mired in the thick of the garbage mess. All but two of the state's landfills were closed by 1988. Three years later, the state ordered cities to reduce their waste stream by 25 percent, creating an immediate need for regional recycling programs.

The Worm Tunnel

Nineteen cities and towns in southwest Connecticut attacked the problem by stepping up recycling efforts and by turning to their school-age residents for guidance. In 1994, a regional recycling committee opened The Children's Garbage Museum in order to educate youngsters about trash and the benefits of reducing waste production through recycling.

Learning about trash here is good clean fun. There are 15 hands-on exhibits, a learning laboratory where kids can make crafts out of trash, and an amphitheater that screens many educational films about recycling.

To enforce its message, the museum is located adjacent to the region's main recycling plant. Visitors can watch the process in action by stepping out onto the glass-enclosed skywalk that extends over the plant's "tipping floor"—the area where recycling trucks unload their haul of recycled trash to be sorted and processed.

The museum is geared to kids from kindergarten to grade eight, but offers useful information and displays for those older and younger as well.

Children's Garbage Museum and Education Center
of Southwest Connecticut

The Trash-O-Saurus in all its glory

Young Educators

"Children are the best ambassadors for recycling that we have," insists museum director Valerie Knight-DiGangi. "They put a great deal of pressure on all of us to do the right things in life. They will go back and tell their families how important it is to recycle and how much it really makes a difference. They're really the ones teaching the adults."

Apparently, it's working. The museum opened in the fall of 1994 before it even had any exhibits. People came just to observe the recycling trucks come and go. The displays were ready by the fall of 1995 and that same year the region recycled more than 57,000 tons of garbage, surpassing its goal of a 25 percent reduction in trash production.

Leading by Example

The museum is designed like a factory building. Materials used in its construction include recycled steel.

There is energy efficient lighting that draws less power to provide standard lighting. And you may not even notice, but as you walk about you step over carpet made from recycled plastic bottles.

"It looks like regular carpeting," Knight-DiGangi points out. "You would not be able to tell the difference. It's held up real well."

Museum Highlights

One of the most striking exhibits is the Trash-O-Saurus. It's a one-ton dinosaur sculpture that's 24 feet long and more than 11 feet tall. It was made by artist Leo Sewell of Philadelphia, who often works with found art. He used "dumpster divers" who scoured the city to retrieve trash for the work, including discarded sporting equipment, household garbage, car scraps, a kettle grill and old toys and dolls. He used found pennies as washers and old steam irons for toenails.

The sculpture's weight of one ton is a significant measure because it equals the amount of garbage each person generates annually. It's an entertaining and striking way to make kids more aware of the need for recycling and conservation.

Trash Talking

At the Trash Bash station, knowledge about trash isn't wasted. Rather, you can put it to good use in a unique quiz game that Knight-DiGangi says is part "Jeopardy!" and a bit of "Wheel of Fortune." But there's a twist. Contestants don hard hats and goggles and enter special trash booths where they are asked questions about garbage. If they answer incorrectly, they are showered with trash from players who stand above them ready to deliver the messy load. Talk about pressure!

"We dump 'clean' garbage on them, soft stuff like paper and tissue," says Knight-DiGangi.

Squirming to Knowledge

The Worm Tunnel is a crawl-through compost pile that illustrates how leaves and other organic material decompose in soil. Adults can fit in the tunnel too, and they seem to enjoy the wriggly passage as much as kids. As you slither along you see giant-size worms and other bugs in the compost pile of leaves, egg shells, apple peels and cobs of corn. The bugs in the soil are of a massive scale to illustrate how vital they are to this process.

The Problem with Packaging

At the General Store, kids learn how merchandising has changed through the years and increased trash levels. The exhibit is set up like a well-stocked general store of 1870 and explains, for example, how shoppers would buy flour and then use the leftover sack to make clothing.

"How many of us would be able to make a shirt out of the packaging that we have now?" Knight-DiGangi asks.

Instead, clothing today, especially men's shirts, comes wrapped in plastic, cardboard and pins, which are all discarded, she observes. In addition, other modern goods are taken home in shopping bags which are also thrown away. "Transporting things has become more convenient, but by the same token we have more garbage," Knight-DiGangi explains.

Turning Trash to Treasures

Classrooms at the museum offer kids the chance to make art out of trash. During fall, for example, kids are shown how to make masks and jack-o'-lanterns out of simple household garbage such as empty cereal boxes and old magazines. Lessons on making basic compost heaps are also offered.

How Trash Savvy are You?

Here are sample questions from the Trash Bash game to test your knowledge. Remember, if you answer incorrectly, you are subject to becoming a human landfill.

1. How much garbage does each of us make every day?

2. What are the four "R" words that help us save our natural resources and produce less garbage?

3. By volume, paper makes up what percentage of our garbage?

Answers:
1. Five pounds. 2. Reduce, Reuse, Recycle, Rethink. 3. Fifty percent.

How did you do? Are you covered with trash? Or did you come clean with the right answers?

The Energy Cone is part of an exhibit that shows the amount of resources that go into making aluminum cans

As you slither along you see giant-size worms and other bugs in the compost pile of leaves, egg shells, apple peels and cobs of corn.

By. Francesca Benedetto

Cave

Thank you!
Thank you very much for teaching me about
compost and how to recycle. I liked it when we
went under the cave because we went under a
real compost.

Wobnelia

I went to the trash museum and
I saw a trshasaurus.

National Lighter Museum

107 South 2nd Street
Guthrie, Oklahoma 73044

405-282-3025

10 A.M. to 6 P.M. daily.

Free.

Guthrie is located
about 25 miles north
of Oklahoma City.
Take Interstate 35
North to exit 157
and head west.

Ted Ballard owns more than 30,000 lighters, yet he's never smoked anything in his life. His interest in lighters stems more from their form than their function. His fascination with fire-starters began in 1939 when his grandfather returned from his great-uncle's funeral with a bag of coins and three cigarette lighters—a Zippo and two Regents. The Regents given to Ballard sparked his curiosity and he began collecting and repairing any lighters he could find.

Ballard made a living as a television and radio repairman. He also found time to make jewelry, and trade guns and other collectibles, including toys and knives.

Ted Ballard, with some of his 30,000 lighters

Meanwhile, his lighter collection grew by the hundreds every year. When he retired and moved to Guthrie, Oklahoma with his wife Pat, it was with the intention of opening a lighter museum. The couple did that in 1993 in an historic building located, appropriately enough, next to the town fire station.

The Ronson bulldog lighter:
An exotic way light up

One of Ballard's favorites is a jukebox lighter that plays a tune while you light up.

"Anything that you can imagine as a lighter actually exists as one."

Museum Highlights

Ballard's lighter collection is presented in jewelry display cases. Some lighters date back hundreds of years. Exhibits chronicle the history of fire-starting and society's shifting attitudes about smoking.

While many items in the collection look like traditional devices used to fire up a smoke, others do not. Instead, they tend to resemble art pieces or household knick-knacks. These lighters date from a time when smoking was more fashionable and a well-crafted mechanical fire-starter could be a showcase item in the home, office or business.

Lighters in the museum come in all shapes and sizes. Some look terribly weighty, while others were meant to be carried in a pocket. Name an object, Ballard says, and somebody probably designed a lighter that looks like it. There are lighters shaped like pianos, animals, modes of transportation, mechanical devices and even former U.S. Presidents.

"Anything that you can imagine as a lighter actually exists as one," Ballard states.

To prove his point, he shows a lighter shaped like a pool table with pool cue attached. Or how about a working slot machine that fires up when you pull its handle? In addition to getting a light, you get a chance to be lucky, too.

There's also a brass crawling cherub, the Kupie Doll Wonderlite made by Ronson in 1916 that has a lighting device sprouting out of the doll's head. A companion piece is a Ronson bulldog lighter that sports a lighter projecting out of the dog's head. That's from the 1930s, Ballard says.

One of Ballard's favorites is a jukebox lighter that plays a tune while you light up.

Back When a Smoke was Something More

The heyday of lighter making in the U.S. was from 1930 to 1950, Ballard points out. That's when smoking was socially acceptable and even glamorous. It was common for the average person to own up to 20 lighters. Most sets of silverware sold during this period included an elegant table lighter, and Ballard has many fine examples of these. In this era, pocket lighters were often given away as gifts to mark special occasions or accomplishments. Many of these "historical documents," as Ballard calls them, are in the collection.

Long Lasting Lights

Ballard showcases a number of perpetual lighters which burn methane and remain lighted when fueled. Cigar stores often placed decorative ones on a counter for their customers. Some of the perpetual lighters displayed by Ballard are fanciful, exotic figures that blow flame from their

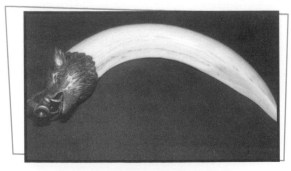
Boar's Tusk cigar cutter

This reclining damsel, from the 1880s, cut cigars with her legs

mouths. Others are of more traditional figures, such as the bronze image of the well-dressed businessman with a handlebar mustache.

Other Museum Highlights

The oldest lighter in Ballard's collection dates back to the 15th century. It still works. To fire it up, you strike a flint with a piece of steel to ignite a pouch's tender. The tender can be anything from fuzz balls to something organic, such as mushrooms, thistle leaves or even bat manure.

Ballard's collection of military-themed lighters is astounding. There are lighters shaped like canons, bullets, aircraft carriers, fighter planes, grenades and miniature tanks. He also has an extensive collection of lighters issued to troops in the U.S. military.

An 1880 rare cigar cutter and ink blotter features a reclining naked woman, hand on head in an expression of either rapture or dread. Smokers lift up

her leg and use it to slice off the end of their cigars.

Ballard also owns a rare Boar's tusk cigar cutter from the 1930s, possibly made in Russia. The cutter has a red-eyed metal boar's head made of metal that chomps down to cut a cigar end. He's looking for the other piece, which was the lighter.

A Ronson lighter from 1934 features Abraham Lincoln, in bronze, seated next to a fireplace. The lighting device sits on top of the fireplace where Lincoln's hand rests, as if he's testing it for heat.

The oldest lighter in Ballard's collection dates back to the 15th century. It still works.

Fanciful lighters from Ballard's collection

International Museum of Surgical Science

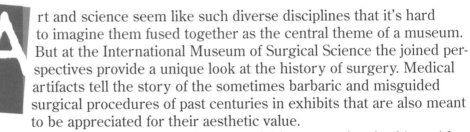

1524 North Lake Shore Drive
Chicago, Illinois 60610-1607

312-642-6502
Fax: 312-642-9516

10 A.M. to 4 P.M. Tuesday
through Saturday and
11 A.M. to 5 P.M. Sunday.

$2 suggested
donation.

Accessible by public
transportation on 151
bus route or by car off
Inner Lake Shore Drive
between East Burton
Place and North
Boulevard.

Art and science seem like such diverse disciplines that it's hard to imagine them fused together as the central theme of a museum. But at the International Museum of Surgical Science the joined perspectives provide a unique look at the history of surgery. Medical artifacts tell the story of the sometimes barbaric and misguided surgical procedures of past centuries in exhibits that are also meant to be appreciated for their aesthetic value.

Displays range from gallbladder stones laid out on velvet backing with the care afforded to gems, to lithographs illustrating horrid skin diseases of the mid-19th century. Murals depict key moments in surgical history, such as one of the earliest human medical dissections and the discovery of anesthesia. Medical relics include a working iron lung from the time of the polio epidemic. There is an antique, massive bone-crushing device in the orthopedic wing that was once used to correct bowlegged children.

The museum was opened in 1953 as a division of the International College of Surgeons, an association formed to promote the understanding of surgical science. The museum offers training programs for students and teachers, and maintains a research library with more than 5,000 volumes, some dating to the 15th century.

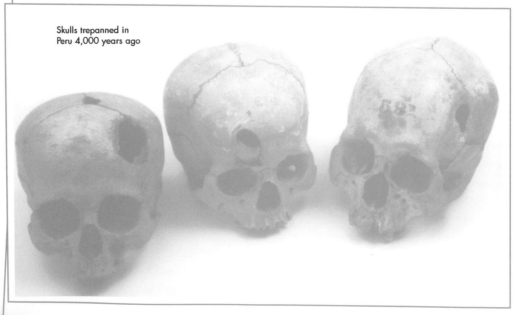

Skulls trepanned in
Peru 4,000 years ago

Shave and a Bloodletting

Museum exhibits reveal that, until the 20th century, surgery was a fairly crude craft. Early medical tools on

19th century amputation kit

display, in fact, include many kits for amputation, since this was once the most widely performed surgery, explains Linda Schubert, Manager of Programs and Collections for the museum.

"They didn't know how to repair things, so they just cut them off," Schubert says. It wasn't until the late 15th century, when taboos against dissection were eased and the Church relaxed bans on the practice, that doctors began to learn exactly how the body functioned. Before this, surgeons were most often clergy, and later, even barbers, who offered bloodletting services along with their more traditional clipping duties. The red-and-white swirls of the barber pole were originally intended as a beacon to those in need of a bloodletting, Schubert points out. Red represented blood, and white signified the bandages applied after the procedure.

"They didn't know how to repair things, so they just cut them off."

Museum Highlights

One display features a small-scale replica of the first anatomical theater. Built at Padua, Italy in 1446, the theater was a circular auditorium with an operating table at its center. It was here that many medical pioneers of the 15th century recorded observations that would lay the framework for modern medicine. It was a revolutionary time for medicine, Schubert says, when many early misconceptions about medicine were corrected by direct examination of the body.

"So much of what doctors had been basing their theories on had been all wrong," Schubert explains.

Skull Boring

To appreciate just how far surgery has come, visitors need only view the museum's display of trepanned skulls. Trepanning, which dates back 4,000

One artist's interpretation of an amputation

years and was common to many cultures, involved boring into the skull of the unfortunate patient. "No one knows why anybody did this, but it was happening all over," Schubert points out.

Researchers believe the procedure was used to relieve skull pressure or to release evil spirits trapped in the body. Devices on display include drills and other metal and stone boring tools. Dozens of skulls subjected to the gruesome surgery are also shown—their missing chunks painfully obvious. Not surprisingly, many patients died while having their skulls excavated. But one skull here shows new bone growth, indicating that the patient survived the operation.

Surgical Stones

Another of the oldest forms of surgery is the removal of gallstones and bladder stones. It's a procedure that dates back thousands of years, Schubert says, and often had a high mortality rate.

Patients usually agreed to it after enduring excruciating pain.

The hundreds of stones on display can be appreciated for their historic value and admired as medical oddities of interesting shape and design as well. Some stones are quite large, almost an inch-and-a-half in diameter. Other displays feature unusual sets removed from a single patient, such as a cluster of 20 or so miniature pyramid-shaped rocks.

Miracle Cures

An apothecary shop, with items that were offered for sale in two turn-of-the-century pharmacies, offers an amusing look at medical quackery. An assortment of powders, liquids, lotions and pills stock the shelves, all contained in original packaging that boasts of magical healing powers. A celery product claims to cure all ailments of the blood, while the Pilgrim Vegetable Prescription promises to ease symptoms ranging from depression to "female weakness."

While these fraudulent claims may seem to belong to a remote period, Schubert points out that it wasn't until 1966 that a federal law required that all claims for medications be subject to scientific proof.

Changing Exhibits

In 1992, the museum opened a special gallery for temporary exhibits that showcase artistic aspects of the medical profession. "Skin Disease," for example, presented lithographs made from 1860–1884 that documented gruesome skin diseases during that period, ranging from leprosy to severe acne, "and everything in between," Schubert says.

"Resonance From Within" offered a stunning series of photographs by Howard Sochurek. These are medical images, recorded by sophisticated equipment such as magnetic resonance machines, and then enhanced by Sochurek to create effects that render them much like abstract art. One work, "Miro's Eyes," shows what looks like two white and blue circles accentuated with slanting white lines. It's actually a composite of 52 medical scans of a tumor on an optic nerve marked for radiation therapy.

Trepanning, which dates back 4,000 years and was common to many cultures, involved boring into the skull of the unfortunate patient.

Left: kidney, gallbladder and bladder stones

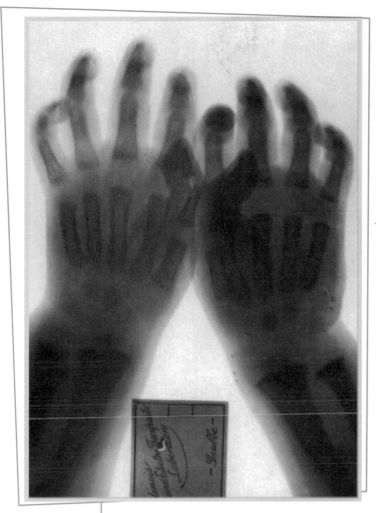

Grubbé frequently placed his hands in front of the radiation pathway. As a result he suffered severe burns and blisters before he realized that he needed to protect his skin. The painful experience did have one positive effect—it led to the use of radiation as a treatment for certain diseases, such as cancer.

The X-ray as art, from "Images from Within"

A Glimpse Inside

While X-rays are a vital medical tool today, a recent gallery exhibit showed that they can be appreciated for their artistic quality as well. "Images From Within" presented dozens of early X-ray images taken by a pioneer in the field, Emile Grubbé.

Some of the 21 images in the exhibit had an obvious medical purpose, including one X-ray revealing a bullet in a patient's leg. Other images taken by Grubbé suggest that he was experimenting with the device, and not necessarily engaged in treatment. Some of these images include X-rays of hands with rings on them and shadow portraits of women's hair—images that reveal hairpins and other accessories.

INTERNATIONAL MUSEUM OF SURGICAL SCIENCE CHICAGO

A Division of the International College of Surgeons

The Barnum Museum

820 Main Street
Bridgeport, Connecticut 06604

203-331-9881

10 A.M. to 4:30 P.M.
Tuesday through Saturday,
Noon to 4:30P.M. Sunday.

$5 adults, $4 seniors and students,
$3 ages 4–18.

Take exit 27 off Interstate
95 and bear right onto
Lafayette Boulevard to State
State. Make a right Main
Street and the museum is
two blocks down on the left.

P hineas Taylor Barnum said many things during his career as master showman, politician and civic leader. But the one remark remembered most is a cynical line he may never have uttered—"There's a sucker born every minute."

Robert Pelton, curator of the Barnum Museum, suggests that rival circus operators attributed the quote to Barnum to tarnish his image with the paying public. "Barnum did not treat his audiences lightly. He would never mention them in that tone," Pelton insists. "He was a shrewd operator, a master of human psychology, and he cultivated his audiences."

If the misquote was just a savvy publicity stunt, Barnum would surely have appreciated its effectiveness. He was a pioneer in the field of mass-marketed amusements, and a deft practitioner of publicity ploys to attract crowds to them.

Barnum is best known for the circus he founded in 1871, which still performs today. But during his career he was more famous for his American Museum in New York City, a cultural emporium that enticed crowds with displays of scientific curiosities and sensational oddities. Barnum lured museum visitors with such exhibits as Egyptian mummies, a two-headed calf, and a piece of wood that Barnum claimed came from Noah's Ark.

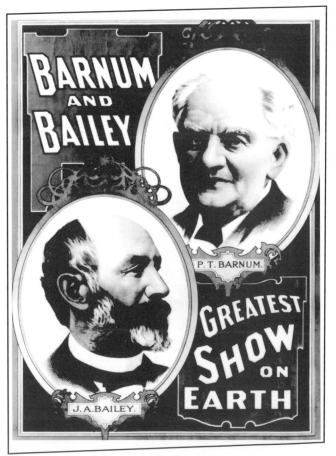

A vintage poster from Barnum's circus, 1897

One of Barnum's most daring stunts was inviting the public to view a creature he called the Feejee Mermaid. Once inside, museum visitors discovered not a beautiful sea nymph, but a freakish creature that was actually the top half of a monkey sewn to the bottom half of a fish. A ghoulish replica of the original Feejee Mermaid is exhibited at the Barnum Museum as a tribute to Barnum's skills as a master promoter.

A Show Palace

The building that houses the Barnum collection was the showman's last great project, and a fine example of his exorbitant tastes. Completed two years after his death in 1893, the building housed his Institute of Science and History. The structure's architectural jumble of Byzantine, Gothic and Romanesque flourishes has prompted critics to label the resulting style "Barnumesque."

The institute closed in 1936, and the building was re-opened in the 1960s as a museum. Now run by the city of Bridgeport, the museum is dedicated to documenting Barnum's public and private life, as well as mounting displays of local history.

Three floors of exhibits include a replica of a drawing room from one of Barnum's four ornate mansions, as well as artifacts from the career of his most celebrated entertainer, Tom Thumb, the 35-inch high vaudeville performer.

The museum captures the spirit of Barnum's own wide-ranging amusements by offering such displays as Victorian-era toys and an Egyptian mummy, believed to be 2,500 years old. The mummy was donated to the original Barnum museum by his second wife, Nancy Fish Barnum. Other exhibits trace the history of Barnum's circus, "The Greatest Show on Earth."

Barnum was more than an impresario. He dabbled in politics, serving as both mayor and state legislator, and played a pivotal role as a real estate developer, helping to transform Bridgeport into a manufacturing center.

One of Barnum's most daring stunts was inviting the public to view a creature he called the Feejee Mermaid...that was actually the top half of a monkey sewn to the bottom half of a fish.

Exterior view of the museum

"He was the Donald Trump of his day," Pelton says. The museum documents Barnum's business career with displays of typewriters, buttons and corsets—examples of goods made in Bridgeport in Barnum's time.

Little Man, Big Draw

A major display chronicles the life of entertainer Tom Thumb, Barnum's most prized attraction. Barnum immediately saw the potential to create a public sensation when he first met Charles Stratton, who at the time was a perfectly proportioned five-year-old dwarf standing 24 inches tall.

"What appealed to Barnum was that he could tell this boy had an outgoing and pleasant personality," Pelton explains.

With the blessing of Stratton's parents, who were paid handsomely, Barnum turned the boy into Tom Thumb, a midget vaudeville performer who sang, danced, and charmed audiences with comedy skits.

Tom Thumb's walnut carriage is a favorite with children of all ages

"There were other midgets around, but none as well managed as Tom Thumb," Pelton contends.

As Stratton grew older, he became General Tom Thumb, the central act of Barnum's traveling show, which often toured Europe. Barnum eventually added another star, singer Jenny Lind, the "Swedish Nightingale," and in 1862 he also signed three other performing midgets, including Lavinia Warren.

"There were other midgets around, but none as well managed as Tom Thumb."

The suit and boots worn by Tom Thumb during his visit with Queen Victoria

80

Barnum planned and promoted the wedding of Tom Thumb and Lavinia Warren

During their first year together, Tom Thumb and Lavinia Warren fell in love. Barnum planned their 1863 wedding, a spectacle that drew 2,000 guests from around the world, and garnered Barnum valued publicity.

"Barnum probably wanted them to remarry," Pelton chuckles.

The museum displays artifacts from Thumb's life, including several of the tiny carriages Barnum provided for him. The most unique of these vehicles is a walnut-shaped two-seater. When not used for transportation, the carriages were used to attract crowds to one of Barnum's shows.

Visitors can appreciate the tiny aspects of Tom Thumb's life when viewing items from his home, including furniture, clothing and personal mementos. A wedding photo of the small couple is displayed, along with Thumb's court suit, which he wore when he called upon Queen Victoria in 1844.

"Ladies and Gentleman . . . "

Circus artifacts include vintage posters and a life-size photographic cut-out of Jumbo, once billed as "the world's largest elephant." Barnum bought Jumbo in 1882 from the London Zoo to be an attraction for his circus. The clown trade is represented with several gag items, including a drum with a satirical portrait of a mother-in-law on its shell, colorful wigs, and props such as an oversize wrench and a tiny canon.

The highlight of this exhibit area is a miniature re-creation of Barnum's

Cut-out of Barnum's giant elephant, Jumbo

Barnum insisted that an elephant be used to plow his estate in yet another brilliant publicity stunt

"He was the Shakespeare of advertising."

circus. It was crafted by William Brinley over a 50-year period, beginning in 1927 when he was 9 years old, and includes more than 3,000 figures. Visitors view the scale-model circus from above.

Anything to Sell a Ticket

Pelton says Barnum often wrote to a fellow museum operator in Boston discussing ways to best use publicity stunts, like the Feejee Mermaid, to draw crowds.

"The letters would say things like, 'I'm getting a lot of mileage out of the mermaid,' or 'It's starting to wear out, I'd better give it a rest,'" Pelton laughs.

Never one to miss a chance for a promotional ploy, Barnum insisted that an elephant be used to plow his Bridgeport estate. Barnum knew that this spectacle would be seen by passengers on trains heading to New York City. The sight invariably created such a buzz of excitement that, by the time the train pulled into the city, passengers were primed to make their first stop Barnum's American Museum.

"He was," Pelton marvels, "the Shakespeare of advertising."

Famous Siamese twins Chang and Eng

Barnum and Tom Thumb

Leila's Hair Museum

815 West 23rd Street
Independence, Missouri 64055

816-252-4247 (HAIR)

8:30 A.M. to 4:30 P.M.,
Monday through Saturday.

$3 adult, $1.50
seniors and child under 12.

From Interstate 70,
exit at Noland Road
(exit 12) and head
north to 23rd Street.

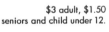

When Leila Cohoon tells people about her hair museum, she is often greeted with blank stares and confused looks. "I get a funny response," she admits. Some wonder if she's crafted something odd from the hair snippings generated at her cosmetology school, housed in the same building.

But initial skepticism quickly fades once visitors step inside the Hair Museum. On display are hundreds of antique examples of how hair was once used as the centerpiece for family mementos, jewelry, and even memorial tributes.

"It's genealogy done in hair," Cohoon explains. Before camcorders and disposable cameras, family history was preserved with craft items made from hair. Long wreaths woven with strands from each family member were displayed in the home. Hair rings were worn either as memorials to loved ones or as a way to keep absent ones close to your heart.

Cohoon exhibits more than 1,000 pieces of hair jewelry, including bracelets, watch fobs, necklaces, earrings, chains, brooches, hat pins and cufflinks. Most of the pieces are at least 100 years old, and some date back to the 17th century, when people did more with their hair than just shampoo and comb it. "People ask me, 'Is this the hair of dead people?' Well, I'm sure it is," Cohoon laughs.

Hair bracelet

84

A Kodak Moment with Hair?

Cohoon believes that this art form was a forerunner to photography. It captured the essence of a person at a point in time. Receptacles at a dressing table would collect hair "drippings" which would be made into flower wreaths or jewelry. Family members could create hair pieces themselves or have artisans do the work for them.

Even after the development of photography, early portraits were often combined with locks of hair from the subject. These cuttings would be woven into a flower pattern and framed with the picture. Today the craft is all but forgotten. Parents clip the first locks of their children's hair, stick them in a photo album, and then pull them out occasionally to reminisce. Cohoon believes that this custom is left over from earlier times when hair crafts flourished.

"This is the only part of those human beings that is still here."

Right: Hair art

On Her Way to Buy Shoes

Cohoon picked up her first piece of hair jewelry around 1960. She had gone out to buy Easter shoes but first stopped in an antique store where she spotted a gold-framed wreath featuring woven hair from two girls. The piece was 6 inches by 6 inches, she recalls, and on it were inscribed the date of 1852 and the words "Mama" and "Papa."

Cohoon went without new holiday shoes that year. She bought the hair wreath instead. During the next several years she acquired hundreds of hair art pieces, usually in antique stores, which would stock one or two as part of their collection. "People ask me which piece I like best," she reflects. "I've fallen in love with every piece. It's like one of your kids. How can you say you like one better than the other? This is the only part of those human beings that is still here."

Little Miss No Name

Many of the items are deeply personal. One, a memorial to a small girl, features a picture of her in her casket and a wreath of her hair shaped into a flower. Cohoon took the items out to re-frame them and didn't find her name anywhere. "I call her 'Little Miss No Name,'" she smiles. "I hope someone will come in one day and identify her."

Before she opened the museum, Cohoon was so attached to these items that she would wear some of the

Little Miss No Name

antique jewelry. Once she wore a 17th century hair brooch while visiting the Victoria and Albert Museum in London. A horrified curator wasn't pleased with Cohoon's fashion statement.

"The lady had a fit," Cohoon grimaces. "She said, 'You don't wear 17th century pieces and you don't carry them in your purse.'"

Cohoon did have one mishap with an antique hair ring. Many times these rings were made from the hair of someone who had just died. They were sent to people who couldn't attend the funeral, Cohoon points out. She was wearing one and went to wash her hands.

"Long hair stretches when it's wet. I should know that. The little ring went down the drain," she says sadly. "It broke my heart when I lost that one."

Cohoon almost lost her entire collection when a fire broke out in her house, where she had stored all the artifacts before opening the museum.

"I had so many under my bed and in my closet. I almost lost my life trying to get them out of my house," she remembers. "They are a part of history and you can't duplicate that."

After that scare, Cohoon opened the museum in 1992. It's been a popular attraction. Sometimes a busload of tourists will come to her place and skip the Harry Truman museum nearby.

"I don't think Mr. Truman would like that," she jokes.

Museum Highlights

The museum features dozens of watch fobs. These are tightly woven strands of hair used to support a man's watch. Fobs were often embellished with other designs, such as a compass, to make them more attractive.

Simple hair accessories on display include a pair of hair buttons, a dime-size cape fastener that has hair woven into its tortoise shell frame, and a hat pin four inches long that has brown and blond hair in a spiral around the pin.

Hair trees are also a part of the hair craft tradition and a few examples are displayed. One, about a foot tall, features a marble base and a glass dome top that covers a tree made of hair. Cohoon says it looks rather like a palm tree. Hair threads draped around the base rise upward to form the tree.

The museum also has a children's section which features rings and bracelets made from children's hair. These were probably worn by a child's mother, Cohoon explains. Cohoon has studied these pieces and figured out how to make them. She's now creating a wreath using hair from her grandchildren. It's a dying art, but some are trying to revive it. A book on the subject is due out soon.

Once she wore a 17th century hair brooch while visiting the Victoria and Albert Museum in London. A horrified curator wasn't pleased with Cohoon's fashion statement.

Hair watch fob with pocket knife

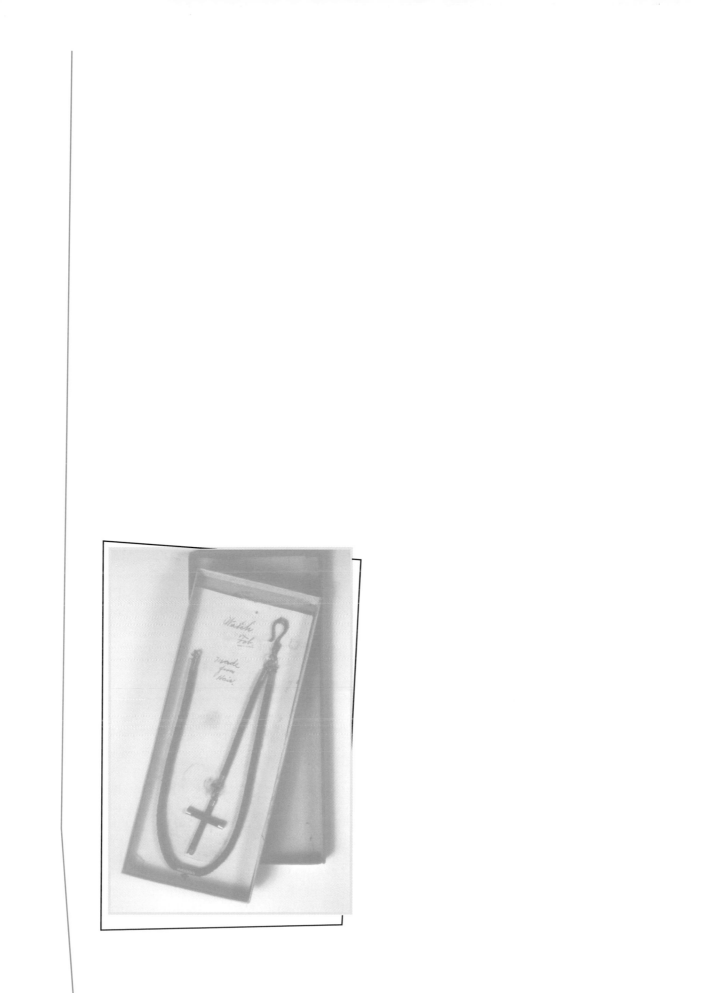

The National Farm Toy Museum

1110 16th Avenue SE
Dyersville, Iowa 52040

319-875-2727

8 A.M. to 7 P.M. daily.
Closed Christmas Day,
Thanksgiving, and
Easter Sunday.

$4 adults, $1 ages 6–11.
Free for children under 5.

Dyersville is at the
intersection of Interstate
20 and Highway 136.

The motto of this town in the heart of rural America is: "Where dreams come true." That enticing slogan refers to the area's prime tourist lure, a baseball diamond carved from a corn-field and featured in the popular 1988 film, *Field of Dreams*. Now this community of 4,000 annually welcomes thousands of tourists who flock to the landmark field to watch ballplayers in baggy uniforms emerge from the stalks and to experience the magic and novelty of the site.

Long before this heavenly field was created, Dyersville was making dreams come true for another group of fans—avid collectors of die-cast metal farm toys. Popular in rural regions, these scale model replicas of farm vehicles and tools became hot collectible items in the mid-1980s. An annual trading show for these farm toys is held in Dyersville.

The motto of *Field of Dreams* was, "Build it and they will come." In the case of The National Farm Toy Museum, it was "Build it because they are already here." Thousands of farm toy enthusiasts have been coming to Dyersville since 1978, when Claire Scheibe of North Dakota organized the first farm toy convention and held it in a school auditorium. As more collectors began turning up, the entire school was used. Finally, Scheibe explains, he and others began kicking around the idea for a museum so that the town could house the show in a permanent location.

Four local companies that dominate the farm toy industry lent their sup-port and the museum opened in 1986. Its collection includes more than 30,000 farm toys, from miniature tractors to tiny manure spreaders. In addition, the museum pays tribute to rural life with several scale model representations of typical farms, an exhibit that includes tiny examples of farms from 1920 to the present.

A scale model of a working farm

Injection molding die-cast machine
used by the Ertl company in the 1950s

within the region surrounding Dyersville, were receiving his publication.

The farm toy show is held the first weekend in November. Scheibe's arrival in Dyersville for the annual event marks the beginning of the winter season for residents.

"When I come to town they say, 'Put down the lawnmowers and put away the rakes because that crazy farm toy guy is here,'" he laughs.

Nostalgia-Driven Trend

Scheibe's interest in farm toys began in the mid–1970s, when he went to an antique show and searched for toys he had played with in his youth. It was common practice for rural children to play with tiny versions of the tools used to perform farm chores.

"When dad was out in the field, you made believe that you were doing the same thing," Scheibe recalls. "You'd be plowing and later on in the year you'd be harvesting. It was a breakdown in miniature of what your father was doing."

When Scheibe first began collecting the toys as an adult, they were hard to find. They were not featured items at antique shows and were often stuffed into boxes under tables. Sometimes dealers insisted that Scheibe buy an entire box of toys rather than just the few he actually wanted.

As he traveled around, though, he noticed others with a similar interest and jotted down their names. In 1978, he used this list to enroll his first 17 subscribers for a magazine dedicated to farm toy collecting. By 1996, more than 28,000 collectors, most living

History of the Industry

The museum tour begins with a 20-minute movie documenting the development of the local farm toy industry. In 1945, Fred Ertl of Dubuque, Iowa began making die-cast farm toys in his basement using war surplus aluminum aircraft pistons. Within four years he was so successful that he was producing more than 5,000 toys a day. He moved to Dyersville and opened a farm toy factory, today the largest company of its kind.

An opening exhibit is the first tractor ever produced by the Ertl company. "For people who are collectors, that's a highlight," says Kari Wittmeyer, the museum's director.

Right: A depiction of
rural family life

Left: Actual pedal tractor

Farm Life in Miniature

The museum displays several dioramas of typical farm life from the 1920s to the present. Set against a painted backdrop, these small-scale scenes of rural life feature miniature farm tools and thumb-size animals such as horses, pigs and chickens.

By studying the dioramas, visitors can see how farms changed through the years to accommodate such developments as electricity and the telephone. For a larger-scale glimpse into rural life, visitors can peer into a kitchen window and see a simulated tableau of a family enjoying life on the farm.

Corn Harvesting

It's hard to imagine life in rural Iowa without mentioning corn. The museum has mounted a major exhibit that traces corn cultivation throughout history. The displays range from scale replicas of thousand-year-old hand tools to modern combines. One

It's hard to imagine life in rural Iowa without mentioning corn.

Exhibit Highlights

One of the more coveted toys for kids growing up on a farm is a pedal tractor, a kid-size version of the standard rural vehicle.

"I remember riding on one as a kid at my grandmother's house," Wittmeyer says. "It was the coolest thing. It wasn't a bike. You actually sat in it. It was twice the size of a tricycle. It was just like driving a tractor."

The museum exhibits several of these mini-tractors and also displays one that young museum visitors can climb aboard and use to plough through their own field of dreams.

On the museum's first floor there's a replica of an assembly line at a farm toy factory, complete with a massive die-cast machine. Mannequins outfitted as factory workers busily pour molds and create the final product.

Also on the first floor are rare antique farm toys, including some built in the 1920s. There are tractors, wagons, hay balers and other tiny replicas of harvesting equipment.

Toy tractor

device, called the sledder, dates to 1884. It contains a front blade and would cut down stalks as two work horses pulled the device through rows of corn.

A Popular Offshoot

A related industry to farm toys is the production of toy money banks. The museum displays hundreds made in the shape of cars and trucks and featuring company logos. Designed to store loose change, these banks have become highly collectible in recent years, making them more valuable than any amount of coins that can be stuffed inside them.

Houdini Historical Center

Houdini

330 East College Avenue
Appleton, Wisconsin 54911

414-733-8445

10 A.M. to 5 P.M. Tuesday through Saturday and Noon to 5 P.M. Sunday. Additional summer hours include 10 A.M. to 5 P.M. on Monday during June, July and August.

$4 adults, $2 children aged 5–17.

Take College Avenue exit east from Highway 41. The museum is at the intersection of Drew Street and College Avenue.

Every Halloween, on the anniversary of Harry Houdini's death, a group of his fans gathers for a seance, seeking to make contact with the master escape artist. So far, not a peep has been heard from the beyond. If Houdini has wriggled free of death—the ultimate confinement—he's not talking.

For those who want to explore Houdini's life within the limits of this temporal world, there's always the Houdini Historical Center. No seances here. Just dozens of fascinating artifacts, photographs, film clips, handbills and assorted documents relating to Houdini's life.

Houdini was born Ehrich Weiss in 1874 in Budapest. He moved with his family from Hungary to Appleton, Wisconsin so that his father, Rabbi Samuel Mayer Weiss, could lead a congregation there. Houdini lived in Appleton from age four to 10 before his family moved on.

Appleton residents never forgot him. They named a school after him, a nightclub, and even a root beer concocted in a local brewery.

Harry Houdini in the movie, *The Grim Game,* 1919

In 1986, they dedicated Houdini Square with tributes, a magic performance by Doug Henning, and the unveiling of a mysterious artwork called "Metamorphosis." The sculpture, according to museum spokesperson Nancy Broeren, mystifies passersby in the way that Houdini's

Attending the dedication ceremony was Sidney Radner, an escape artist himself. He had inherited dozens of Houdini artifacts from Houdini's brother, Theodore Hardeen. For decades the collection had been stored in Radner's basement in Holyoke, Massachusetts. But Radner

Houdini answered every escape challenge

feats puzzled his audiences. One-and-a-half stories high, the work features a partially opened box with interwoven chains, and is precariously perched on a street corner.

"It looks like it's impossible to balance there," Broeren marvels.

was impressed with what he saw in Appleton that day, especially the careful way the town exhibited its history at the local museum. So he decided to donate his collection to Appleton, and the Houdini Center was launched.

Magic and More

Houdini began his career by performing magic acts in turn-of-the-century circuses, sideshows and vaudeville theaters. Many magicians had mastered various sleight-of-hand tricks that mildly amused audiences, but Houdini, Broeren explains, added another level to his act by performing daring, death-defying escapes.

There were imitators and rivals, but Houdini set himself apart early in his career by staging a sensational escape from Scotland Yard in 1900. Through the years, many highly publicized challenges were issued and Houdini answered every one of them, clamping on handcuffs and leg irons and dutifully climbing into vaults, jail cells and sealed steamer trunks. For good measure he was often tossed into water. No matter how improbable escape seemed, Houdini always found a way out.

"Houdini changed what people thought of as traditional magic. Instead of using rabbits, his tools became restraints and locks. He created his own brand of magic," Broeren points out.

Museum Highlights

As you might expect, the museum displays many of the restraint devices that failed to hold back Houdini during his extraordinary career. There are handcuffs, locks and the various picks he used to open them. Among the handcuffs on display are those that were once slapped onto the wrists of President Garfield assassin Charles J. Guiteau. Houdini wore them and was able to free himself from their hold.

There's also a straight jacket known as the "Punishment Suit." The jacket has arm restraints and leg bands and "looks impossible to escape from," observes Broeren. Not only is the jacket an interesting artifact, it also offers museum visitors a guide to gauging Houdini's size.

"Houdini had such a commanding presence, but he really was only 5-5 or 5-6. He was rather compact," Broeren states.

Many of Houdini's escapes took place underwater, so the Alliance Dairy of England challenged Houdini to escape while submerged in milk. The dairy believed that Houdini's

Left: An early photo of Houdini performing a traditional magic act

Among the handcuffs on display are those that were once slapped onto the wrists of President Garfield assassin Charles J. Guiteau. Houdini wore them and was able to free himself from their hold.

A decade later, Houdini had created a unique stlye of performing

escapes were aided by his ability to see underwater. It didn't hurt that the staged event garnered publicity for Houdini as well as the dairy company.

Houdini was handcuffed and dunked in a 60-gallon milk tub that was sealed with locks.

"Of course he was able to escape," Broeren laughs.

The museum displays the milk tub in question, as well as other handbills and newspaper ads challenging Houdini to similar stunts.

The museum has recently added an interactive exhibit that allows visitors to try on handcuffs and a straight jacket. They can also practice a simple magician's ploy known as the "French Drop." This allows magicians to hide objects without the audience taking notice.

If you want to see a master do it, you can watch the museum's short video which includes film clips of escapes Houdini performed in the 1919 movie *The Grim Game*.

Houdini was handcuffed and dunked in a 60-gallon milk tub that was sealed with locks. "Of course he was able to escape."

Right: The milk tub from which Houdini escaped

Spiritual Debunking

When Houdini's mother died in 1913, he was so upset that he consulted spiritualists who claimed that they could contact the dead. Houdini easily saw through their tricks. The experience led him on a crusade to debunk other spiritualists. He had a standing $10,000 offer to any spiritualist who could produce an effect that he couldn't duplicate.

Houdini was so consumed by this battle against mediums that he exposed many of their techniques in 1924 by writing a book, *A Magician Among the Spirits*.

As an example of one way Houdini exposed these frauds, the museum displays photographs he produced that duplicated "ghost images." These photos included images of ghosts and were offered as proof of a medium's ability to raise spirits. Houdini produced his own examples to show that it was not supernatural power but a knowledge of trick photography that created these images. The museum offers two humorous photos Houdini made. One shows him with Abraham Lincoln, and another depicts him kneeling in front of a floating image of himself.

Houdini: King of the iron locks, circa 1902

THE HOUDINI HISTORICAL CENTER

Original   Harry Houdini   Original
Original   König der eisernen Fesseln.

A Magician Never Tells . . .

The museum doesn't give away any of Houdini's secrets. Houdini did that himself in his own writings. He did this partly as a way of throwing off his competitors, as he would sometimes mention only basic elements of his methods. He also revealed some techniques in order to counter claims by spiritualists that he was really a medium using supernatural powers.

Exhibits cite some of Houdini's writings in which he apparently explains how to escape from handcuffs. Or does he? "He was pretty good at talking around things and making you feel that you'd learned something when you really hadn't," laughs Broeren.

"After escaping, his second genius was PR."

His Second Genius

Houdini was a masterful self-promoter and the museum offers testimony of this skill, including photographs depicting his many publicity stunts. In one, he is seen dangling in a straight jacket above a street filled with staring people. He would stage similar events to promote his show, which would be playing in the town that very evening.

To drum up enthusiasm for his performance in Paris, he spelled out his name on the heads of seven bald men, and then had them tip their caps around town in unison.

"After escaping," says Broeren, "his second genius was PR."

Havre de Grace Decoy Museum

PO Box A
215 Giles Street
Havre de Grace, Maryland 21078

410-939-3739
Fax: 410-939-3775

11 A.M. to 4 P.M. daily.

$4 adults, $2 seniors and children.

From Interstate 95 north or south take exit 89 to Route 155 East. Follow the signs to Route 40. Cross Route 40 at Otsego Street and follow Otsego until it ends. Make a right on Union Avenue and follow until it ends at Tydings Park. Make a left and follow the museum signs.

Creating an elaborate hoax to fool your opponent is usually considered poor sportsmanship. But in hunting the use of decoys to lure ducks and other waterfowl into firing range is a time-honored and respected tradition. Well-crafted decoys not only determine the success of a hunt, they can also be judged as great works of art.

So the folks at Havre de Grace take pride in proclaiming their town the duck decoy capital of the world. The scenic upper Chesapeake Bay region of Maryland is home to thousands of ducks and other waterfowl. Some are actually living. But a great many are beautifully crafted fakes displayed at the Havre de Grace Decoy Museum, located on the edge of the Susquehanna flats.

The heyday of duck hunting here was the 1930s. Flocks of birds were so dense that they sometimes blotted out the sun, recalls Connie M. Daub, a museum assistant. As hunters flooded the area, they created a demand for decoys that was answered by local carving legends. The museum specializes in these works, some dating back to the 1800s. There are also plans to showcase decoys made in other regions of the country.

Re-creation of decoy carving legends shooting the breeze

Re-creation of master decoy carver R. Madison Mitchell at work

"I had a real fondness for hunting, too. But the problem was, with running my funeral business and making all those birds, I never could find the time to put it in."

A Master Decoy Carver

One of the most prolific decoy makers in the area was Madison Mitchell. The museum has hundreds of his works, and as a tribute it features a life-size, wax figure of Mitchell standing in a carving shop next to a pot-bellied stove along with wax statues of other local carving greats. This opening exhibit features a voice recording of Mitchell, taped in 1993 when he was 91 years old. As you study the wax figures, Mitchell both describes the scene and sets the tone for the visit.

"There was me, next to Paul Gibson, wearing my bow tie as always," Mitchell says as he begins a three-minute speech that expresses the quaintness not only of the museum but also of the surrounding region. "I had a real fondness for hunting, too. But the problem was, with running my funeral business and making all those birds, I never could find the time to put it in."

Museum Highlights

The main display area features decoys that reflect the variety of waterfowl hunted as well as the different styles of decoy making. To be more effective as lures, decoys were made in a variety of poses, including preening, nestling and swimming. "Dippers" were weighted decoys that showed only a duck's backside to make it look like it was feeding underwater. They would attract ducks who would drop by to join the feast, only to become a meal themselves when shot by nearby hunters.

One unusual exhibit shows a devious hunting device called the "sink box." Shaped like a coffin, the sink box was weighted down with cast-iron bird decoys so that it floated along at water level. The hunter would lay down inside and wait for unsuspecting birds to approach. Then the hunter would rise up and shoot to kill.

The "Gunning the Flats" exhibit displays guns used by hunters to shoot ducks drawn within range by the decoys. Looking at these powerful weapons, it's easy to imagine how many species of ducks were hunted out of the region. Punt guns were 10- to 12-feet long and were more like canons, holding up to two pounds of shot. Recoils from these guns would knock the hunter's boat back in the water.

Another heavy-handed weapon was a shotgun that could fire six barrels with the pull of one trigger. It would be aimed at a flock of birds.

The exhibit, not surprisingly, goes on to point out how regulations were imposed after the 1930s to help conserve the duck population and make waterfowl hunting more of a sport and less of a massacre.

Not All Decoys are Ducks

Although not as widely known as those used for hunting waterfowl, animal and fish decoys have also been used with some success. The museum's display of these includes an antique deer decoy made of foam rubber that folds up into a hunter's pack. When spread out it looks like a doe resting on the ground.

Ice fishermen use decoys of small fish to lure larger fish. They also use decoys of turtles, frogs and even small beavers. They pull these decoys through the water and spear fish swimming over to examine them. The museum has examples of all of these decoys.

Another heavy-handed weapon was a shotgun that could fire six barrels with the pull of one trigger. It would be aimed at a flock of birds.

The real R. Madison Mitchell

GUNNING THE FLATS

Decoys in the Environment

While decoys have traditionally been used to hunt waterfowl, they have more recently played a valuable role in conservation. Biologists looking to re-introduce certain birds to their former habitats have used carefully crafted decoys to make this happen. A recent article in the museum's newsletter documents the use of decoys to lure small seabirds known as puffins to an island along the Maine coast. Birds see the decoys and conclude that the habitat is a good place to nest and feed. Sometimes sounds of the birds are piped in to enhance the effect of the decoys!

Havre de Grace Decoy Museum

Havre de Grace
DECOY MUSEUM

The Museum of Death

ames Dean Healy is fascinated with death, but not the peaceful end that comes to some in their sleep, or the drifting away that claims others after a long illness or in old age.

Healy is drawn to the sensational demise—murders, executions, horrendous car crashes and other gruesome accidents.

So Healy, an artist who owns a gallery in San Diego's Gaslamp district, turned the basement of his building into a museum that shines a light on a dark topic: ghastly death. The Museum of Death displays execution devices, artwork by serial killers, mortician's equipment and coroner photographs of murder and accident victims. The museum also screens a six-hour video that showcases plane crashes, executions, and other horrid ends.

"We show the heavy, heavy stuff," Healy says, talking enthusiastically about his favorite subject. "We show the deaths that people want to see. The things that the media are afraid to show."

Healy says that despite all the carnage that visitors encounter, they climb back up to street level with lifted spirits. "I've never had one complaint. People love it," he claims. "It's their way of defeating death. When you go down and come back up, you feel happy to be alive. It's a positive thing."

548 Fifth Avenue
San Diego, California 92101

619-338-8153

Noon to 10 P.M. Tuesday through Sunday. Closed on Mondays.

$4.

Take I-15 south to Front Street (Second Street exit). Stay on Front Street until Market Street. Turn left on Market. Turn right on Fifth Avenue.

Execution devices such as this electric chair are prominently featured

102

Some people have suggested to Healy that his museum might be more at home in cities with more eccentric tendencies such as San Francisco or New Orleans. Instead, he's located smack in the middle of San Diego's fashionable historic quarter of shops, restaurants and nightclubs. But Healy points out that the location is entirely appropriate. It once housed the city's first mortuary.

Moreover, Healy believes he's especially needed here, amid all the bustle, to put things in perspective for people.

"Death is the last taboo. It's the one thing that everyone thinks won't happen to them," Healy says. "But it's like lunch. It's coming."

"Death is the last taboo. It's the one thing that everyone thinks won't happen to them," Healy says. "But it's like lunch. It's coming."

Morticians Headrest

17-foot high guillotine

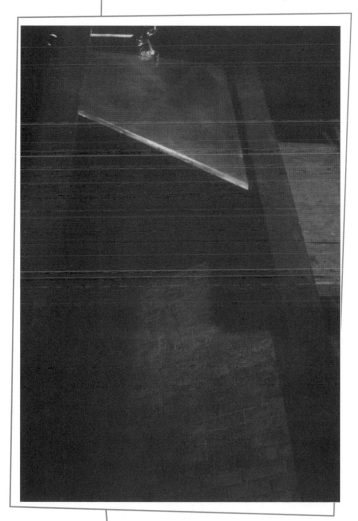

Serial vs. Cereal

Healy had always collected death memorabilia. But he didn't think of a death museum until he presented a gallery exhibit where he juxtaposed images of serial killers with cereal boxes. Healy's aim, he says, was to make people compare the nature of two evils: serial killers and the manipulative marketing tactics of cereal manufacturers.

It was a novel concept and the show proved popular. Healy noticed how people were especially drawn to the art of the serial killers. He had collected the pieces by corresponding with several infamous killers and receiving the works directly from them, sometimes after a visit to Death Row.

When the show ended, he moved the serial killer art pieces to the basement with the idea of opening a permanent death museum. He brought in other artifacts he had collected over the years, including a 17-foot-high guillotine he had built for another gallery show. After he opened the museum in 1995, appreciative visitors came forward to donate or sell additional items. A mortician friend, for example, offered many tools of his trade.

"Once you start doing stuff like this, the word goes out and people start remembering that they have something in their closet that they'd rather have in The Museum of Death," he points out. "This started out as a collection of artwork, but it's evolving. It was an idea that I thought of, but now it's bigger than I am."

Day of the Dead altar honoring airline disaster victims

The serial killer exhibit features works by Charles Manson, Lawrence Bittaker, "Night Stalker" Richard Ramirez, John Wayne Gacy and "Son of Sam" killer David Berkowitz.

Museum Highlights

Visitors are meant to feel that they are entering a coffin as they step down into the museum. The walls are covered with satin and display cases are lined with red velvet.

The serial killer exhibit features works by Charles Manson, Lawrence Bittaker, "Night Stalker" Richard Ramirez, John Wayne Gacy and "Son of Sam" killer David Berkowitz. There are also a denim work shirt and baseball autographed by Manson. Healy plans to display letters written to him by the killers which, he says, reveal a key aspect of their personalities.

"They are all power-trippers," Healy speculates. "It's not the murders with them, it's having power over the other person. When you start corresponding with these people, their thing is control. They want to control every aspect of the relationship."

Instruments of execution and torture include a guillotine, an electric chair, a gallows and an ax-shaped pendulum. Displayed along with these exhibits is the prison uniform worn by Wayne Robert Felde when he was executed by electric chair at Angola Prison in Louisiana in 1988. It has one leg cut off at the knee and shirt stains that Healy identified as "purge marks."

A mortician's exhibit features antique and modern mortuary tools, including body viewing tables, embalming fluid bottles, pressurized embalming tanks and many other devices used in the corpse preservation trade.

After Healy first opened he was approached by a man who said he was the grandson of Orange County

The Coffin Theater

The museum has one of the most unusual movie screening rooms in the world. It features six chairs placed in front of an opened coffin. A six-hour video featuring actual footage of executions and deaths is shown, with the coffin lining used as the screen.

"We've had people who've sat there and watched the whole six hours," he says proudly.

The Freak Farm

One of Healy's next projects is to open an exhibit he plans to call Freak Farm. It will feature biological oddities from the animal world, including many live specimens. He already displays a live two-headed turtle and plans to add "Albino Swamp," featuring many albino critters who dwell in swamps.

A six-hour video featuring actual footage of executions and deaths is shown, with the coffin lining used as the screen.

coroner photographer Mel Killpatrick. The man then offered to sell Healy a 100 photographs of accident and murder victims taken by Killpatrick during the 1940s and 1950s. Healy bought them for $1 each and they now line the walls of the museum.

One of his favorites is of a car crash victim whose twisted vehicle ended up embedded in a billboard sign above an advertising slogan that reads: "It's Lucky When You Live in America."

THE MUSEUM OF DEATH

THIS HALLOWEEN
BE AFRAID,
BE VERY AFRAID

LOCATED IN THE HISTORIC HEART OF SAN DIEGO'S GASLAMP QUARTER AND HOUSED IN SAN DIEGO'S FIRST MORTUARY, THE MUSEUM OF DEATH IS THE FIRST MUSEUM IN THE UNITED STATES DEDICATED SOLELY TO DEATH

548 FIFTH AVENUE
SAN DIEGO, CALIFORNIA 92101
619.338.8153
4.00 ADMISSION

The Museum of Jurassic Technology

9341 Venice Blvd.
Culver City, California 90232

310-836-6131
Fax: 310-287-2267

museumjt@rhythm.com
www.mjt.org/

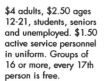

2 P.M. to 8 P.M. Thursday,
Noon to 6 P.M. Friday
through Sunday.

$4 adults, $2.50 ages
12-21, students, seniors
and unemployed. $1.50
active service personnel
in uniform. Groups of
16 or more, every 17th
person is free.

From Interstate 10,
exit at Robertson
Boulevard and head
south to Venice
Boulevard. Turn right
and travel about four
blocks west. The
museum is located on
the north side of the
street.

Visitors to the Museum of Jurassic Technology are led to a small cushioned bench in front of a circular viewing area as a way of introduction. A slide and audio presentation offers a brief overview of museums throughout history. You are told, for example, that the term "museum" originates from "a spot dedicated to the muses," a place where people are lifted above everyday affairs.

In addition, the explanation continues, museums are sites offering "rational amusement" that guide visitors from the "familiar to the unfamiliar."

With these remarks, visitors embark on an unusual journey filled with wonder, curiosity and, sometimes, confusion.

Although the museum claims to offer the general public a "hands-on experience of 'life in the Jurassic,'" just what this means is never fully explained. Its real purpose is to compel visitors to ponder the meaning of museums in general and even to question the nature of their own everyday experiences.

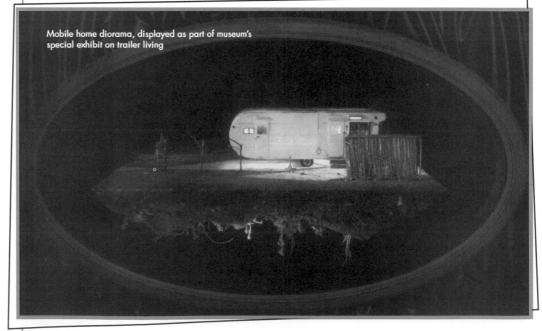

Mobile home diorama, displayed as part of museum's special exhibit on trailer living

"Duck's Breath" exhibit, a surreal representation of an ancient folk cure

The museum is nestled amid a commercial stretch of a busy boulevard, housed behind a bland door that doesn't hint at the treasures contained within. Visitors who stumble in here—including bus passengers killing time before their ride comes along—often depart in an amused and frequently perplexed state of mind.

An Ever Uncertain Reality

At the center of this institution is David Wilson, an enigmatic character who, just like his museum, is hard to pin down. In Lawrence Weschler's best-selling book on the museum, *Mr. Wilson's Cabinet of Wonder,* the author notes that Wilson was at times sketchy when discussing his life and role in developing the museum.

"Occasionally we'd talk about his own life story and it's my impression that everything he told me was more or less true-as-stated, although, as with many of the displays, a wealth of solid detail early on began to fog over somewhat as one approached

the present," Weschler writes in the book.

An avant-garde filmmaker, Wilson once made a 13-minute movie called "Stasis" which consists of one long-distance shot of a mountain stream. The camera pulls back slowly for the duration of the shot as the film image changes ever so slightly throughout.

In an earlier interview, Wilson explained that the museum began with the donated collection of two midwestern botanists who had amassed an array of curiosities and artifacts, including some botanical fossils from the Jurassic era. Included, for example, was an exhibit on a "Child's Call," which Wilson says was a membrane that covered the face of some infants and was believed to give them the power of second sight.

Wilson added his own dioramas that illustrate elements of folklore or natural phenomena that he found interesting. The museum's collection

At the center of this institution is David Wilson, an enigmatic character who, just like his museum, is hard to pin down.

was temporarily displayed at various sites in Los Angeles until it opened at its present location in 1988.

Natural Metaphor

"We have a motto here that is *trans-latia natura*, which means 'nature as metaphor,'" Wilson says. "If there is a thread that ties together the obvious eclectic nature of the museum, it is that. By looking at nature we don't just mean flora and fauna. We include humankind and all of its endeavors. It's a metaphorical understanding of natural phenomena."

Revealing too much about the exhibits would spoil the experience for the visitor. The best way to discover it is to wander in knowing nothing at all.

"We don't know how to explain things. Generally we always try our best to answer questions that people might have," Wilson offers. "We are more interested to hear from people about what they think of their experience than for us to tell them what kind of experience they should be having."

One exhibit is of a spore-inhaling stink ant and features a leafy plant and vine inside a glass display case, with a petrified ant crawling up the plant's trunk. Pick up a phone next to this case and you'll hear an authoritative voice explain how this large ant of West Central Africa is sometimes "infected by inhaling a microscopic spore from a fungus of

One exhibit is of a spore-inhaling stink ant and features a leafy plant and vine inside a glass display case, with a petrified ant crawling up the plant's trunk.

THE MUSEUM OF JURASSIC TECHNOLOGY
TRANSCRIPT SERIES

THE STINK ANT

PURIFICATION BY SUBLIMATION

VOICE OF THE AMERICAN GREY FOX

published by the trustees

The Museum of Jurassic Technolo 9341 Venice Blvd., Culver City, CA

SUPPLEMENT TO A CHAIN OF FL

THE MUSEUM OF JURASSIC TECHNOLOGY
TRANSCRIPT SERIES

ON THE FOUNDATIONS OF THE MUSEUM

published by the trustees

The Museum of Jurassic Techno 9341 Venice Blvd., Culver City, C

SUPPLEMENT TO A CHAIN OF F

THE MUSEUM OF JURASSIC TECHNOLOGY
TRANSCRIPT SERIES

THE DELANI/SONNABEND HALLS:
MADELENA DELANI

A BIOGRAPHICAL NARRATIVE

published by the trustees

The Museum of Jurassic Technology 9341 Venice Blvd., Culver City, CA 90232

SUPPLEMENT TO A CHAIN OF FLOWERS

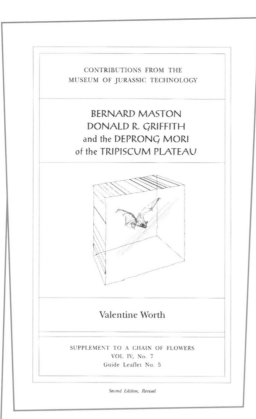

CONTRIBUTIONS FROM THE
MUSEUM OF JURASSIC TECHNOLOGY

BERNARD MASTON
DONALD R. GRIFFITH
and the DEPRONG MORI
of the TRIPISCUM PLATEAU

Valentine Worth

SUPPLEMENT TO A CHAIN OF FLOWERS
VOL. IV, No. 7
Guide Leaflet No. 5

Second Edition, Revised

"We have inhaled something that causes us to behave in aberrant ways and to do this whole crazy project, a museum where no one even comes close to making a living."

the genus *Tomentella*.

"After being inhaled, the spore seats in the ant's tiny brain and begins to grow, causing changes in the ant's patterns of behavior. The ant appears troubled and confused, and for the first time in its life the ant leaves the forest floor and begins to climb."

Driven onward by the spore's effects, the ant climbs until, exhausted, it dies.

"The stink ant is a good exhibit to talk about," Wilson says. "On the one hand, it's an interesting piece of biology that this ant would inhale this spore and become a servant to the fungus. That's an interesting piece of science.

"By further extension, there's a second and third level in that we ourselves at the museum feel as if we have inhaled a spore. We have inhaled something that causes us to behave in aberrant ways and to do this whole crazy project, a museum where no one even comes close to making a living."

Museum Highlights

The museum's interior is dark, and exhibits are lit by the occasional spotlight placed throughout the space. Some exhibits feature sound effects such as running water or opera music that can be heard as you wander about. What you'll also detect are comments from visitors that include: "I wonder if that's true," and "I haven't figured that one out yet." Laughter is also frequently audible.

The museum consists of rotating special exhibits and permanent displays such as an array of mounted horns, a detailed exploration of neurophysiologist Geoffrey Sonnabend's theory of memory and microminiature sculptures mounted on pinheads. One room contains a collection of letters written to the Mount Wilson Observatory from 1915–1935.

In 1996, the museum mounted a special exhibit called "Garden of Eden On Wheels." It consisted of collections from people living in trailer parks around Los Angeles. In odd-shaped cases visitors could view, for example, collections of unusual bottles, pin cushions, and one woman's

"Mice on Toast" exhibit, an unusual cure for bladder control problems ("Take two mice and call me in the morning")

handmade jewel trees. Interspersed with these cases were panels of photos of trailers along with pertinent writings about trailer living. As a final touch, the exhibit included several dioramas of small-scale trailers at night in secluded spots.

In another exhibit area, several examples of animal horns are placed along a wall. In the center of these is a peculiar, furry hard protrusion that looks like a long, bony finger covered with black hair. The accompanying text relates the story of a woman named Mary Davis who apparently grew a horn from the back of her head.

Unusual Treatment

In a rear exhibit area are several examples of folklore cures and displays that animate these cures in sometimes grotesque ways. For example, one alleged cure for loss of bladder control was the consumption of mice on a piece of toast. In a

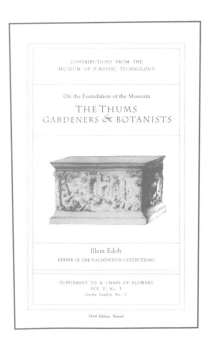

case you can see two dead mice laid neatly upon a piece of toast. Other cures are similarly represented.

One popular exhibit is the miniature sculptures of Hagop Sandaldjian. The Soviet-Armenian violinist and music teacher crafted minuscule portraits

Miniature Goofy perched on top of a pinhead, one of Hagop Sandaldjian's minuscule gems

of famous images on either a taut strand of hair or in the eye of long sewing needles. These works are displayed inside acrylic cylinders and include such images as Disney characters, Pope John Paul II and Napoleon.

You need to view them through a magnifying glass placed outside the display case. When you look directly at the sculpture without this aid, you can't really discern any image at all. It might be an elaborate hoax—but then again it might not.

The accompanying text relates the story of a woman named Mary Davis who apparently grew a horn from the back of her head.

Kam Wah Chung & Co. Museum

N.W. Canton Street
John Day, Oregon 97845

541-575-0028

9 A.M. to Noon,
1 P.M. to 5 P.M. Monday
through Thursday, 1 P.M. to
5 P.M. Saturday and
Sunday. Open from May 1
to the end of October.

$2 adults, $1.50 seniors
and $.50 children.

John Day is located
at the intersection of
Interstates 26 and
395. At the stop light,
head two blocks west
to Canton Street. The
museum is located one
block north in the city
park.

In the mid-19th century thousands of Chinese, facing harsh living conditions at home, were lured to the United States by the Gold Rush and the prospects of a better life. Most ended up enduring equally hard times in America building railroads, working in fisheries and performing menial labor at mining camps.

By the 1880s, Chinese following the Gold Rush trail were led to eastern Oregon. After a fire destroyed most of the Chinese community in a town called Canyon City, members experienced the persecution that was part of the Chinese experience on the western frontier: They were not allowed to rebuild.

They moved on instead to the tiny town of John Day, where gold beckoned, as well as a chance for a fresh start.

It was here that two Chinese immigrants purchased a wood and stone military trading post. It was an unlikely partnership between Ing "Doc" Hay and Lung On. Hay was an herbal healer and spiritual leader, while On was a businessman, gambler and ladies' man.

But what they created in Kam Wah Chung & Co., which opened in

Opium den

112

For those needing special comfort, there was an opium den in the back with smoking apparatus and four bunk beds...

1887, was more than just a general store and pharmacy. It became a religious and social center for the local Chinese community for the next several decades.

The store, whose name translates roughly as "desert flower" or "golden flower of prosperity," must have seemed like a cultural oasis for the local Chinese. Gathered in the cramped, dark confines of the store, immigrants could experience the sights and rituals of their homeland. For those needing special comfort, there was an opium den in the back with smoking apparatus and four bunk beds clustered together where they could escape into a hazy dreamland and then sleep it off.

Natural Preservation

The building was boarded up and closed in the late 1940s. After Hay's death in 1952, a nephew deeded the building to the city on condition that it be turned into a museum honoring the Chinese community.

City officials didn't even realize they owned the property until 1969, when they made a startling discovery upon opening the building. Because of the cold, dry climate and the building's stone exterior, the contents were

extraordinarily well preserved.

In 1975, with almost every item in place exactly as it was during its turn-of-the-century operation, the building was opened as a museum.

Researchers have praised the collection as the most vivid portrait of Chinese immigrant life in the American West of the late 19th century. Included are hundreds of herbal remedies stored in tins and bottles, canned goods, pre-Prohibition liquor bottles, religious shrines, Hay's bedroom furnishings and clothes, as well as the kitchen where he cooked up his healing compounds on a wood stove. The environment is so authentic that the wallpaper covering the back room is blackened with the opium smoke of several decades.

Doc Hay's bedroom

Hidden Signals

Hay diagnosed patients by reading their pulse. Museum curator Carolyn Micnhimer says that she's spoken to a few visitors who were children when Hay was still practicing and they vividly recall their visits to see him.

"He had a pillow on a table," Micnhimer says. "If you came to him for medical reasons you would put your hand on the pillow and he would take your pulse and tell you what was wrong. Then he would go back and get the herbs and boil it up. Everyone said that it smelled awful and tasted

as far away as Idaho and Nevada to offer his services.

On was also a notorious gambler, and the store often doubled as a gambling hall. In letters, Hay complained about his partner sometimes going on the road to buy needed supplies, only to return empty-handed after losing their money in a gambling debacle. Supplies did make it into the store, however, and many are on display today, often in unopened jars or other containers, exactly as they were at the turn of the century.

On was also a notorious gambler, and the store often doubled as a gambling hall.

The kitchen where Hay cooked up his herbal remedies

even worse. But after you drank it you did get better."

At first Hay saw only local Chinese patients. But other residents, sometimes out of desperation after their own doctor had failed, began coming to see him as well. His cures were offered to many sick people throughout the region.

Hay's partner, Lung On, also developed a regional reputation. He specialized in helping other Chinese deal with immigration problems, often acting as a mediator and translator as they dealt with the U.S. government about their resident status and other legal woes. On often traveled

From Gizzards to Cocoa

There are at least 500 herbal cures exhibited. About half have been analyzed and researched to determine how they were used. But no one is sure how Hay used the remainder as medicine.

The herbal cures include bear paws, rattlesnake, chicken gizzard, tiger's bone, turtle shell, deer antler, dried lizards, algae, pomegranate bark, and various animal gall bladders. These are all displayed in carefully labeled tins, bottles and boxes, just as Hay arranged them. Some of the supplies came from local residents,

The herbal cures include bear paws, rattlesnake, chicken gizzard, tiger's bone, turtle shell, deer antler, dried lizards, algae, pomegranate bark, and various animal gall bladders.

From baking powder to mousetraps, the store was well-stocked

When the building was first opened up, more than $23,000 in uncashed checks were found under Hay's bed.

who knew the items he needed, while others were imported from China.

If residents didn't believe in Hay's remedies, traditional medications were also available, including laxatives, liniments and aspirin. These are also on view.

Much of the store's general merchandise is also exhibited in its original packaging. Items include tobacco, coffee, baking powder, lard, syrups, mining equipment, and specialty goods such as canned marshmallows, peanut butter kisses and mousetraps.

In the back room you can see large brass tins that contained opium shipped to the United States when it was still legal to do so.

Daily Offerings

Several shrines located throughout the building were maintained daily by Hay, who would burn incense at them and leave offerings. Micnhimer says that fruit left by Hay at several of these shrines remains today where he placed it, although in a dried state after decades of lying at the altar. People who recall the store when it was open often mention the omnipresent aroma of incense.

Hay's bedroom is set up as if he's about to walk through the door and climb into bed. There is a nightstand, Chinese chest, iron bed, box alarm clock, wooden stool, and some of his clothing on display. When the building was first opened up, more than $23,000 in uncashed checks were found under Hay's bed, a strong indication of the operation's high volume of business.

Kam Wah Chung & Co. was one of the first buildings to add electricity in the area. Even so, it was a dark place and still is, Micnhimer says. There aren't many windows and when it's cold, she has to leave the front door shut.

"People often ask how I can stand being in there," she admits.

The cloistered, dark environment is a fitting symbol of an immigrant's excluded experience.

115

The Liberace Museum

1775 East Tropicana Avenue
Las Vegas, Nevada 89119

702-798-5595

10 A.M. to 5 A.M. Monday through Saturday, 1 P.M. to 5 P.M. Sunday.

$6.50 adults, $4.50 seniors, $3.50 students, $2 children under 12.

Two and one half miles east of Las Vegas Boulevard, at the corner of Tropicana and Spencer Boulevards.

If Wladziu Valentino Liberace had followed his father's wishes, he would have been an entertainer of a much different sort. As a boy he showed great promise as a classical pianist, debuting at the age of 14 as a soloist with the Chicago Symphony and later earning a scholarship to the Wisconsin College of Music.

But the young Liberace betrayed his classical education early on, much to his father's dismay. As a teenager he made the rounds playing popular tunes in speakeasies, ice cream parlors and movie theaters, billing himself as Walter Busterkeys.

By 1940, when he turned 21, he entered the New York City nightclub circuit and began to promote himself by his last name only. By then he was making a mockery of his early training, offering audiences shortened versions of classical pieces embellished with crowd-pleasing flourishes. Borrowing from a Hollywood movie about the life of Chopin, he began placing a candelabrum upon his custom-made piano when he performed, a touch that would become his trademark.

When it came to cars, jewelry, pianos and costumes, Liberace showed flamboyant tastes. To say that his fashion statements were excessive is an

Liberace had a dazzling stage presence

understatement. With rhinestone-studded coats, feathered capes and glittering jewels, Liberace dazzled his fans throughout his career, establishing himself as an entertainer like no other.

A Living Museum

Liberace owned 11 homes, and it was his desire to open one of them to the public as a museum, says his longtime publicist, Jamie James. In 1975, his Hollywood Hills mansion was opened to tourists who were brought to the location by a fleet of limousines. The estate's 11 dining rooms were set up to entertain, complete with crystal and silver service. Visitors could also gawk at his gold leaf bedspread and other extravagant household items.

"Liberace always said that he didn't feel that these possessions were his," James says. "He was just the caretaker so that someone else years from now could enjoy them. He wasn't possessive. He enjoyed sharing everything."

Neighborhood complaints forced the closure of the Hollywood museum after only a few months, and a search for a new location was soon underway.

Modest Beginning

In 1979, The Liberace Museum opened in a nondescript shopping center located a few blocks from the Las Vegas Strip, where Liberace performed several weeks a year during his career. It contained only a few items from Liberace's massive collection, including a couple of cars, some of his miniature pianos, and several of his costumes, which were exhibited on hangers in unremarkable fashion.

After Liberace died in 1987, the museum acquired the bulk of his prime possessions. Today, three major exhibit areas highlight his career, which included a syndicated television show, sold-out Carnegie Hall performances and several gold albums. Proceeds from the museum go to the Liberace Foundation for the Performing and Creative Arts, which provides scholarships to arts students around the country.

Knowing How to Make an Entrance

During his career, Liberace's performances began well before he took the stage. His mode of transportation was part of the show. He amassed a fleet of expensive and elaborately adorned vehicles that were designed to create a splashy entrance.

Included in this collection, and displayed in the Car Gallery, are a Rolls Royce covered with thousands of mirror tiles etched with galloping horses, and a 1934 Mercedes Excalibur coated with Austrian rhinestones. As a salute to the national Bicentennial in 1976, Liberace cruised to a show in a red, white and blue 1954 Rolls convertible that is also parked in the gallery. Other custom cars here are the Volks Royce, a Volkswagen built to look like a Rolls, and an English taxi cab made especially for Liberace.

Glittering Clothes

In the Costume Gallery visitors can ogle the most glamorously dressed mannequins in the universe, who model the most extravagant of Liberace's performance outfits.

The silver-headed mannequins seem impassive to their glittering clothes, but they are impressive, from the black diamond mink lined

"Liberace always said that he didn't feel that these possessions were his. He was just the caretaker so that someone else years from now could enjoy them."

Faceless mannequins display some of Liberace's most outrageous costumes

with more than 40,000 2.5 karat rhinestones, to the red, white and blue hot pants ensemble and feathered cape Liberace donned for a Radio City Music Hall performance.

Topping Himself

Liberace's showy wardrobe dates back to a Hollywood Bowl concert early in his career. Until then he had worn a black tuxedo when performing. For this concert, however, in order to set himself apart from the orchestra, he donned white tails and created a sensation.

From then on, says James, he sought to top himself with each new costume.

"He called all of his costumes an expensive joke," laughs James. "When he would come out with the black mink cape it would be closed. Then he would spin around and open it and the spotlights would hit the rhinestones and they would be flashing everywhere. The audiences loved it."

Each costume took about six months to make, from initial drawing and fabric selection, to the detailed hand-stitching required to complete the work. James says there is film footage of women sewing jewels on Liberace's outfits while wearing sunglasses to ward off the glare.

A King Neptune outfit covered in sea shells and pearls was designed for the 1984 World's Fair in New Orleans. It weighs 200 pounds and is the heaviest non-fur outfit in the collection.

"When he wore it he made it look so light," James marvels.

If you stare at these costumes and can't imagine someone putting them on, much less performing in them, there are pictures of Liberace draped in the jeweled outfits to make you a believer.

"He called all of his costumes an expensive joke."

Just a few of Liberace's elaborately adorned fleet of vehicles

Just Jewels

How do you accessorize a bejeweled cape and trousers? The answer is in the jewelry display cases that also appear in the wardrobe gallery.

Among the items are a candelabrum ring with platinum candlesticks and diamond flames, a piano-shaped watch with diamonds, rubies, sapphires and emeralds, and a piano-shaped ring with 260 diamonds and black jade keys.

Oh Yeah, Pianos Too

Visitors may be so overwhelmed by the car and costume galleries that they may forget the central element of Liberace's career —his piano playing. Of course, he wouldn't think of banging away on any instrument. He owned 39 pianos, all unique, and half of them are available for viewing in the museum. They are just as expensive as his other possessions.

There's a rhinestone-covered Baldwin that he used in his last Radio City Music Hall performance, and a con-cert grand piano covered with etched mirror tiles. Historical pianos include Chopin's French Pleyel, a Broadwood grand made in England in 1788, and a Chickering grand once owned by George Gershwin.

Chance to Regroup

The rest of the museum includes antiques that were part of Liberace's collection, including a monogrammed set of dinner plates that once belonged to President John Kennedy, and an inlaid desk that was used by Czar Nicholas II of Russia.

With a collection of this size, it's not surprising that one room can't hold it all. The exhibit areas are not directly connected, so visitors have to step into the parking lot to reach the other galleries.

After staring at so much opulence, the short walk between the showrooms is a welcome respite.

Liberace's pianos were equally grand in style

The National Cryptologic Museum

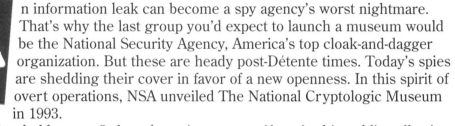

DIRNSA
Attn: S542
Ft. George Meade, Maryland
20755-6000

301-688-5848/9
Fax: 301-688-5847

http://www.nsa.gov:8080/

9 A.M. to 3 P.M. Monday
through Friday, 10 A.M. to
2 P.M. on Saturday. Other
times by appointment.

Free.

Take Route 295 or
Interstate 95 to Route
32. The museum is at
Fort Meade's Colony 7
Road, north of Route 32.

An information leak can become a spy agency's worst nightmare. That's why the last group you'd expect to launch a museum would be the National Security Agency, America's top cloak-and-dagger organization. But these are heady post-Détente times. Today's spies are shedding their cover in favor of a new openness. In this spirit of overt operations, NSA unveiled The National Cryptologic Museum in 1993.

It's a bold move. Only a short time ago, artifacts in this public collection were vital secrets that agents guarded with their lives. The exhibits in the museum focus upon a key element of secret activity: communicating in code. Visitors can gawk at giant encrypting computers made obsolete only a few years before the museum opened. Other machines date from World War II-era code-breaking activity. There is also one of the oldest secret code machines in existence, which may have even been used by Thomas Jefferson.

If the collection whets your appetite for more secret information, the museum offers a rare book collection which contains ancient texts on spy codes, some dating back to the 16th century.

The Cipher Wheel, an early encoding device possibly used by Thomas Jefferson

Secrecy Lingers

To be sure, there's a lingering reluctance on the part of NSA to step into the public spotlight. The museum isn't listed in the phone book. There's been no advertising, says curator Jack Ingram. There are road signs pointing to the museum, but they're partially obscured by weeds. The museum doesn't exactly beckon visitors. It's surrounded by a 10-foot chain-link fence topped with rows of barbed wire.

The museum doesn't exactly beckon visitors. It's surrounded by a 10-foot chain-link fence topped with rows of barbed wire.

NCM Curator Jack Ingram

The building showcasing the nation's spying secrets is a former motel, bought by NSA in 1989. The exhibits are set up in the motel's former dining area. NSA spent about $10,000 to open the museum, a tight budget that had its staff foraging for display cases. They secured these by repairing damaged ones tossed out by the Smithsonian Institution.

To its credit, NSA hasn't rushed to cover up after its initial wave of disclosure. The agency has a website where anyone worldwide can embark on a virtual tour of the museum. The website also offers access to declassified materials made available under NSA's new OPENDOOR policy. The available material is being made public as the result of an Executive Order in 1995 that ordered NSA to review for declassification all classified documents 25 years or older.

The web page, along with the museum, have proven to be popular, says Ingram.

"This was always a black, hidden world, the most secretive agency in the government. To have anything go public fascinates people," he points out. "People who work in intelligence never thought they'd see it in a museum. But a lot of World War II

veterans love it."

Ingram got a taste of these new open times when he recently played host to an unlikely visitor: the last general to run the Russian spy agency, the KGB. The former KGB chief now runs a security firm and called ahead to announce his visit.

"For me, I never thought I'd be in the same room with someone from the KGB," admits Ingram, who's been with NSA since 1963. "Did he like it? Are you kidding? He stayed much longer than he thought he would."

One of the items that stunned the general and his Russian escort was a World War II Soviet code machine that is probably the only one of its kind in existence. It was captured after the war.

The Russians also presented the museum with a significant artifact—a piece from the spy plane flown by Gary Powers that crashed in Russian territory at the height of the Cold War.

Ingram has no intention of returning the gesture and making a trip to the KGB museum in Moscow.

"I don't plan on going to Russia," he says emphatically.

Museum Highlights

The Cipher Wheel, believed to be the oldest coding device in the world, is a wooden wheel with rotating disks containing 42 characters. A bar on top contains a disk that lines up plain language to decode secret messages.

The first recorded reference to the wheel, by Francis Bacon, dates to 1605. Thomas Jefferson mentions it in his writings. The Cipher Wheel turned up in a West Virginia antique store in 1983, brought there by a woman who had found it in her attic when she was a little girl. No one knows how it got there.

"I never thought I'd be in the same room with someone from the KGB . . . Did he like it? Are you kidding?"

Left: A 1518 1st edition of one of the oldest known books on cryptology

Another exhibit, consisting of pictures and text, tells the story of the Black Chamber, also known as MI-8. This was a U.S. Army and State Department agency that broke the diplomatic codes of other countries, including Japan.

Decrypted messages intercepted by the Black Chamber were used by the U.S. Secretary of State, Charles Evans, to enhance his position in trade talks during the Washington Naval Conference of 1921–22. Evans knew before each meeting what the Japanese negotiating positions would be because of the information supplied by MI-8.

In 1929, the closing down of the Black Chamber so angered its director, Herbert Yardley, that he wrote a book exposing the agency's secrets. Needless to say, Japan quickly changed its diplomatic codes.

An example of a German Enigma Cipher machine

Among encoding machines on exhibit is the Sigaba, a World War II-era machine built and employed by American forces. It looks like an antique typewriter and has a system of levers and rotating wheels housed in a large metal box extending behind the keyboard. Called the "Big Machine" by the Germans, it produced the only coding system not broken during the war.

The Enigma also looks like a typewriter and was Germany's main coding machine during World War II. Its codes were broken by the Allied machine called the Bombe, also on display here. Visitors are allowed to encode their own message on the Enigma.

The Harvest machine looks like a giant reel-to-reel tape recorder and was produced by a joint venture between NSA and IBM. Many modern computers owe their development to these types of research projects involving the spy agency and private computer firms.

This high-level cipher machine, used by the U.S. Government in WWII, produced a code that was never broken by the Axis powers

Beware Russian Children Bearing Gifts

In 1946, a group of Russian school kids offered what seemed like a friendly gesture when they gave American U.N. Ambassador Averell Harriman a wooden replica of the Great Seal of the United States. He hung it in his office and it stayed there until the 1960s. Then, a security check revealed that the seal contained a secret listening device. The museum offers an exhibit that includes a replica of the seal with the hidden microphone.

Are You Spy Material?

The museum hands out puzzle books to visitors. Here's a brain teaser included in that book which tests your ability to solve logic problems, a skill closely tied to that of breaking codes.

Carol's ideal man is tall, dark and handsome. She dates Fred, George, Hank and Joe. One of them is her ideal.

A. Each of the four has at least one desired trait.

B. Fred and George have the same complexion.

C. George and Hank are the same height.

D. Hank and Joe are not both tall.

E. Only three of the men are tall, only two are dark, only one is handsome.

Who is Carol's ideal man?

A. If George and Hank are the same height, they must be tall. Then Joe is short and the third tall man is Fred. Joe must be dark or handsome or both. Suppose that Joe were handsome, he would be the only handsome man. Joe can't be the ideal man because he is short, so someone else is handsome. Joe is dark, and one other man is dark. Then Fred and George have the same complexion (fair). So only Hank is dark and tall. Hank must also be handsome and the ideal man.

Left: This U.S. Cryptoanalytic "BOMBE" machine was used in WWII to break Enigma key settings

Carol's ideal man is tall, dark and handsome.

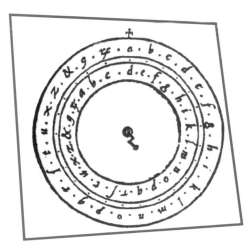

Silvestri's cipher wheel

The U.S. Border Patrol Museum

4315 Transmountain Road
El Paso, Texas 79924

915-759-6060
Fax: 915-759-0992

9 A.M. to 5 P.M. Tuesday
through Sunday.

Free.

Turn off Highway 54
South to Loop 375
(Transmountain Road)
heading west. Take the
first right into the
museum.

I f you visit the Ellis Island National Monument, you learn about the historic stream of legal immigration into the United States from the late 19th century to the present.

The flip side of that story, of course, is the flood of illegal immigration during this same period, a topic that has been the source of much political and social debate. The issues surrounding immigration aren't hashed over at The U.S. Border Patrol Museum. Rather, exhibits are designed to show one part of that story: the job performed by agents who guard our nation's borders.

As the introductory text to the museum explains, an organized patrol intended to monitor illegal entry into the country was established as early as 1904. However, it was a somewhat ragtag bunch that wasn't properly funded or trained to handle the overwhelming number of people crashing the borders. The need for a more effective patrol became evident as the federal government sought to enforce new closed-door policies designed to restrict immigration, laws that came into vogue at the turn of the century.

In 1924, more than $1 million was provided for a land-border patrol within the Bureau of Immigration, and the modern Border Patrol was launched.

In 1995, the Border Patrol arrested 1.3 million people making illegal crossings into the United States.

Right: Historic photo of an early border patrol

Tremendous Responsibility

Today the U.S. Border Patrol monitors more than 8,000 miles of international boundaries. Agents keep watch from the air, at sea, in cars, on horseback and even on foot. The Border Patrol's duties include the investigation of drug trafficking and other smuggling, as well as tracking organized crime activities and violent, foreign criminals seeking entry into the United States.

"There are a lot of people who know that there is a Border Patrol, but they don't know a lot about it. We can give them an education," explains museum curator Michael Kirkwood. "The Border Patrol isn't just sitting around waiting for someone to cross the border. They do a lot more."

In 1995, the Border Patrol arrested 1.3 million people making illegal crossings into the United States. Agents believe that for every three people they catch, five to seven others get through.

Transportation Exhibits Dominate

Kirkwood has been curator since the privately funded museum was opened in 1992 by retired agents who wanted to pay tribute to the patrol. It was originally housed in the basement of an existing building, but the space was too small so money was raised to build a freestanding museum. The new windowless structure is located on the eastern slopes of the Franklin Mountains in an area that is one of the hot spots of illegal immigration.

The museum is still in an initial stage of collecting. Early attention has been focused upon the different ways agents get around when monitoring an area and moving in to make arrests.

An OH-6 helicopter on display was originally built for use during the Vietnam War and was later flown by border agents during surveillance missions until 1989. A neighboring Piper Super Cub plane was built in 1969 and used in the Tucson area. Visitors can get up close to both of these crafts and peer inside.

Also featured is a 1988 Firebird, one of three cars used for the "Roadrunner Project," which brought to the patrol a fleet of rocket-fast cars for high-speed road pursuits. The idea was to use cars that were so fast that vehicle chases would end quickly, Kirkwood says.

"If you can shorten the time of the pursuit then everybody is better off," he points out.

Vessels of Desperation

More poignant are the transportation artifacts on display that were used by illegal immigrants trying to get into the country. There are two crude boats that reveal the ingenuity, determination and, most likely, desperation of

Tie Tack
Blue logo on gold 1/2" $5.00 #225

"I Love My Federal Agent"
Brass key tag for spouses
$500   #228

3" Brass Key Tag
Badge $5.00   #230

the people who used them.

The first vessel is made of two truck hoods welded together. It was used for several years to ferry passengers across the Rio Grande until agents finally captured it and arrested the people who were using it to transport people at $500 a head.

A more intricate handmade vessel is a raft used by Cubans to reach Florida in June, 1994. The boat's flotation device consists of tire tubes sliced in half and placed under a metal floor. In between another sheet of metal there is a layer of Styrofoam to add buoyancy. A piece of blue canvas was mounted in the front to prevent the ocean spray from splashing in the boat. It has a Russian outboard motor and paddles made of

metal piping with pieces of wood attached at the end.

As primitive as this boat sounds, Kirkwood says that it was better developed than many of the other crafts used by people to make that same crossing from Cuba. Even so, when the boat landed everyone was arrested.

Other Museum Highlights

Another display features weapons issued to border agents through the years to do their job, including a variety of pistols, rifles, and shotguns. There are mannequins outfitted in historic Border Patrol uniforms, including examples of one worn in 1924. This army-green outfit features a "Smoky the Bear" wide-brimmed hat that gives the agent the look of a Canadian Mounted Policeman.

One of the oldest objects in the museum is a historic marker that was originally placed along the Texas border in 1896. It's marker number four and looks like a stone obelisk.

If you want to get an overview of the immigration problem along the California border, there is a 25-foot relief map that shows the border and includes red lights that represent the sites of the most frequent crossings. There are also many photographs placed around the museum that highlight the history and development of the patrol.

More poignant are the transportation artifacts on display that were used by illegal immigrants trying to get into the country.

Left: The museum catalog offers unique gift items

Below: This crude craft was used to ferry illegal immigrants into the U.S.

The Martin and Osa Johnson Safari Museum

111 N. Lincoln Ave.
Chanute, KS 66720

316-431-2730

10 A.M. to 5 P.M.
Monday through Saturday,
1 P.M. to 5 P.M. Sunday.

$2.50 adults,
$1 students,
free for children
12 and under.

From U.S. Route 169
take State Route 39 to
the Cherry Street exit
and go east to Santa
Fe. Turn right onto the
overpass and museum
will be on the right at
next light.

When Osa met Martin, it was hardly love at first sight. The year was 1909, and Martin Johnson, 25, had just returned from a year of traveling with adventure writer Jack London aboard his ship, *The Snark*. Johnson had organized a show about his experiences as a crew member on the voyage and was traveling to midwestern towns to present it.

Osa Johnson (pictured) and her husband Martin pioneered the Safari film genre

He stopped in Chanute, Kansas, where teenager Osa Leighty walked in and promptly walked out, disgusted by scenes of barely-clothed South Seas tribesmen prancing about. Mutual friends arranged a date between

Martin and Osa Johnson with chimps

Leighty and Johnson, however, and this time sparks flew. A few months later the couple married. For the next three decades they lived a life of romantic adventure worthy of a Jack London novel.

The couple made dozens of journeys to the South Pacific and Africa, destinations unknown to most Americans and considered to be mysterious and exotic. The Johnsons produced more than a dozen film documentaries about their travels, which not only thrilled audiences back home, but also pioneered the wildlife genre of filmmaking.

In addition, they shot thousands of photographs of native tribes, their rituals, and the surrounding environment and wildlife, perfecting many techniques in this field as well. They wrote hundreds of magazine articles and more than a dozen books, providing Americans with a window to foreign cultures that at the time were little understood. Their life story is told in the biography *They Married Adventure* (Rutgers University Press) by Pascal and Eleanor Imperato. The museum, which opened in 1961, was dedicated by Osa's hometown as a tribute to the couple. Visitors can see their many films and photos, as well as study artifacts from their journeys.

Expanding Collection

The museum has grown considerably since it first opened and has broadened its focus to include other collections of African cultural items and arts, such as ceremonial masks. One new wing showcases wildlife art from around the world.

Osa Johnson and friends

For the researcher, a library with more than 10,000 books covering topics such as natural history and travel is also open to the public.

A Perspective of Their Work

The Johnsons were more than just innovative filmmakers and photographers. They were also savvy when it came to using publicity to generate funds to pay for their travels.

When they first began, the Johnsons hooked up with the vaudeville circuit, presenting stories of their travels in a unique way. They showed slides and told occasionally embellished tales of danger and adventure, while Osa danced in a grass skirt and sang Hawaiian songs. They would perform on the same bill with entertainers such as Houdini and W.C. Fields, says museum director Conrad Froehlich.

"Osa would dress up in a leather skirt with a fringe on it," he says. "It really didn't look like what you would think of as Hawaiian, but I think people back then didn't know any different. This was something exotic. She sang Hawaiian songs, but that didn't last long."

You can decide for yourself how realistic the skirt is, since it's displayed at the museum.

As they progressed in their careers, the Johnsons' public presentations became more polished. In fact, major movie studios handled the distribution of their travel films. Posters for one of their early films, *Simba*, lured audiences with teasers such as "A drama of desperate realities picturing indisputably wild beasts of jungle and veldt," and "Naked men against fangs and claws!"

"It's easy today to flip on the television and see a lot of exceptionally done wildlife programs. But before television these films were the way that people found out about the world," explains Froehlich.

Wildlife Celebrities

A major attraction of these films was Osa herself, who nabbed considerable screen time as the films not

"Naked men against fangs and claws!"

The Johnsons traveled to many exotic locales

Taking a break from a day of hunting

only documented native people and the surrounding wildlife, but the Johnsons' own travel methods as well.

"Osa was the attractive girl-next-door figure from middle America," says Froehlich. "It was kind of a 'beauty and the beast' type of thing to see this pretty girl next to a South Seas headhunter or next to these wild animals. She looked so neat dressed up in her safari outfits. They really inspired a lot of people to want to go to Africa."

Dreamy Figures

The filmmakers at work

A main focal point of the museum are the life-size sculptures of Martin and Osa depicted in a safari setting, including a tent and other camping equipment. Osa was the one who organized their safaris, which sometimes included more than 100 native guides and helpers. She was also a deadeye with a rifle and often provided cover for Martin while he approached dangerous jungle animals with his camera.

In the full-scale diorama, Martin is pointing his camera at Osa. She stands by the tent and gear, which includes a folding chair, luggage and camera equipment.

"We didn't want it to be super-realistic," admits Froehlich. "We went to flea markets and bought stuff that could have been used in a safari. Then everything was covered with a white paint and glue mixture to give it a dreamy look."

Other artifacts on display are real, however, ranging from Martin's christening gown and cigar holder to Osa's fishing hat. There are also stock certificates that were issued to investors who backed their journeys. These backers would be paid out of

Respresentation of two natives the Johnsons encountered

1937, the Johnsons were aboard a flight to Burbank, California from Salt Lake City when the plane crashed into the San Gabriel Mountains. Osa survived, but Martin, who had spent decades in dangerous travel around the world, died the following day, the victim of a commercial plane crash.

Osa survived, but Martin, who had spent decades in dangerous travel around the world, died the following day, the victim of a commercial plane crash.

profits from the sale of the Johnsons' movies, photos and books.

Safari Theater

The museum has a 30-seat theater where visitors can screen any of the Johnsons' films, which have been transferred to video. These films contain many images of wildlife areas that no longer exist.

From 1933 to 1935, the Johnsons piloted two Sikorsky planes and shot aerial footage over Africa and Borneo, logging more than 60,000 miles in the air. This aerial footage made up what proved to be their final film. In

Natives help Martin Johnson fill up the gas tank

The Johnsons in the center of an African village

The Shrine to Music Museum

The University of South Dakota
414 East Clark Street
Vermillion, South Dakota 57069-2390

605-677-5306

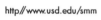

http//www.usd.edu/smm

9 A.M. to 4:30 P.M.
Monday through Friday,
10 A.M. to 4:30 P.M.
Saturday and 2 P.M. to
4:30 P.M. Sunday.

Free.

From Sioux Falls, take
Interstate 29 south to
Highway 50. Travel
west on Highway 50
for about five miles
and look for signs. The
museum is located on
the university campus
at the intersection of
Clark and Yale streets.

In the 1930s, Arne Larson, a public school music instructor in South Dakota, began collecting instruments made obsolete by the development of newer ones tuned to more modern pitch standards.

He'd read about these antique instruments and wondered what they sounded like, so he found a few of them, fixed them up, and began playing them. Larson's collection soon expanded when he developed international contacts who sent him instruments from Europe, Asia and Africa.

After World War II, when food rationing continued in England, Larson mailed tea and Spam to hungry Britons in exchange for instruments he needed to broaden his collection. He discovered a simple joy in playing these outdated instruments, and he questioned whether the music produced by more modern instruments was an improvement.

"When he grew up after the turn of the century, there was the feeling that everything would get better and better," says Larson's son, Andre. "Well, he was not so sure. Changes made to instruments meant that we lost a lot of different sounds that we used to have with old instruments."

Those lost tones were revived by Larson. He developed a touring program where he would demonstrate several dozen antique instruments. When not in use, they were stored at home.

"It was a big house, but there were rooms that you couldn't walk into because of all the instruments," recalls Andre Larson.

19th century Burmese zither in the shape of a crocodile

Beautiful Sights and Sounds

In 1979, Larson donated 2,500 instruments to the University of South Dakota, where they formed the basis for the school's Shrine to Music Museum. The collection has greatly expanded since then and now totals more than 6,000 instruments dating from the 16th century to the present. It is the only institution in the United States devoted entirely to the collection of musical instruments. From all regions of the world, these instruments are compelling not only for the sounds they produce, but for their stunning beauty as well.

Andre Larson, now the museum's director, says that instruments made before mass production in the 20th century were valued as much for their craftsmanship as for the music they produced. "All the way up to World War I, even things like band instruments were beautifully engraved," Larson points out. "They used to put mottoes on harpsichords that said, 'Pleasing to the ear and the eye.' It's only in the 20th century that instruments have become utilitarian objects."

From Tiny to Exotic

Exhibits range from the tiniest of harmonicas to a colossal organ built in Pennsylvania in 1808 that stands almost 12 feet high. Exotic instruments include an arched harp from Burma with silk strings that is richly decorated with gilt and mica, and a Burmese zither carved in the shape of a crocodile.

Also featured are violins made in Italy in the 16th century, including models designed by Andrea Amati, whose shop is credited with developing the shape of the modern violin.

Among contemporary instruments on display is the 1993 limited edition Presidential Model tenor saxophone built by the L.A. Sax company of Illinois. It was donated by President Bill Clinton and features a red, white and blue body with stars on the curved end section.

Other recent acquisitions are nine-foot-tall slit drums from the South Pacific and a two-headed carved harp, most likely made in the Belgian Congo in 1910. The instrument's full-figured female torso serves as the harp's neck.

Visitors are fascinated by instruments from Tibet, Larson says, because some are made of human parts. There is a clarinet, for example, made from a hollow leg bone and there are drums made with human skulls. The skulls are placed back to back and cat skin is drawn tautly across the skulls to create the surface of the drum. Larson asserts that there's nothing morbid about this tradition. It's based on a tribal belief that ancestral voices are preserved

Right: Donnu (detail), by Mangbetu people, Belgian Congo (now Zaire), circa 1910–1920

Visitors are fascinated by instruments from Tibet, because some are made of human parts.

Exhibits range from the tiniest of harmonicas to a colossal organ built in Pennsylvania in 1808 that stands almost 12 feet high.

Shofar, Poland, 17th–18th century. A mystic, Kabalistic text is carved on both sides

by turning human parts into instruments.

In a gallery dedicated to the musical age of Louis the XIV, there are decorative harpsichords from many European countries. Each region was known for adding its particular decorative flourish to these instruments.

"You can tell where they are from by the way they are decorated," Larson says. Flemish harpsichords were made with wallpaper pasted on the inside, for example, while English ones were constructed mostly of mahogany woods. The Italians preferred ivory while the French were renowned for painting soundboards with images of birds, flying animals and flowers.

Eerie Sounds

One of the more unusual instruments in the collection is the theremin, considered to be the first synthesizer. The museum's theremin was produced in the 1930s. When it was introduced, the theremin was likened to black magic because it was played by hands moving through an electromagnetic field produced by two antennae projecting from the instrument's box. It sounded at times like a cello or a bassoon, but in the upper ranges was compared to the sound of a person humming.

Some composers were intrigued enough by the theremin to write music for it, and it proved an effective instrument in producing eerie soundtracks for suspense and horror movies, such as Alfred Hitchcock's *Spellbound.* Recently, Larson says, there is renewed interest in the instrument and musicians are learning to play it.

Obsolete Saxes

While many brass and woodwind instruments used today seem well-established, many were not set in their designs until the late 19th century. Some, such as the saxophone, were not even invented until then. Early versions of these instruments no longer made but on display here include a set of saxophones by the C.G. Conn company of Elkhart, Indiana. The museum has a Conn-O-Sax in F made by the company in 1920. It features a round bell on the lower end and an Art Deco engraving of a woman with long wavy hair and bare shoulders. Although music historians said that the instrument performed and played well, it wasn't a hit and was quickly discontinued. The museum's sax, in mint condition, is one of the last of its kind.

Left: Conn-O-Sax in F, circa 1929

This 19th century African arched harp features an ivory neck and pegs

Portuguese grand piano, 1767, one of the earliest, best-preserved pianos known to survive

Seen and Heard

While most of the instruments here are strictly preserved and no longer played, some are dusted off for regular concerts. These instruments are housed in the "Golden Age of Bands" section, which exhibits a variety of horns and woodwinds. You can also view a unique "Raincatcher" Sousaphone built around the turn of the century. It features a bell that points upward, hence its name. This section also displays a number of harmonicas, including miniature and decorative examples, and one shaped like a concert piano.

Museum concerts featuring these instruments provide a unique opportunity to hear sounds long forgotten. The performances are an appropriate event for the museum because they hark back to the museum's roots and to Arne Larson's touring shows of the 1930s.

While most of the instruments here are strictly preserved and no longer played, some are dusted off for regular concerts.

Disc Music Box, circa 1900.
Still plays for a nickel!

House organ, Switzerland, circa 1786

Tragedy in U.S. History Museum

7 Williams Street
St. Augustine, Florida 32084

904-825-2389

9 A.M. to 5 P.M. every day.

$3.50 adults,
$3 seniors,
$1 children under 11.

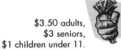

Take the U.S. 1 about 35 miles south of Jacksonville to St. Augustine. The museum is just down the street from the Fountain of Youth.

As the oldest city in the United States, St. Augustine is a natural tourist mecca. Attractions include 18th century homes, churches and a jail, as well as the Fountain of Youth Archeological Park, the site of Ponce de Leon's landing on April 3, 1513.

In addition to these historic centers, the city is home to a number of more exotic institutions. These include the Alligator Farm, where you can view a giant crocodile from New Guinea, and Zorayda Castle, a replica of a Moorish palace that exhibits a mummy's foot and an Egyptian rug woven from the hair of prehistoric cats. And of course there's Ripley's Believe it or Not! Museum, where you'll find a two-headed calf and a pinhead used as a canvas for an oil painting.

The car Lee Harvey Oswald drove to the assassination

Clearly, when it comes to museums in St. Augustine, anything goes. This was true, at least, until Buddy Hough came along with the Tragedy in U.S. History Museum.

Hough's plans for a museum were launched within hours of the assassination of President John F. Kennedy. Hough heard the news as he drank coffee in the office of his gas distributorship business. Right away, he recognized the event as a tragedy, and one of obvious historical significance.

140

In the months following the assassination, Hough made several trips to Dallas to buy artifacts related to Kennedy's death.

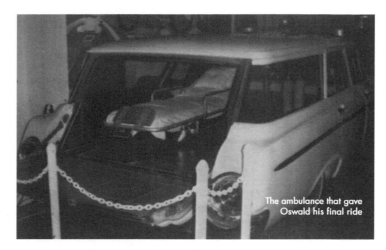

The ambulance that gave Oswald his final ride

In the months following the assassination, Hough made several trips to Dallas to buy artifacts related to Kennedy's death. His purchases included the ambulance that drove the fatally wounded Lee Harvey Oswald to the hospital, as well as the car Oswald drove to the assassination.

Hough's interests spread to other tragedies. He bought cars allegedly involved in the deaths of Jayne Mansfield and Bonnie and Clyde. He acquired rusted, antique torture devices, a train whistle from a disastrous 1903 rail wreck, and a copy of Elvis Presley's will.

By 1965, Hough had so many historical items stored at his wood frame house that he decided to open a museum. To round out the collection, he displayed items not necessarily tragic, but of historical merit, including vintage tools, antique furniture and a miniature steam engine.

The day before the museum was to open, the St. Augustine City Council revoked Hough's operating permit after an emergency hearing, declaring that the museum was not related to local history. Hough opened his doors anyway—and was promptly

Bonnie and Clyde took time off from robbing banks to pose for these portraits

arrested. And so began a four-year legal battle that cost him $60,000 before he ultimately prevailed in Florida's Supreme Court.

Hough was prone to calling civic leaders opposed to his museum "a bunch of sore-heads." He suspected that their main objection was that they considered his museum to be in bad taste and not a bona fide institution.

Hough kept a leather scrap-book documenting his battles with city officials. Some of the clippings detailing this conflict are framed and displayed on the wall of the museum, an example of yet another tragedy in U.S. history.

Hough always maintained that by opening the museum he was just satisfying people's curiosity. He was also offering a bit of history. Instead of turning away from adversity, he believed, we need to confront it and learn from bad times.

Tragedy, he was fond of saying, is what makes America great.

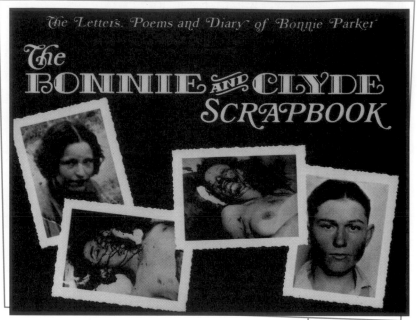

The Letters, Poems and Diary of Bonnie Parker

The BONNIE AND CLYDE SCRAPBOOK

An Uphill Battle

Hough wanted to make the museum a success in his lifetime, but there were further obstacles. It was years before the Chamber of Commerce included his museum on its free tourist maps. The local tourist trolley shuttles visitors to nearby attractions such as the Old Jail and the Fountain of Youth, but it's never turned into Hough's driveway.

Tragedy, he was fond of saying, is what makes America great.

And tragic, too

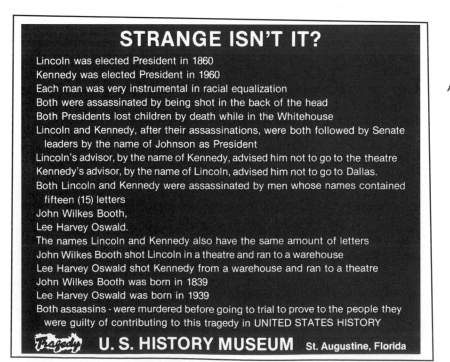

STRANGE ISN'T IT?

Lincoln was elected President in 1860
Kennedy was elected President in 1960
Each man was very instrumental in racial equalization
Both were assassinated by being shot in the back of the head
Both Presidents lost children by death while in the Whitehouse
Lincoln and Kennedy, after their assassinations, were both followed by Senate leaders by the name of Johnson as President
Lincoln's advisor, by the name of Kennedy, advised him not to go to the theatre
Kennedy's advisor, by the name of Lincoln, advised him not to go to Dallas
Both Lincoln and Kennedy were assassinated by men whose names contained fifteen (15) letters
John Wilkes Booth,
Lee Harvey Oswald.
The names Lincoln and Kennedy also have the same amount of letters
John Wilkes Booth shot Lincoln in a theatre and ran to a warehouse
Lee Harvey Oswald shot Kennedy from a warehouse and ran to a theatre
John Wilkes Booth was born in 1839
Lee Harvey Oswald was born in 1939
Both assassins - were murdered before going to trial to prove to the people they were guilty of contributing to this tragedy in UNITED STATES HISTORY

Tragedy **U. S. HISTORY MUSEUM** St. Augustine, Florida

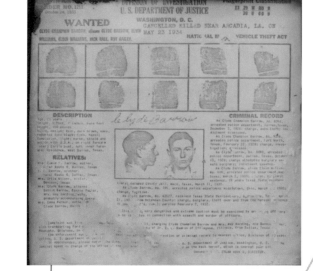

Clyde Barrow's wanted poster

This was my husband's dream.

Buddy Hough's four-year battle to open his museum went all the way to the Florida Supreme Court

The long legal fight ate up Hough's budget. He couldn't even afford to run the air conditioning. News reporters who stopped by invariably described the musty, stale air that hung about the exhibit rooms. Hough couldn't hire staff members, so he ran the museum with his wife, Debra. Sometimes, she'd emerge from the kitchen in a robe to admit visitors.

Hough died in March, 1996, never seeing the museum achieve the acclaim he thought it deserved. His wife has vowed to keep the museum open.

"This was my husband's dream," Debra Hough says. "I'd like to keep it going. People who come in are so enthusiastic about different things and so appreciative, that it makes me feel good.

"I don't push anybody who wants to come in. People ask me at the front, 'Will I like it?' I say, 'Well, you've read the brochure. You know what's here. If it's something that you think you'd like, come in.'"

Museum Highlights

Visitors are beckoned from the road by massive signs, such as one that reads: "See Jayne Mansfield's death car. Learn the truth."

You don't even have to go inside to see one exhibit. In a picture window above the garage, there is a mannequin of Oswald, rifle in hand, taking aim at his target.

Inside, the main attractions are several historic cars that Hough purchased, among them the ambulance that transported Oswald to the

Hough wrote Oswald's widow a letter asking for her assistance in putting together the exhibit. She wrote back saying that she didn't want to be associated in any way with the museum. Not fazed by the rejection, Hough framed the letter and made it part of the exhibit.

Death Cars

There are two other notable death cars in the museum. One is the gray 1966 Buick Electra 225 in which screen star Jayne Mansfield was riding when it crashed (she was decapitated by the back of a semitrailer). This exhibit includes a poster-sized, framed version of the police report detailing her beheading.

The bullet-riddled 1934 Ford that Bonnie and Clyde were driving when they were ambushed and killed is also here. Actually, at least five other people claim to have this car. The car displayed here could possibly be the vehicle used in a movie about Bonnie and Clyde.

The car is accompanied with a bloody morgue photo of Bonnie and a letter from Clyde to Henry Ford company that reads: "While I still got breath in my lungs, I will tell you what a dandy car you make. I have drove Fords exclusively when I could get away with one."

hospital after he was shot. It includes a gurney with a crumpled white sheet, and a framed picture of Red Yager, the driver. Behind the ambulance is a mural of Parkland Memorial Hospital.

You can also view the 1953 Chevy that Oswald borrowed from a friend to drive himself to the Book Depository. Hough always considered this one of his most important items. Without it, he claimed, Oswald could not have arrived at the assassination site.

Behind glass is the furniture from the Dallas room where Oswald stayed before the assassination. It includes a bed, bureau, and a framed painting of Kennedy. There's a letter of authenticity from Mary Bledsoe, owner of the boarding house, who sold the items to Hough.

"I believe he planned the assassination in this room, on this very furniture," the letter says. As part of the sale price for the furnishings, Hough had to repair Bledsoe's porch.

There are also enlarged photographs from the Zapruder film of the assassination, and yellowing newspaper headlines of the event.

INSIDE
TRAGEDY IN U.S. HISTORY MUSEUM
7 Williams St., St. Augustine, FL

YOU WILL SEE:

* President Kennedy's Car * The Ambulance used to carry Lee Harvey Oswald to his death * The Car Oswald used to transport the murder weapon to the Texas Book Depository * Lee Harvey Oswald's Bedroom Furniture as it was in Dallas * Bonnie and Clyde's bullet riddled get-away Car * The Car Jayne Mansfield (famous movie star) lost her life in * The Whistle, Speed Recorder and the Dead Engineer's Watch from the "Wreck of Old 97" and how the famous song was inspired * Original Human Bill of Sale * Antique Horse-drawn Wagon * Civil War Wagon * Old Spanish Jail built in 1718 with Human Skeletons Inside * Little Toot - Live Steam Engine built in 1875 * See and read Elvis Presley's Last Will and Testament * See the Horses on Parade with their Antique Farming Equipment * See the names of all the 58,000 brave men and women that lost their lives in Vietnam * Antique Hall with Shackles, Knives, Indian Treasures, Antique Gun Collection and much more * Old Blacksmith Shop * Antique Torture Equipment - Headstock, Neckbreaker and Whipping Post * Read of the Flagler Tragedy * Things of Yesteryears - Beartraps, Saddles, Whiskey Still and Working Tools * One of the Oldest Gasoline and Diesel Engines in existence * Documents and Statements pertaining to the Assassination * The Famous Zapruder film showing each bullet as it struck the President * The fight between "Hoss" Manucy and Martin Luther King in St. Augustine. Read the letters from all over the world pertaining to this conflict * Read of the opposition the City of St. Augustine has given this museum, over 20 years.

THIS IS THE MUSEUM THAT WAS ON NATIONAL T.V.
DON'T MISS SEEING IT!

Spinning Top Exploratory Museum

533 Milwaukee Avenue
Burlington, Wisconsin 53105

414-763-3946

By appointment only.

$5.

From Milwaukee, take Highway 36 south for about 30 miles. In downtown Burlington, the museum will be on the right hand side.

J udith Schulz remembers the first three spinning tops she ever bought. And she recalls the last two as well.

It's the 5,000 or so in between she's a little fuzzy about. But you can't blame her. Her collection spans two centuries and includes gyrating toys from all over the world.

Everything began to spin out of control for Schulz in the mid-1970s.

That's when she paid a nostalgic visit to an old dime store in Racine County, Wisconsin, where she had often shopped as a little girl. As she stepped over the creaking wooden floor, she spotted three snake tops—spinning toys with magnets that cause a toy snake placed under them to move as they twirl.

"They were hysterical" she recalls. Thinking they might make fun gifts, she bought them and took them home. People noticed.

"They would say, 'Oh, you collect tops,'" Schulz says. "They said that because there were three tops. I guess that's the magic number."

So she became a collector. The hobby fit in nicely with her love of toys and her role as director of an educational resource center. Kids discovered that playing with the tops—and creating their own—was good fun. And if

Press Lever Top set, a Louis Marx toy

146

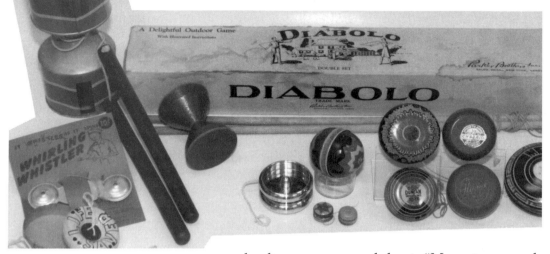

Schulz could slip in a little education on the side, using the tops to explain math, science

smiles—kids, or the parents who brought them here.

Schulz says that these group tours

The museum began with only two display cases. Now it's moved to a larger location where dozens of displays showcase up to 2,000 of Schulz's spinning tops on a rotating basis.

and culture, so much the better.

By 1987, her collection of tops was substantial. The staff at the resource center wanted to mount an exhibit for Burlington's annual chocolate festival, so they turned to Schulz and her tops. The display of antique and modern tops, along with demonstrations and the opportunity to play with a variety of different spinning toys, were major attractions for kids as well as adults. The response was so favorable that Schulz was compelled to open a permanent museum.

The museum began with only two display cases. Now it's moved to a larger location where dozens of displays showcase up to 2,000 of Schulz's spinning tops on a rotating basis. In addition, there are tables in the middle of the museum where visitors can experiment with dozens of tops.

You must make reservations to visit. Ever the educator, Schulz turns the museum into a classroom, leading tours herself on scheduled days. The visit begins with an introductory video on the history of the top. Then Schulz demonstrates how to use different varieties of twirling toys. Visitors are then invited to wander about and enjoy them on their own. At this point it's hard to tell who has bigger

work best. "My pet peeve about many museums is that there isn't anyone around who can answer questions and give you more details about the exhibits," she explains.

Museum Highlights

Schulz's collection includes tops, gyroscopes, yo-yos, dreidels, and even bubble blowers. Yo-yos, she says, are included because they are a type of "return top." There are several on display from the early days of the yo-yo in the 1930s and 1940s that include the term "return top" on their packaging.

Although they can be enjoyed by themselves, tops are also used as focal points of games. One of the oldest top games is called Put-N-Take. It's from 1790 and uses a four-sided top with letters on each side. Players

HUMMING TOP

acquire or give away tokens according to which side the top lands on.

The museum has several examples of box games that utilize spinning tops. One game is a kind of gladiator competition for tops, and calls for players to spin their pieces in a contained board area in an attempt to knock over an opponent's piece. The object is to have the last top still spinning.

A horse racing game using a top may not conjure up the thrill of a real racetrack, but it still manages to provide a great deal of amusement. A top with the names of famous race horses on its many sides is spun, and a player's horse advances along the track if his horse's name comes up. The same concept is used for a baseball game where players "bat" by spinning a top and having it land on different sides, awarding them either hits or outs.

One of the newest acquisitions at the museum is a Malaysian, five-pound top that has a metal rim and center along with an ornate cap. It requires an 11-foot rope to spin. Used in ceremonial contests, this gigantic top can spin for several days.

In fact, games featuring tops are common to many countries, which leads Schulz to make a social observation tied to spinning toys.

"These are used in so many cultures, cultures that you would think wouldn't have anything in common," she offers. "Which shows how we're all pretty much the same."

Aside from its role as a popular toy, tops are also a favorite marketing device. The museum exhibits many examples of so-called "spinning ads," including several for shoe companies and familiar American products such as Coca-Cola and Cracker Jack.

The Spin Doctor

Spinning a top seems like a simple proposition, but there are so many techniques and specialty tops that successful twirling is considered to be somewhat of an art form. One of the most difficult tops to spin is the peg variety, amply displayed in many forms at the museum. Peg tops are spun when a string is wound around them and then the top is

A Malaysian, five-pound top... requires an 11-foot rope to spin. Used in ceremonial contests, this gigantic top can spin for several days.

A variety of peg tops (the two in the upper left were featured in the film version of *Of Mice and Men*)

Judith Schulz, with a handful of her 5,000 tops

Secret Spin

The museum displays and also sells the "Top Secret Top." It can spin for up to several days. It's advertised that it will stay whirling for seven days, but Schulz says that customers have written back to say that theirs kept spinning for up to two weeks.

How does it work? Schulz won't say. That's why it's called the "Top Secret Top!"

The museum displays and also sells the "Top Secret Top." It can spin for up to several days.

carefully thrown. The top spins only if the throw is performed correctly.

Schulz was taught the technique by her father, and the training has paid off well. When MGM film studios needed an instructor to teach child actors how to spin tops for a film project, they called upon Schulz. Not only did she show the three boys in the movie *My Summer Story* how to spin tops, but Schulz also built the tops used in the film.

During filming, she earned the name "The Top Lady" when she executed a ten-foot toss over the head of a cameraman and on to the exact mark on the set where the boys were positioned.

"There are different styles of wrapping the string around the top. Then you swing back your arm and throw the top out and yank the string and hope that it spins," she points out. "The hoping part is important. It's a timing thing and you have to release the top at a certain moment. If you can throw a baseball, you can throw a top."

Unusual metal tops (the one on the extreme left was a souvenir of the United States' 100th anniversary celebration)

American Sanitary Plumbing Museum

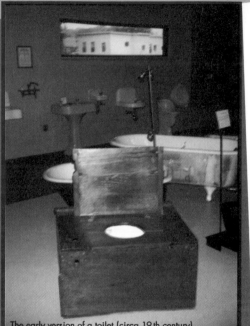

39 Piedmont Street
Worcester, Massachusetts 01610

508-754-9453

10 A.M. to 2 P.M. Tuesday and Thursday. Closed for July and August.

Free.

About 40 miles west of Boston. Take Interstate 290 west to exit 18. Follow the signs to the south end of Main St.

Pull a lever, the toilet flushes. Turn a faucet, water flows out. That's as deep as it gets for most people when it comes to understanding modern plumbing.

Plumbing is not a sexy science. But the development of modern sanitation equipment revolutionized the way we live. Without it, there'd be no indoor bathroom, for starters. The advancement of modern plumbing meant bathtubs, sinks and showers, greatly improving the level of national hygiene. The introduction of the indoor toilet greatly enhanced domestic comfort.

The American Sanitary Plumbing Museum brings plumbing artifacts out from underneath the sink and

The early version of a toilet (circa 19th century) was simply a wooden box with a hole

into the display case. Hundreds of items trace the history of modern plumbing from the mid-19th century to the present. Exhibits range from an enamel cast-iron prison toilet from the late 19th century to one of the first crude attempts at the modern dishwasher. There are antique plumbing tools, pipes, early tubs, sinks and showerheads—even an exhibit of antique toilet paper (unused).

The museum has found a ready audience within the plumbing industry. "People in the plumbing business revere this as being next to utopia," insists B. J. Manoog, the museum's administrative director.

For older visitors, the exhibits trigger memories and elicit stories of experiences with early plumbing devices. For some, however, the idea of strolling along and judging rows of urinals and toilets as if they were fine art is a bit much to ask.

"Little kids come and they snicker and laugh. But they go out very knowledgeable about how water comes into the house," Manoog asserts.

Museum Origins

The museum was created by B.J. Manoog's father-in-law, Charles Manoog, who had built a successful plumbing wholesale business. When Charles Manoog retired, he wanted to pay tribute to the industry, so he started a museum. His collection got off to a rousing start when he came upon an extraordinary artifact—the spigot end of a wooden water main dating to 1652. The main had supplied water from Jamaica Pond to Faneuil Hall in Boston and was uncovered in 1956 when engineers were digging a highway tunnel.

"After that he got together with several old crony friends, plumbing contractors, and suggested that they might have stuff hidden away in the basement. And material started coming in," recalls Russell Manoog, Charles Manoog's son. The material was initially displayed in the lobby of the family's plumbing supply store. In 1986, to carry out the wishes of his father, Russell and his wife built a separate two-story building that became the plumbing museum. Russell conducts many of the museum's tours. It's clear that he has as much enthusiasm for plumbing as his father. He has even traveled abroad to attend toilet bowl symposiums. And when he contemplates history, he does so with an eye toward how different civilizations handled their sanitation needs.

He'll point out that moats built around castles in the Middle Ages

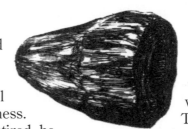

were used not only as barriers against enemies, but also as receptacles for human waste. Turrets, he says, were ancient toilets. They had openings that could be used for wastes. These slits emptied out into the surrounding moat. Wealthy families who owned more than one castle rotated among them, allowing time for each moat to "sort of clean itself out," Manoog says.

Showering, standard practice today, was decidedly abnormal before the 20th century.

"It was considered a mild form of torture," Russell Manoog says. "The idea of getting into a small cubicle and being pelted by cold water from every angle was pretty frightening." It took water heaters, gentler showerheads and closer attention to personal hygiene to change that old attitude.

Showering was heavily promoted following World War II, when it was suggested to the public that regular bathing and washing of hands would help prevent the spread of germs and deadly diseases.

Museum Highlights

A 19th century water closet, what the Manoogs call an "outhouse in-house," is featured in one display. This crude interior toilet is typical of some of the early models, which lacked a key feature of the modern commode.

"The first toilets didn't contain any water. That was the unfortunate thing about them," Russell Manoog explains. "They were

He'll point out that moats built around castles in the Middle Ages were used not only as barriers against enemies but also as receptacles for human waste.

crude wooden boxes that opened up to somewhere underneath the house."

Eventually, someone had to go under the house and clean up the wastes that had trickled down from the toilet. On a positive note, this arrangement made the soil around the home very fertile, providing nourishment for plants and flowers.

There are several examples of bathtubs, including some early 19th century models that could be taken outside after use and hung up on a peg to dry. It wasn't until a technique was developed to enamel large pieces of iron and steel that permanent tubs could be brought into the home and used without rusting. One of the museum's best pieces is a copper-lined bath tub topped by an oak rim and supported by decorative claw feet.

There are also several examples of antique showerheads, some up to a foot in diameter, and many of exquisite design, including some made of porcelain and others of copper.

A dishwasher from 1920 is exhibited. It has a motor and propeller that was placed on the bottom of the deep side of a double sink. Dishes were placed in a wire basket and, supposedly, washed by the spray of water deflected by the propeller. But the idea of machines performing simple household chores was ahead of its time.

"It was a complete failure," observes Manoog.

There are two examples of prison toilets on display. One enameled iron seat bowl dates back to 1898. A modern prison toilet made of stainless steel is offered for comparison, and features many safety devices so that the bowl cannot be used as a weapon.

A Toilet Paper Primer

Toilet paper is a bathroom accessory that has seemingly been around forever. Actually, it's a modern development. During tours Manoog points out that ancient Romans wiped up with sponges attached to sticks stored under running water when not in use. Before the advent of toilet paper, a variety of materials were used for this purpose, including corn cobs, sea shells, and pages from catalogs and newspapers.

The English, Manoog explains, were the first to develop a tissue paper specifically designed for the wiping function. It came in packages with individual sheets that were hung within easy reach. Rolls of toilet paper came along in the 20th century.

A modern prison toilet made of stainless steel...features many safety devices so that the bowl cannot be used as a weapon.

Trustees Russell Manoog (left) and Phillip Masterson (right)

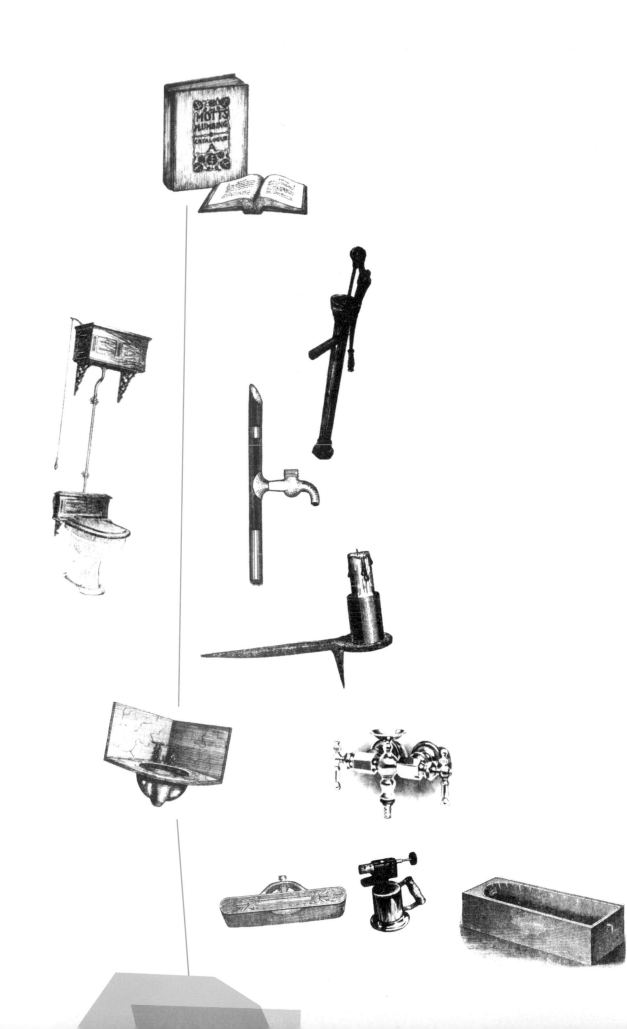

153

Mister Ed's Elephant Museum

6019 Chambersburg Road (US Route 30)
Orrtanna, Pennsylvania 17353

717-352-3792

10 A.M. to 5 P.M. daily.

Free.

From Gettysburg, travel about 12 miles east on Highway 30. Look for the large white elephant sign on the right.

E d Gotwalt is a showman. He tells you that up front. And if he can squeeze a few dollars out of it too, why not? That's why one day Ed wants to have a live elephant frolicking outside his mountain top museum and gift shop.

"Can you just imagine the cars coming up and reaching the crest of the hill, and then their brakes screeching? I'd love to train it and teach it to do tricks," he smiles, the publicity wheel turning inside his head.

But then there's the plan's downside. An elephant, after all, eats like one, so there's the staggering feed bill. Then you can add the cost of medical care.

"If an elephant has to get a shot for anything, you're talking three, four hundred dollars," he explains.

So scratch the live specimen idea. But no problem. Gotwalt's Elephant Museum already boasts quite a tourist lure in the massive shape of a 10-foot-tall fiberglass elephant statue. The white elephant with pink toes wiggles its ears and tail. It talks some, too, strongly urging that you head into the museum, or sample some of the delicious roasted peanuts sold in the gift shop. At Mister Ed's, they don't miss an opportunity for a pitch. Once inside, visitors encounter what Gotwalt says is the world's largest collection of elephant-related items, a claim that so far has gone uncontested.

Ed Gotwalt and his talking, fiberglass elephant

The museum offers fresh-roasted peanuts

154

Right: The elephant potty chair

*The collection...
includes more than
5,000 examples of
elephants featured as
toys, knick-knacks,
sculptures and
appliances...there's
even an elephant
potty chair.*

Everywhere an Elephant

The collection is as vast as a pachyderm's appetite. It includes more than 5,000 examples of elephants featured as toys, knick-knacks, sculptures and appliances, as well as elephant images appearing on movie posters, clothing and lighters. There's even an elephant potty chair.

Gotwalt began collecting in the late 1960s with a simple wedding gift from his sister-in-law. It was a small elephant sculpture so nondescript that now he can't recall what it looked like. Then his wife, Pat, bought him another elephant figure on their honeymoon. On the same trip Gotwalt himself picked out five elephant pieces in antique shops, and the stampeding hobby was off and running.

The collection quickly grew by the hundreds. Surprisingly, though, Gotwalt the showman was slow to capitalize on its marketing potential.

Instead, in 1975 he left a job as a supermarket manager to open a general store along Lincoln Highway, a tourist gateway to Gettysburg lined with beckoning attractions. Gotwalt made his mark by staging promotional events at the store, including Civil War battle reenactments on the Fourth of July. He grabbed the spotlight during Bicentennial festivities in 1976 by announcing that he was going to man his store for 76 straight hours. If anyone could catch him napping at his post, they'd win $100.

"I thought I'd get a couple hours sleep in the middle of the night," he recalls, "but it's amazing how many people stopped by to try and catch a man sleeping!"

One of his best publicity ploys was a scheme that literally came crashing down. At the store's annual Christmas party, he always made a dramatic entrance as Santa. One year he attempted an arrival in a hot air balloon, but a severe downdraft deflated the balloon and his plan. The balloon crashed into a tree 12 miles from the store. Gotwalt and the pilot dangled there for four hours before they were rescued.

It may have spoiled his entrance, but the crash succeeded as a publicity stunt—news of the event was carried worldwide.

MISTER ED'S
PEANUTS AND MORE
Since 1975

Spread a Little Sunshine

Gotwalt initially stored his elephant collection in boxes at home. "There were elephants in places where most people don't have places," he jokes. Collectors who eventually open museums often reach this critical point. They either have to get rid of their collection, or find a way of displaying it.

In 1984, when the Gotwalts moved their store two miles up the road, an opportunity opened up. They turned their new store into an elephant museum. Since its debut, Gotwalt has realized that he might have been keeping his best attraction packed up for all those years.

"There are thousands of elephant collectors," he beams. "When they come here they are blown away. They leave teary-eyed. I become a reverend to them."

This is not a natural history museum. You won't come away with a lot of knowledge about elephants. But Gotwalt doesn't make those claims, anyway. He's here to spread a little joy, he says. When visitors leave, they become ambassadors for his museum.

"I have a huge collection, and anyone with the magnitude of this collection should share it with the public," he declares. "People leave here with a smile in their hearts. It makes for a pleasant experience. Sometimes in life we have to stop and smell the roses, and this is one of the places where you can smell the roses."

Oh, and if you also pick up an elephant item in the gift shop, or some candy or roasted peanuts, that's all right too.

Museum Highlights

Gotwalt likes to search antique shops and flea markets for elephant bargains to add to his collection. He's shopped around the world, and re-members markets the way others recall monuments. He excitedly recounts a visit to an antique market in Rio de Janeiro.

"They had some nice pieces there and there was one made out of porcelain, a lamp, that was an elephant with a serpent wrapped around it. It was garish-looking. Ugly, actually, and I knew I had to have it," he laughs. After bargaining through an interpreter, he bought it for $35.

One of his most prized elephant items is worn on his finger. It's a cus-tom-made ring featuring an elephant with diamond eyes.

Other items include an elephant hair dryer from the 1940s. An elephant head sprouts a hose for a trunk and you dry your hair with hot air funneled through the trunk. "It works," Gotwalt boasts. "It has a little heater and fan. I found it at a flea market for five bucks."

A swagger stick that once belonged to a German general is carved from mahogany and includes an elephant head and tusk. Gotwalt bought it at a police auction. The elephant potty chair was made by a local crafts artist. She specializes in animal-shaped potty chairs, but this was her first elephant creation.

There's one item in the collection that had to be explained to Gotwalt.

"These two college kids said, 'Hey man, you've got a bong.' I said I didn't know what it was, but it might be fun!"

"There are thousands of elephant collectors," he beams. "When they come here they are blown away. They leave teary-eyed. I become a reverend to them."

Circuses, Peanuts and other Elephant Facts

Gotwalt never ran away with the circus. But years ago while working at a supermarket in Richmond, Virginia, a friend arranged for him to ride an elephant from the visiting circus. He rode atop the elephant's head in the circus parade as it passed from the railroad station and down the city's main street.

"They don't have a saddle," he points out. "You sit on the head and hold on. You balance. When they walk in a parade it's a kind of lope, a motion that you can get into, like riding a horse. You roll with it."

Obviously, he had a ball.

For years, Gotwalt sold roasted peanuts at an annual fair. One year, he fed peanuts to three elephants at the fair. They seemed to enjoy the treat, sucking five pound bags up their trunks in one quick motion. Next year, as Gotwalt was setting up his stand, he looked up to see the same elephants standing there, awaiting their snack.

"Which shows you, they never forget," he laughs.

Some facts that Gotwalt has learned about elephants that he finds fascinating:

They have lines on the front of their legs that are like fingerprints on humans; they're unique to each elephant.

Elephants in the wild grow six sets of teeth. When elephants lose their last set of teeth, they die.

"Elephants are family-oriented," Gotwalt explains. "There are stories of herds of elephants coming to an elephant graveyard where bones are and standing in a circle and passing the bones from one elephant to another, moaning and crying about a loved one. That's really happened."

Elephants in the wild grow six sets of teeth. When elephants lose their last set of teeth, they die.

Warther Carvings

331 Karl Avenue
Dover, Ohio 44622

330-343-7513

9 A.M. to 5 P.M. every day.

$6.50 adults,
$3 seniors,
under 6 free.

From Canton, take Intersate 77 south for about 20 miles. At exit 83, make a left. After the first stop light, make a right at 9th Street, which ends at the parking lot.

If Ernest "Mooney" Warther inherited his fantastic gift for carving, he certainly didn't get it from his father. Warther's dad, his mother pointed out, couldn't even carve a shaving.

Ernest Warther, on the other hand, took to whittling as a boy to pass the time while herding cows. The son of Swiss immigrants, Warther dropped out of school after the second grade to help support his family when his father died. He earned a penny a day herding cattle from his hometown of Dover, Ohio to surrounding areas during the day, returning them by nightfall.

To pass the time, he began carving with a penknife he had found on his daily trek. One day he met a hobo who showed Warther how to carve a pair of pliers out of wood using 10 cuts. Warther copied the hobo's technique, but added his own twist: he carved two additional pliers out of the first tool's handles.

Later he extended that vision to carve a tree of 511 interlocking pliers made from a single piece of wood. It required 31,000 cuts and took two months to complete in 1913. When the pliers sculpture was displayed at the Chicago World's Fair in 1933, a group of professors commented on how someone would need a math degree to design the intricate work. Warther, who of course had a second-grade education,

Ernest "Mooney" Warther at work

A replica of the steel mill where Warther worked for 23 years

When he retired after 23 years he created a replica of the old mill out of ivory and walnut. It contains moving equipment and 17 animated workers performing their mill jobs.

told the academics that he was relieved to learn this *after* he had made his tree of pliers.

No schooling made Warther a master carver. It was something within.

"He'd just start and know what he was doing. He pictured it all in his mind," says David Warther, the youngest of Ernest's five children.

Museum Highlights

Ernest Warther worked in a mill, bundling and shaping steel. At night he'd carve in walnut, ivory and pearl, using knives with interchangeable blades that he designed himself. To earn money after leaving the mill,

Warther sold kitchen knives he designed and made by hand. This practice would later grow into a lucrative family cutlery business, which still thrives today.

When he retired after 23 years he created a replica of the old mill out of ivory and walnut. It contains moving equipment and 17 animated workers performing their mill jobs. There's even a replica of a sleeping worker being chewed out by his irate boss. The mill carving is the first example of Warther's work on display in the museum.

A replica of the Great Northern locomotive, carved from ivory, ebony and pearl

Warther's main interest, however, was the steam locomotive. He carved dozens of historic locomotives, starting with a large block of wood or ivory to create a detailed, functional engine with hundreds of moving parts. In 1930, he gathered up 17 ivory billiard balls and one long elephant tusk. Eight months later, Warther had carved a working model of the New York Hudson locomotive, so painstakingly crafted that it looks like it could pull away at any moment.

In 1933, he produced his favorite piece, the Great Northern locomotive, made of ivory, ebony and pearl. It took seven months to complete and consists of more than 7,700 moving parts.

Other notable works include the Nashville Engine, which pulled the Lincoln funeral train, and a carving dedicated to the driving of the "golden spike," which marked the completion of the first transcontinental railroad. His largest work is the Empire State Express, an 8-foot ivory train that stands on a stone arch bridge.

In 1965, on the 100th anniversary of Lincoln's assassination, Warther completed the Lincoln funeral train made from ebony and ivory.

Warther died in 1973 at age 87, leaving his last work, The Lady Baltimore locomotive, unfinished.

1,100 Knives and 73,000 Buttons

During World War II, Warther handmade more than 1,100 commando knives for American serviceman. Each soldier's name was stamped on a brass plate inset on the knife's handle. When told the war had ended, Warther put down the commando knife he was working on and never finished it. It's displayed in the museum along with other examples of his knife work. Museum visitors can tour the shop where family members carry on Warther's tradition of making high-quality knives.

You can also visit Warther's small workshop, an 8' by 10' frame building

The Empire State Express

His largest work is the Empire State Express, an 8-foot ivory train that stands on a stone arch bridge.

Portrait of the artist as a young man

She started collecting buttons when she was 10 and amassed more than 73,000 of them by the time she entered her 90s.

that Warther himself built in 1912. The shop's fireplace was used to heat the room, and doubled as a forge when Warther made knives. Warther also created custom overhead lights on a rolling system so that he could direct a bench lamp at the part of the table where he was working.

Near the shop is the button house of Warther's wife, Freida. She started collecting buttons when she was 10 and amassed more than 73,000 of them by the time she entered her 90s. The buttons, displayed on boards in geometric patterns, can be enjoyed as a bonus treat to the carving museum.

An Independent Spirit

Warther would never sell one of his carvings, and he has been displaying them to the public since the 1930s. Henry Ford was so impressed when he viewed the carvings, that he offered Warther $75,000 up front and an annual salary of $5,000 to create carvings for him.

Warther's response?

"He told Henry Ford to go to the devil," laughs David Warther. "He said, 'My roof doesn't leak, my family is not hungry, and my wife has all her buttons.'"

Freida Warther and some of her 73,000 buttons

The Great Blacks In Wax Museum

1601-03 East North Avenue
Baltimore, Maryland 21213

410-563-3404
Fax: 410-675-5040

www.usbol.com/bnn/gbiw/gbiw.html

January 15 to October 15:
9 A.M. to 6 P.M. Tuesday
through Saturday,
Noon to 6 P.M. Sunday.
October 16 to January 14:
9 A.M. to 5 P.M. Tuesday
through Saturday,
Noon to 5 P.M. Sunday.

$5.75 adults,
$5.25 seniors and students,
$3.75 ages 12 to 17 and
$3.25 ages 2 to 11.

Take Interstate 95 South
to Interstate 695. Get
on Interstate 83 South
(exit 23). Exit on North
Avenue and turn left.
Travel east to the 1600
block of North Avenue.

Joanne and Elmer Martin were college students during the sixties, an intense period of activism and awareness for young black Americans. There were struggles over civil rights, and a Black Power movement that sought to promote an appreciation of African-American culture.

That's why it was hard for the Martins as middle-aged adults to accept what was happening in the black community. Joanne, a college administrator, and Elmer, a professor of social work, saw that much of what had been accomplished during the sixties was being undone only one generation later. Drugs and gang violence were major problems among young African-Americans. And young blacks fortunate enough to escape these traps seemed more interested in blending in with mainstream America than in learning about their own heritage.

It was particularly galling for Elmer Martin when one day he heard a six-year-old boy complain about the quality of his team's Little League picture. The boy thought it made him look too black.

Rosa Parks is escorted off the bus

162

James Hubert "Eubie" Blake
Jazz Performer and Composer
(1883-1983)

and stock Hollywood characters and are usually designed as low-brow tourist amusements.

But the Martins believed in the idea.

"My husband said that if you put a wax figure across the room, people are naturally going to gravitate to it," Joanne Martin explains. "They are going to ask questions like, 'Who is that?' and 'What is that?' Then you are in a position to teach. Particularly with this generation, you've got to get their attention."

In 1980, the Martins began with a traveling show of four wax figures which they displayed at schools, churches and shopping centers to test the public's curiosity and interest. The response was positive, and after raising additional funds they opened a museum in a Baltimore storefront in 1983 with 21 wax characters.

Today, with city and state grants, the museum is housed in an historic funeral home and includes more than 130 wax figures. The Martins prefer to call the stately building a mansion, and not refer to its past use as a mortuary, a tidbit that might reinforce the public's inherent fears of wax museums.

"There are actually people who believe we've dug up Frederick Douglas's grave and dipped his body in wax," Joanne Martin laughs. "This doesn't just come from children. There are adults who are leery of wax figures. They often believe that the figures are wax, but that the eyes are real, because they seem to be following them around."

"We convinced ourselves that we should be black and proud and that black is beautiful. But it wasn't taking hold in our young people."

"Here we were, still clinging to the belief that it was possible to be too black, instead of looking within and finding the beauty in yourself," sighs Joanne Martin. "We thought we had gotten away from all that. We convinced ourselves that we should be black and proud and that black is beautiful. But it wasn't taking hold in our young people."

Something needed to be done, the Martins decided. During a trip to Spain, they observed how one museum presented massive figures to honor the country's war dead. This visit led to the unconventional concept of promoting black culture and history through wax statues.

It was certainly a risky idea. Wax museums tend to feature horror creatures

The Great Blacks In Wax Museum

UP FROM SLAVERY
AN AUTOBIOG
BY BOOKER T. W

Booker T. Washington and Mary McCleod Bethune

3,000 Years of History in Wax

What is real is the history that is taught using these wax figures. The exhibits cover African history, slavery, the Underground Railroad, the Harlem Renaissance, the Civil Rights Movement, religious leaders and educators. Figures such as Jackie Robinson, Booker T. Washington, Billie Holiday and Malcolm X may already be known to visitors, but the museum also intends to highlight achievements by blacks not often recognized in history books or by mainstream media. Included in this group is Lewis Latimer,

Community Effort

Joanne Martin says that a great deal of research goes into each figure before it's completed. Various artists and crafts people work on sections of the overall project. Some, for example, design costumes, while others may provide the hairpiece or the wax face.

Marcus Garvey (left) and Paul Robeson (right)

who was asked by Alexander Graham Bell to design the first telephone.

A statue of Jocko, the maligned lawn ornament deemed racist for its caricature features of a black jockey, seems an unlikely exhibit at this museum. Accompanying text, however, points out that the statue has an historic significance that is often overlooked. During the Revolutionary War, a black youth named Jocko froze to death while keeping a dedicated watch on George Washington's horse. The general was so impressed that he ordered a statue built in his honor. During the era of slavery, a statue of Jocko placed in front of a building symbolized that it was a safe house for escaping slaves.

"It's a process where you might receive a head in the mail, you do your work, and then you pass the head on," Martin explains.

Even when a figure is finished and put on display, the museum's staff still considers changes suggested by the public. For example, Nation of Islam visitors objected to the bow tie placed on the figure of Elijah Mohammed, because they said he would have worn a clip-on tie to avoid being grabbed and choked. The change in attire was duly made.

A group of school children wasn't satisfied with the uniform placed on the figure of Jackie Robinson, who broke baseball's color barrier. So they made a more authentic uniform and presented it to the museum.

Nation of Islam visitors objected to the bow tie placed on the figure of Elijah Mohammed, because they said he would have worn a clip-on tie to avoid being grabbed and choked. The change in attire was duly made.

Slave ship display

ways. An escaping slave is seen stretching his body through an old-fashioned stove to be greeted on the other side by Underground Railroad leader Harriet Tubman. Martin says that this display represents many of the secret passages that were part of the slave escape route.

Rosa Parks is depicted stepping off a bus, escorted by a white patrol officer after she refused to give up her seat to a white passenger. This simple act of defiance in 1955 helped spark the Civil Rights Movement.

Dred Scott is presented in a court-room suing for his freedom, while black aviation pioneer Bessie Coleman—seated in a replica of a prop plane—soars by overhead.

Former U.S. Congresswoman Shirley Chisholm donated two suits to the museum to dress her figure. One is for summer, the other for winter.

Members of the Oblate Sisters, the oldest order of black nuns, insisted on making the habit worn by the figure of Mother Mary Lange, founder of the order.

These contributions are welcome, Martin says. "Our suggestion box is always filled. We want people to feel a connection to this museum."

Museum Highlights

Billie Holiday

Martin says that one of the most profound exhibits is the slave ship display. Visitors step down into a replica of a cramped cargo hold, designed to re-create the oppressive conditions under which the voyage to America took place. Disturbing sounds—clinking chains, screams and moans—enhance the realism of the exhibit. The life-size diorama includes 30 figures. Other exhibits also feature wax fig-ures presented in theatrical

It's in the Skin

When the Martins studied other black wax figures before opening their museum, they were disturbed by what they saw. They were all of one color—a dark, shiny black. They were determined to design their fig-ures to reflect the many shades of skin color present in real black people.

To do this, they would often stop strangers on the street and photo-graph them if they matched a certain skin tone they wanted to capture in a wax figure. Some people were skeptical at first, but cooperated when told of the project, Martin says.

"Skin color is very important. That's a key identifying characteristic of African-American people," Martin points out. "There *are* shiny black people in the world, but we come in a range of colors."

National Museum of Dentistry

31 South Greene Street (at Lombard)
Baltimore, Maryland 21201-1504

410-706-0600
Fax: 410-706-8313

10 A.M. to 4 P.M. Wednesday through Saturday, 1 P.M. to 4 P.M. on Sunday. Closed Mondays, Tuesdays, major holidays, and the week between Christmas and New Year's Day.

$4.50 adults; $2.50 ages 7 to 18, senior citizens and students; free for children 6 and under.

From I-95, take Route 395 (downtown Baltimore) and exit onto Martin Luther King Jr. Blvd., staying in the right lane. At the fourth traffic light, turn right onto Baltimore Street. Turn right at the first traffic light onto Greene Street and the museum is on the left.

The dentist's office would probably win a contest for anyone's least favorite place to visit. A dental museum might come in a close second.

"The first question we always get is, "Who would come to it?'" admits Ben Swanson, director of the National Museum of Dentistry. "But there's a curiosity value because of its novelty. It's kind of, 'What the heck would they put in a dental museum?'"

The answer is more than 40,000 artifacts relating to dentistry, including antique dental tools, famous dentures, and even Andy Warhol's silk-screen prints of the patron saint of dentistry. Interactive displays and exhibits prompt visitors to ponder aspects of dentistry they hadn't considered before, such as how different cultures view dental hygiene.

They've certainly gone to great lengths here to ensure that visitors will open wide with amazement. "This is a museum for the public," Swanson declares. "Our idea is to tell the story of dentistry, educate people, and to have some fun at the same time."

George Washington's dentures

166

A full-size sculpture of a trapeze artist executing the famed circus "iron jaw" act

George Washington's dentures were not made of wood. Instead, they were constructed of ivory, and animal and human teeth.

Dental Fun

The museum is located on a college campus that is home to the world's first dental school, established in 1840. The museum opened in June, 1996.

You won't hear the disturbing sound of dental drills when you enter, but you will encounter the stunning image of a full-size sculpture of a trapeze artist executing the famed circus "iron jaw" act. The mouth of the female figure supports the sign panel that introduces the first portion of the museum.

The introductory display area deals with representations of dentistry in popular culture. These exhibits include political cartoons containing images of teeth, including a World War II work showing the figure of Uncle Sam extracting a tooth from Adolph Hitler.

The concept of the tooth fairy is also explored in this section. This tradition, Swanson says, is, in fact, a 20th century American invention. To illustrate the power of this myth, there's an amusing letter written to the tooth fairy by a boy concerned that he might not get his full cash award because his tooth was chipped.

Famous False Ones

The museum immediately debunks a popular misconception about historic dentistry by pointing out that George Washington's dentures were not made of wood. Instead, they were constructed of ivory, and animal and human teeth. They were, however, fastened by wooden pegs, which may be the cause of the confusion.

As proof, the museum offers four pairs of Washington's dentures—all of the sets he was known to wear except for the false teeth with which he was buried. The exhibit explains that by the time he was elected president, Washington had lost all but one of his natural teeth, a lower left bicuspid. By 1796, even that tooth was history.

Other fake choppers on display include the tiny dentures of Lavinia Warren, wife of the famous 19th century midget Tom Thumb.

Museum Highlights

Before various dental materials are used on patients to restore teeth, they are tested by a machine for strength and durability. An example of such a chewing machine, developed by dentists at the University of Minnesota, is displayed here. The "Mighty Mouth" is appropriately named. It subjects dental materials used in tooth restoration to the equivalent of many years of chewing in the span of only a few weeks.

Queen Victoria's dental instruments, which look more like elegant table utensils, were made for Sir Edwin Saunders, the dentist responsible for caring for the imperial mouth. The set includes six scalers with mother-of-pearl handles and silver-gilt mounts, a pearl-handled mirror, a silver-plated toothpick and a velvet-lined case featuring the emblem of the crown. The instruments are also decorated with roses, thistles and shamrocks, so that while getting her teeth done the Queen could lie back and think of England, Scotland and Ireland.

Four silk-screen prints made by Andy Warhol in 1984 are based upon a 1740 portrait of St. Apollonia, the patron saint of dentistry. Rather than renounce her faith, St. Apollonia endured the extraction of her teeth by persecutors, a common form of persuasion practiced by the Roman Empire.

The museum displays toothbrushes dating from as far back as 6,000 years ago up to the sleek, motor-driven implements of today. The exhibit explains that the ancient Hindus of India used toothbrushes made of twigs and roots around 4,000 B.C.

A prototype device to fluoridate the home water supply of then Attorney General Robert Kennedy around 1960 is also featured. Unfortunately, it proved to be inefficient and difficult to maintain.

Examples of early tooth extractors on display may give people a better appreciation for modern dental methods. Early models include the pelican, used in the 18th century. It was so named because its claw resembled the beak of a pelican. The claw would yank the tooth out sideways by grabbing hold of it over the crown.

The Cultural Tooth

The exhibit "32 Terrific Teeth" showcases dental aesthetics very different from our own idea of the perfect set of white teeth. In some cultures, blacking out certain teeth is considered attractive, while in others teeth are inlaid with jewels such as jade. Masks that illustrate these various images are displayed.

In contrast, visitors can stop at the Tooth Jukebox, a video center shaped like a large mouth. Select a number and you can view early American television commercials for dental products that promote the benefits of a clean, white smile.

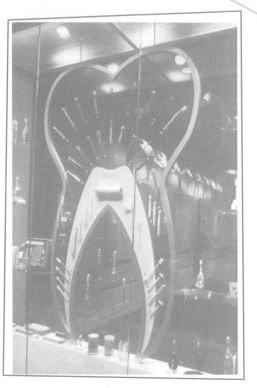

Toothbrushes through history

Sweet Tooth

Cotton candy and chewing gum are the bane of dentists today. But as an exhibit here surprisingly illustrates, both were created by dentists.

In the late 19th century, Nashville's William Morrison invented the Fairy Floss candy machine that made sugar-laden cotton candy. In 1869, Ohio dentist William Semple was the first inventor to patent chewing gum. He anticipated that it would help clean teeth, not rot them away.

"Say 'Aaahh!'"

Rather than renounce her faith, St. Apollonia endured the extraction of her teeth by persecutors, a common form of persuasion practiced by the Roman Empire.

Cotton candy and chewing gum are the bane of dentists today. But as an exhibit here surprisingly illustrates, both were created by dentists.

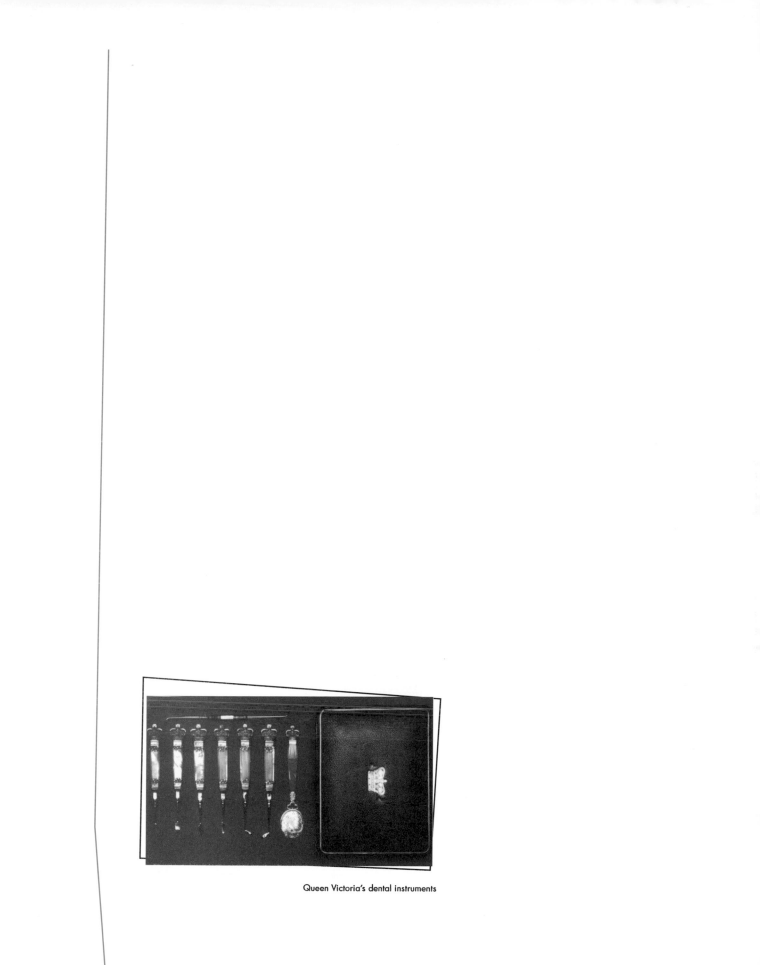

Queen Victoria's dental instruments

American International Rattlesnake Museum

If rattlesnakes were going to hire a publicity agent to spiff up their image, they couldn't select a better person for the job than Bob Myers. In 1990, Myers, a former high school biology teacher, opened the American International Rattlesnake Museum to promote a better understanding of the rattler, as well as snakes and other reptiles in general.

He knew it would be a challenge.

"For whatever reason, there aren't many people who have a good word for the poor rattlesnake," he admits.

To those who would speak ill of the much-maligned rattler, Myers offers the fact that only one person in a thousand bitten by the poisonous snake dies from the wound. The United States averages only eight deaths per year from rattlesnake bites.

"If you compare that to any other way of dying, this is a low number," he says. "You're more likely to die from lightning, bee stings, or a dog attack." Not to mention cancer.

"I try to explain to people that snakes should be the least of their worries," he laughs.

Common Phobia

Yet fears persist, as Myers well knows. He estimates that half of the museum's visitors enter reluctantly. A small percentage can't bear to walk in at all, choosing to wait outside as their friends and relatives sneak a peek at the live specimens on display inside. For that reason, admission tickets double as "certificates of bravery" which praise visitors for having the courage to face their fear of snakes.

You won't be ambushed by any snakes in the museum and, most likely, they won't be surprised by you. More than 30 varieties of rattlesnakes are displayed in glass tanks set up to simulate the snakes' natural habitats. Rattlesnakes are found in North, South and Central America. They vary in size, color and skin patterns. Visitors are often struck by the variety of the snakes on exhibit.

"When people think of rattlesnakes," Myers explains, "they think of the eastern diamondback. That's the one that's most visible in movies. It usually reacts by rattling and is probably our most defensive rattlesnake."

Rattlesnakes in the museum's collection include the canebrake, northern blacktailed, banded rock and the tiger. The largest snake is a 6-foot eastern diamondback. The most unusual is a patternless western diamondback. It was born a solid brown color and has no skin markings, a very rare occurrence. Another unusual rattlesnake on view is an albino diamondback. Because of its blond color, it's been nicknamed Marilyn.

The museum's most famous snake is Joey, who has appeared in movies, videos, posters and other promotional venues.

Shaking With Fear

A snake's rattle is attached to the tip of its tail. When a snake is scared it shakes, and the movement causes the interlocking segments of keratin that make up the rattle to rub against each other and make the distinctive rattling sound.

One myth dispelled at the museum is that you can tell a snake's age by the number of segments on its rattle. Myers says that these snakes shed their rattle two to four times a year, so it's not a gauge of a snake's age. In fact, older snakes may lose a segment or two as they age.

Snakes also don't chase people either, he points out, debunking another popular misconception. They'd rather avoid people and other large, threatening creatures. "All the time we

Admission tickets double as "certificates of bravery" which praise visitors for having the courage to face their fear of snakes.

Certificate of Bravery
awarded to

_____

for showing little or no hesitation and willfully (or with slight encouragement by "friends" or relatives) entering into the previously frightening and now truly fascinating world of the rattlesnake; for having gained insight and knowledge into the rattlesnakes influence on American history, American Indian culture, medicine and other areas, at the

American International Rattlesnake Museum
in "Old Town" Albuquerque, NM - (505) 242-6569

Signed _____Bob Myers_____
Museum Director

Date _____

Every museum visitor receives a
Certificate of Bravery

have people who claim they've been chased by rattlesnakes," Myers says. "I think what happens is that they see a rattlesnake and run away and don't bother to look back to see whether there's a snake on their tail."

Since all of the rattlesnakes here have been born in captivity, they are comfortable with being around people and don't often resort to rattling their tails. Occasionally, however, visitors might surprise one and get to see the defensive reaction up close.

Overcoming Fears

The museum helps people conquer their snake phobia. Museum volunteers sit patiently with nervous visitors outside, calmly educating them about snakes before taking them into the museum to meet them.

"There are people who are paralyzed with fear of taking a walk and coming across a snake," Myers says. "Many times they have heard bad stories but have never had a personal experience with snakes. Almost every fear can be overcome. I've seen people go from hating snakes to wanting to have one for a pet in 20 minutes."

Promoting Conservation

Myers wants to encourage a better understanding of rattlesnakes so that they are not hunted for sport. He's especially opposed to annual events that feature mass killings of snakes for sport.

"Snakes are brought back and weighed, and then thrown into giant pits," he says. "There are hundreds of them, even thousands, slaughtered in public, their heads cut off and skinned, sometimes while they are still moving. You can't imagine the same thing happening with any other animal species."

Museum Highlights

The museum showcases other snakes relevant to the rattler's story. For example, an Egyptian horn viper is on display because it closely resembles the sidewinder rattlesnake. You can also see other venomous animals, including a gila monster lizard, a tarantula and a few scorpions.

Several exhibits showcase snake images in cultural artifacts, commercial products and games. Artworks include a Remington sculpture of a cowboy riding a horse which is rearing away from a rattlesnake, as well as an etching by Audubon, believed to be the only one the famous naturalist made of a snake.

Myers has set up a display case stocked with snake-themed beverages. He's received so many of these containers from around the world, in fact, that there isn't enough room to exhibit them all. The museum also has dozens of board games and toys that feature snakes. For a 1960's game called "Snakes in the Grass," players used rubber

"Almost every fear can be overcome. I've seen people go from hating snakes to wanting to have one for a pet in 20 minutes."

Curator Bob Myers with a display of a rattlesnake skeletal system and fang

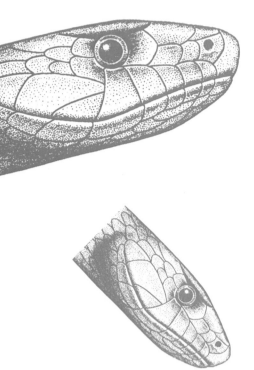

snakes with little scoops at the end to pick up marbles and move them around a board.

Antidotes Galore

Several antique and modern snake bite kits are featured at the museum. Many of these kits once belonged to naturalist Roger Caras, who collected them for more than 50 years during his world travels.

"We've got anti-venom for just about every snake under the sun," Myers says.

Myers and the museum staff are constantly thinking up new ideas for exhibits. There are plans for a display on snake songs, for example. "It's amazing," he marvels. "We're always thinking of something we've missed. Snakes touch our lives a lot more often then we think."

Sculpture of a Minoan fertility goddess. In ancient mythology, the snake represented the cycle of death and rebirth

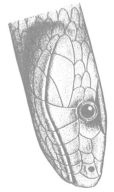

Nut Museum

303 Ferry Road
Old Lyme, Connecticut 06391

860-434-7636

1 P.M. to 5 P.M., Monday,
Saturday and Sunday,
May through November.
(Or call for appointment.)

$2 and one nut adults,
one nut ages 6 to 16.

Take exit 70 off I-95.
Go through the first
light and at the sec-
ond light make a left
on Route 156. Turn
right on Ferry Road.

Elizabeth Tashjian has been called the Nut Lady for years, and it's an identity she assumes with pride and true affection. In her world there is no stigma attached to nuts. She's marveled at their beauty, and pondered the wisdom emanating from within their hard shells. "I've become a nut visionary," she proclaims. She speaks with a lilting, schoolteacher charm that makes you an instant believer, even if you don't always readily follow the thread of her thinking. "I never thought I was going to be a philosopher. I was just an artist and I let the idea lead me," she insists.

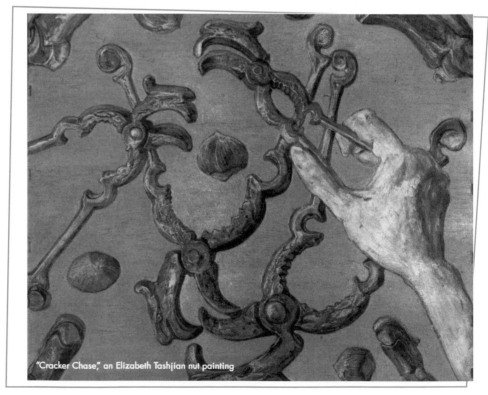

"Cracker Chase," an Elizabeth Tashjian nut painting

Following her nutty instincts led Tashjian to the Nut Museum, which occupies the first floor of her 20-room Victorian mansion. You have to include the grounds as part of the experience, since they feature several nut trees, including sweet chestnuts, walnuts, filberts, pecans and beechnuts.

Inside, amid the chandeliers, antique pipe organ and the dark-wood furnishings, is Tashjian's loving tribute to all kinds of nuts. Exhibits include sculptures, paintings, murals and masks made by Tashjian and inspired by nut shapes and themes.

There's also an assortment of nutcrackers on display, even though visitors have questioned how appropriate that is for a pro-nut museum. "Nutcrackers are enemies of the nut, but here they co-exist in harmony," Tashjian states.

Elizabeth Tashjian, amongst her nuts

When She First Went Nutty

"Our family liked nuts. We liked to eat them and play with them," Tashjian recalls. "I thought of them as more than just edible delights, but also as something paintable. There was a walnut and I thought how beautiful it was when it fell out of the shell."

As a teenager she sketched walnuts on brown wrapper paper and then began creating a series of still lifes with nuts.

In 1972 she decided to open the museum. She called up the local newspaper to make the simple announcement. "I told them that the Nut Museum is opening Saturday at 4:30 p.m.," she says. "The reporter said, 'Will you please spell the first word?'"

The reporter eventually understood and, recognizing a scoop, stopped by to write a full report. Since the opening, word of the Nut Museum has spread like peanut butter over a piece of Wonder bread. Tashjian has been written up in national publications and has also appeared on television with Johnny Carson and David Letterman. She was called back for a second appearance with Carson, and stayed on for 20 minutes.

"When I opened the museum it was a step I took very spontaneously. I didn't think it would get me on television," she admits. "But when I start something I expect good results."

Biggest Nut of Them All

The museum's most impressive artifact is the world's largest nut, the 35-pound Coco-De-Mer, grown in the Seychelles Islands in the Indian Ocean. The colossal nut looks like two semispheres fused together. And, as Tashjian readily points out, it also looks like an anatomically correct midsection of the female body. It was her frankness in talking about how some nuts resemble human sexual organs that so charmed national television audiences, who were obviously not expecting such candid comments from such a demure-looking woman.

"It's nature's own creation," she says of the giant nut, which she displays perched on a cushion on a carved Chinese chair.

Nut Sculptures

Tashjian has made several sculptures out of sheet aluminum upon which she's mounted various nuts that represent parts of the human anatomy. These works are exhibited throughout the museum and on the surrounding grounds. In "Eve with the Forbidden Fruit," a reclining figure of a woman features a giant nut on her pelvis. Tashjian says the title is inspired by the belief that the nut was the forbidden fruit in the Garden of Eden.

The Eden sculpture is a foot and a half long. An 8-foot tall metal nutcracker sculpture stands near the museum's entrance. Each nut sculpture takes months to complete, Tashjian says, and all are created from a single piece of aluminum that she painstakingly cuts with a pair of scissors.

Nut Masks and Other Nut Art

Among other artifacts are several masks carved by Tashjian herself that she says are inspired by nuts. One mask with a cap, for example, was created with a nod to the acorn. Another has almond-shaped eyes.

Among Tashjian's paintings is "Cracker Chase," a somewhat abstract work that features several views of an antique nutcracker given to her by a relative. Tashjian says that the cracker in the painting is not that rare, but another one on display attracts much more interest from nutcracker collectors. It has two pointy ears on the tongs and its shape resembles the mythological figure of Pan.

"The pros really bow down to that one," she says proudly.

Also on display are several art objects not made by Tashjian, but which feature nuts. There's jewelry made out of nut shells, and dollhouse furniture carved from walnut shells. There's also a walnut containing a miniature wedding scene.

Don't Forget Your Nut

Tashjian says she's deadly serious about the admission requirement of one nut per person.

"I don't let them in otherwise. It's very mandatory," she insists.

Most people offer peanuts or pistachios, but a few have been more creative. One man offered his wife as his nut donation, while another visitor, the owner of a hardware store, brought over his entire nut and bolt collection.

Tashjian says she's deadly serious about the admission requirement of one nut per person. "I don't let them in otherwise. It's very mandatory."

"Eve with the Forbidden Fruit," Tashjian's sculpture

176

Tashjian with her pampered, 35-pound Coco-De-Mer, the world's largest nut

"You bear with them," Tashjian says of these visitors.

The nut donations are deposited in a box. Don't expect Tashjian to eat up these offerings. She has a hard time thinking of nuts as food.

"It's difficult, frankly speaking," she admits. "I start hankering for a pecan and I start cracking it open and I see that it's so beautiful that I can't eat it. I crack open another one hoping that it will break into pieces but that one looks so beautiful too. Before long there is a whole row of nuts and not one has come into my mouth."

Recently, though, when a television news crew brought over two bags of fresh filberts, Tashjian put aside all aesthetic concerns.

"These were really fresh, not like the ones in the store that are rock hard," she gushes. "They were so soft. I close my eyes when I eat nuts they are so beautiful."

Musical Tribute

Tashjian has written a short song that she calls the "Nut Anthem." She's also illustrated the song with several pictures that are displayed at the entrance to the museum. The lyrics go like this:

Oh nobody ever thinks about nuts

Nuts can be beautiful if looked at right.

Take some home and handle them properly, artistically,

And feel a new taste being born.

Ah nuts have a curious history and lore.

Nuts once grew in the Garden of Eden.

They've been nourishing man ever since creation began.

Nuts are yearly tokens of primeval life.

American Funeral Service Museum

415 Barren Springs Drive
Houston, Texas 77090

281-876-3063
Fax: 281-876-2961

10 A.M. to 4 P.M.
Monday through Saturday,
Noon to 4 P.M. Sundays.

$5 adult,
$3 children under 12
and adults over 54.

Take Interstate 45
North from Downtown.
Exit at Airtex, go west
to Ella Boulevard and
make a right. The
museum is at the
intersection of Ella
Boulevard and Barren
Springs Drive.

Gary Sanders, director of the American Funeral Service Museum, wants everyone to know that this is not a morbid institution. True, the exhibits are mostly coffins and hearses. There's also a fully equipped, 1920's embalming room thrown in for good measure.

But visitors need not be unduly fascinated with death in order to take an interest in the displays.

"This museum has a lot of history in it," Sanders says. Not only can these antique funeral vehicles and caskets be studied for their historical value, Sanders adds, but they can be admired for their beauty, if you can see past their gloomy function.

Elegant antique hearses dominate the museum's expansive showroom, including a failed attempt at the country's only funeral bus, a 1916 Packard.

The Rockfalls Hearse (1921) is 8 feet tall, over 19 feet long and weighs 4600 pounds

A black sleigh with a plush velvet seat bench looks inviting and quaint, until you realize it's actually a funeral sled from the late 1800s.

A black sleigh with a plush velvet seat bench looks inviting and quaint, until you realize it's actually a funeral sled from the late 1800s. Its cargo is a wood coffin surrounded by flowers.

There are several examples of finely crafted antique coffins made with exotic woods, cast iron and glass.

A special feature is an ornate replica of Abraham Lincoln's coffin—6 feet and 6 inches long—with a silver-beaded design on its sides and decorative handles.

Hearses and More Hearses

The 1916 Packard funeral bus displayed here was designed to carry a casket, flower displays, six pallbearers and 20 mourners. On the way to its first funeral, however, the hearse sagged badly in the rear due to a

design flaw. It was never used again.

There's a restored 1921 Rockfalls hearse made with hand carved maple and a 1925 Dodge Brothers Keystone hearse with curtained windows and a side-riding spare tire.

Other vehicles include the 1934 gold-colored Cunningham hearse which offered an elegant final ride. Another gilded hearse is the 1860 gold-trimmed German hearse. A 1900 white child's hearse carriage features oval glass windows, decorative roof urns and a church-like dome on top.

Coffins and More Coffins

As part of the Lincoln coffin exhibit there is a scale model of the funeral train that carried his body from Washington to Springfield, Illinois. Included is a photo of Lincoln in his casket, and documents and pictures which chronicle his life. A mannequin dressed in an 1860 Honor Guard uniform stands watch over the casket.

The many other coffins on display show how their design changed over the years, Sanders says. There are

Funeral sleigh from the late 1800s

The antique hearse carriage (circa 1860) provided an elegant final ride

solid metal caskets dating back to the Civil War, and some examples of innovative glass models that proved ineffective.

"They were too heavy and the glass would break," Sanders shrugs.

Coffins changed in shape around the turn of the century, Sanders explains, when they were designed with increased shoulder room and a tapered-off look toward the feet.

"Before, you were kind of scrunched up in the coffin. With these, you could spread out," he says.

The museum also showcases what it claims is the world's only casket made for three. It was built for a couple planning suicide after learning of their child's fatal illness. Fortunately, the unhappy parents gave up their plan and the family casket was never used.

The museum also showcases what it claims is the world's only casket made for three. It was built for a couple planning suicide after learning of their child's fatal illness.

1925 Dodge Brothers
Keystone Hearse

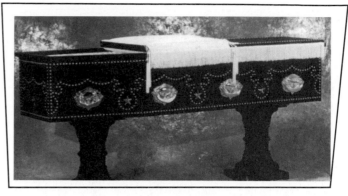

There are newspaper clippings, remembrance cards and booklets from services for such deceased celebrities as Elvis Presley, Judy Garland, John Wayne, Martin Luther King and even John Candy.

Famous Funerals

Another full-size replica of a coffin depicts King Tut's sarcophagus. It's part of an exhibit that tells about the world's first funeral directors—the highly skilled embalmers of ancient Egypt. The Tut coffin leads into a 1920's embalming room that includes a stainless steel table and assorted bottles and tubes used in the process.

Memorial service memorabilia from funerals of the famous are given their due here. There are newspaper clippings, remembrance cards and booklets from services for such deceased celebrities as Elvis Presley, Judy Garland, John Wayne, Martin Luther King and even John Candy. The exhibits are designed to promote the heritage of the mortuary business in the United States. If your interest is piqued, there are three short videos you can watch during your visit which tell you much more. They cover the history of funeral services, embalming and the cultural significance of the American funeral service.

If you are more inclined to go for a souvenir, there are many to choose from, including gold watches, pens, pencils, mugs and even golf balls that feature antique hearse emblems.

Gilded replica of King Tut's sarcophagus

MUSEUM GIFT CATALOG
American Funeral Service Museum

415 Barren Springs Drive · Houston, Texas 77090
(713) 876-3063

Don Brown Rosary Collection

The sickly childhood experienced by Don Brown might have been a curse to some people. To him, it was a blessing.

Overcome by a severe attack of pneumonia in the early 1900s, he was confined at the Mercy Hospital in North Bend, Oregon, where he was nursed back to health. When he was discharged, the head nurse presented him with her personal rosary. It was a gift that he would cherish, and one that would transform his life.

Brown converted to Catholicism and made it his goal to collect thousands of rosaries from around the globe. From that first hospital rosary, he built what is believed to be the world's largest collection of prayer beads, numbering more than 4,000. Not only did Brown collect these rosaries, but he also took great pains to catalog them in detailed fashion.

Rosaries—beads strung together to assist in the reciting of prayers—are used not only in Catholicism but in many different world religions. Although Brown rarely traveled outside his home county, word of his collection reached thousands of miles away. Travelers would bring back rosaries to donate, while others mailed them directly to his North Bonneville, Washington home.

Brown carefully marked each rosary with a jeweler's tag and then created a journal entry that described its origin, design and material.

Don Brown began collecting rosaries as a child in the early 1900s

DON BROWN at his devotions with historic Pre Dieu, a relic originally used by the Most Rev. F. Norbert Blanchet, D.D., first Archbishop to the Oregon Territory. Photo taken in 1972 when collection of rosaries and artifacts was housed in Mr. Brown's North Bonneville home.

"He said that the Lord provided for his needs and he didn't have many wants."

Just Drop By

Visitors were always welcome at his house to view the collection. Brown lived a simple life, managing his family's tract of land and collecting rents from tenants.

"He never owned a car," recalls Sharon Tiffany, director of the Columbia Gorge Interpretive Center, where the rosary collection is now displayed. "He had a telephone, but he did not have a lot of luxuries. When I questioned him about this, he said that the Lord provided for his needs and he didn't have many wants."

Many museums expressed interest in the collection, but Brown felt strongly that it should remain near his home as part of a local history collection. When he died in 1975 at the age of 80, his rosary collection was donated to the Skamania County Historical Society, which maintained a small museum at the time.

In May of 1995, the society opened a much larger museum with a broader focus upon regional history. The Interpretive Center offers a special wing that displays Brown's rosary collection, which now contains more than 4,000 items.

"His collection began out of a curiosity and it grew into a devotion," explains Tiffany. "He told me that he was afraid that the use of the rosary would be totally forgotten and that he didn't want that to happen. He wanted to preserve that portion of church history."

Part of Regional History

The rosary collection is housed on the center's second floor. Among other artifacts in the regional historical museum are the 38-foot high replica of a fishing wheel, used to harvest fish from the Columbia River. You'll also see a logging truck, a steam engine that once powered local saw mills, and a 1929 Ford Model A coupe.

To separate the Don Brown collection from the rest of the museum, designers created a wing outlined with church arches. Rosaries are displayed in tall glass cases that form rows leading up to an altar.

Tiffany says that the rosaries are made of all kinds of material, including precious jewels, wood, peach pits, ivory and even one set of prayer beads made of ping pong balls!

Interior view of the museum

Special Items

Among the many notable rosaries in the collection is one that belonged to President John F. Kennedy. Brown had written a letter to Kennedy when he was a U.S. senator, describing his rosary chapel and requesting a donation. A brown wooden rosary that Kennedy had carried with him while serving in the military during World War II had been given to a small church in Bavaria. After Kennedy's assassination, the German church sent Brown the rosary.

One of the largest rosaries in the collection is 16 feet, 3 inches long. It was used as a prop in a school play. By contrast, there are miniature rosaries with beads the size of pinheads.

A Rosary given to Rev. John M. O'Neill of Newfoundland by Pope Pius XII—just 10 days before the pontiff's death—is featured in the collection. The rosary includes a medal that bears reliefs of the Pope and the Holy Family.

Also on display is a rosary found on a Florida beach after a storm by a visiting nun from Notre Dame College of Ohio. The rosary was discovered entwined on a twig and is displayed exactly in the condition it was found.

You can also see a rosary carved of deer horns by a man in Quebec, Canada, as well as one made of round lead bullets. The bullet rosary uses brass rifle shells as dividers between the beads.

A unique rosary on display is one that glows in the dark. Donated by the Firefly Jewelry Company of Eugene, Oregon, it features black beads

Rosaries, rosaries, everywhere!

separated by hollow glass dividers that contain a mixture of inert gases and mercury. When turned, the glass tubes produce a reddish glow.

If it sounds as if every conceivable material is represented in this rosary collection, it's not. Tiffany says she has yet to see a rosary made of feathers.

Hint, hint.

Also on display is a rosary found on a Florida beach after a storm by a visiting nun from Notre Dame College of Ohio.

John F. Kennedy's rosary

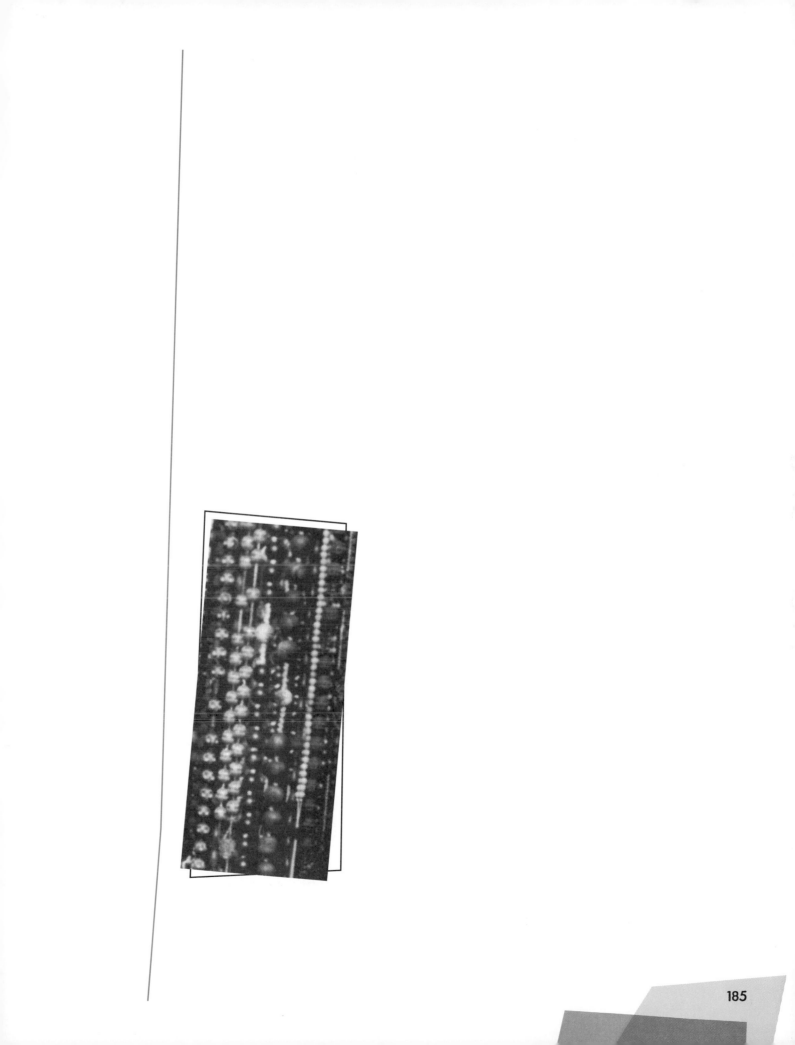

The Time Museum

7801 East State Street
PO Box 5285
Rockford, Illinois 61125-0285

815-229-4199
Fax: 815-398-4700.

10 A.M. to 5 P.M.
Tuesday through Sunday.

$3 adults, $2 senior
citizens, $1 children
ages 6 to 18.

From downtown
Rockford, take Business
Route 20 east for about
six miles. The museum
is at the junction of
Interstate 90 and
Business Route 20.

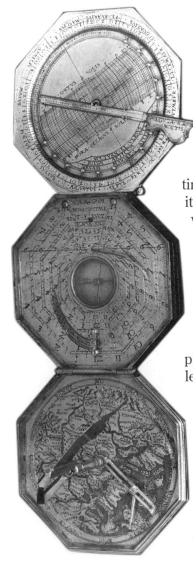

No one's yet figured out how to stop time. But for thousands of years we've used instruments to track its inexorable march.

If you're someone who's continually running late, you'll probably curse the development of timekeeping. At this museum, the history of time measurement is celebrated and explored with thousands of artifacts and historic replicas. They range from early sundials to sleek, modern "talking" wristwatches. Exhibits include water clocks, astrolabes, compendiums, incense clocks, sand-glasses, navigational instruments and modern devices such as the cesium atomic clock.

The collection reflects one man's fascination with time. Seth Atwood, a banker, began by thinking about time in a more abstract way. "My main interest in time was as a theoretical subject. How does it enter into science and our daily lives, and what does the word really mean," he explains. A precise definition of time, Atwood notes, didn't even exist in the dictionaries he consulted. Rather than define the term, dictionaries listed dozens of examples of its use. Looking for something more concrete to study, Atwood began collecting timekeeping artifacts. He didn't set out to pick up a clock or two, but instead challenged himself to amass a collection that would serve to document the history of timekeeping.

"Once I got into it, I discovered that this was a much more comprehensive and wide-ranging subject than I originally thought," he recalls. "I thought I could

16th century German compendium clock includes astronomical maps, a sundial and a weather vane

cover it with 40 or 50 pieces. I ended up with 1,500."

Although Atwood didn't run out of time, he did run out of space at home to house his growing clock collection. Atwood decided to open a museum within a resort hotel he owned. Appropriately enough, the hotel features a landmark clock tower that serves as a beacon to weary travelers.

Exhibits are, of Course, Arranged in Chronological Order

The museum's collection is divided into time periods, beginning with early instruments and leading up to contemporary devices.

Early timepieces include an Islamic astrolabe, dating to 950 A.D., and a Chinese waterwheel—a water-driven mechanism that foreshadowed the modern mechanical clock. There are also historic replicas of the gears and mechanisms that were invented between the 13th and 16th centuries that would provide the basis for modern timekeeping devices. Until the 16th century, timekeeping was closely linked to developments in science and engineering. Wristwatches and clocks in the home were not yet common. Most towns would have a central clock that would sound time at regular intervals. That kept townspeople in sync with each other.

Travelers could carry a device such as a compendium, which would aid their timekeeping while on the road. The museum exhibits one such device from 1556 that was made in Augsburg, Germany, a center for much of the early clock-making industry. The compendium folds out to reveal three octagonal charts which include astronomical maps, a sundial and a weather vane.

Fashion Takes Over

Once the mechanics were worked out, elements of fashion and style began to influence timekeeping instruments, leading to a period of extravagance that is well documented in the collection. A well-crafted timekeeping device in the home was a decided luxury. The clocks of this period are characterized by their flourishes and accessories, frills that often overshadow the clock's main function.

German chariot clock (circa 1600) was designed to move along a banquet table to entertain guests

Time for a Performance

The museum exhibits several amazing examples of performance clocks, devices that not only kept time but also offered staged performances by miniature figures that would dance or otherwise move about beautifully crafted clocks.

One whimsical example of a performance clock is the chariot clock made in 1600 in Augsburg. This clock is designed to move along a banquet table to entertain guests. The gilded work features the mythical king Gambrinus in full state of gluttony, reclining heavily while holding a large cup. At regular intervals the clock becomes animated and Gambrinus takes a swig from his vessel and smacks his lips. Meanwhile, other figures on the chariot play instruments and help drive the vehicle forward.

Another performance clock on display is one that was commissioned by Napoleon. It features two ships that fight a sea battle on the hour to the accompaniment of canons and music sounds from a 72-pipe organ.

A massive German-made astronomical clock crafted by Christian Gebhard between 1865 and 1895 includes figures that stage performances every quarter-hour. A showstopper is performed daily at noon and includes the procession of disciples past the figure of Christ.

Mass Production Takes Over

Eli Terry is credited with introducing mass production to clock-making in the early 1800s after he received an order to make 4,000 clocks. To meet the demand he designed interchangeable parts made of wood. By the Civil War, companies in Connecticut were producing half a million clocks annually. Examples of some of these shelf clocks are displayed, including one box clock from 1815 that features a painted rural scene and a view of the working gears.

Post-World War II wristwatches

Eli Terry is credited with introducing mass production to clock-making in the early 1800s after he received an order to make 4,000 clocks.

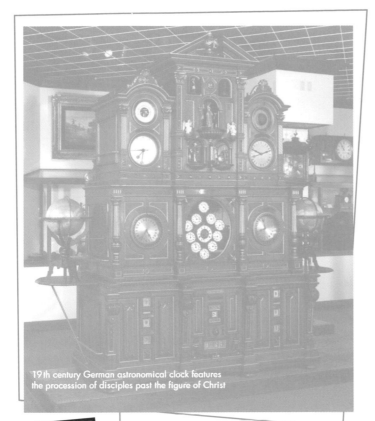

19th century German astronomical clock features the procession of disciples past the figure of Christ

Historic Wristwatches

Hundreds of historic wristwatches are in display cases sunken into tables. You sit in comfortable chairs around the tables to view the watches.

In addition, there are examples of unique alarm clocks, including one from 1750 that released a gun flint-lock to light a candle, and a wrist alarm watch from the 19th century that signaled a set time by poking the wearer in the finger.

Counting Down

One clock, called the Fluxion Clock, is unusual because it counts down from a set time in the future. It was produced in 1988 by Stephen Paul Kaye, and was designed to show the remaining seconds in a person's life. The clock here is counting down the time remaining, in seconds, until New Year's Eve 1999.

Time and Beyond

One of the most intricate timekeeping devices on display is the astronomical clock made by Rasmus Sornes of Norway between 1958 and 1964. It's considered to be the most complicated astronomical clock in the world. Featuring dozens of dials that track everything from astronomical movements to the positions of planets, it calculates sidereal time, which is the measurement of the Earth's movement relative to the stars. This clock will also predict solar and lunar eclipses and measure the rotation of every planet in the solar system.

As an example of the clock's complexity, it simulates the movement of the earth's axis with a cycle system set for 24,800 years!

The most complicated astronomical clock in the world

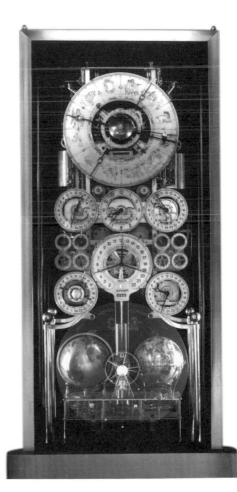

Cockroach Hall of Fame

2231-B West 15th Street
Plano, Texas 75075

972-519-0355

Noon to 5 P.M. Monday through Friday, Noon to 3 P.M. on Saturday.

Free.

Take the I-75 North from Dallas. Exit at the 15th Street off-ramp. The museum is about 1 1/2 miles west at the northwest corner of Custer and 15th Streets.

It is Michael Bohdan's job to kill cockroaches, but it's nothing personal. In fact, the professional exterminator offers his grudging respect for the much-maligned household pest. So much so that he's developed an alternate persona as "Cockroach Dundee." It's his way of acknowledging that no matter how many battles he wins on the extermination front, in the long run the cockroach will emerge victorious.

"They define the word 'survival,'" he admits. "You've got to give them credit. They are going to be around here a lot longer than we will."

The cockroach dates back 350 million years, Bohdan points out. Because they're so hearty and adaptable, it's reasonable to assume that they'll outlive most other species and perhaps one day rule the world.

So it's fitting that they've been given a tribute of sorts at the Cockroach Hall of Fame, housed in Bohdan's pest control business.

Each year the museum sponsors a contest to determine the most creatively dressed cockroach

190

Michael Bohdan a.k.a. "Cockroach Dundee"

So far, animal rights activists haven't registered any complaints.

"I've not come across a society for the prevention of cruelty to cockroaches," he jokes.

Creature Clean

Bohdan says the cockroach's reputation as a filthy creature is undeserved. They are clean and cautious creatures, he insists. They're more careful of where they step with their padded feet than the average person.

"When I watch them I can see how they react with each other and how they use their antennae to test an area before they walk over it," he observes. "They groom themselves continually."

Each year Bohdan sponsors a contest to determine the most unusually dressed cockroach.

Museum Highlights

Live and deceased examples of cockroach breeds are on display. For example, Bohdan exhibits a colony of about 100 Madagascar Hissing Cockroaches. They're registered with a local animal talent agency, awaiting film roles. In the meantime, you can watch them scamper along a four-foot track during weekend races which determine the swiftest of the bunch.

Then there are the cockroach dioramas, featuring ill-fated roaches that have been caught, killed, and then dressed in whimsical attire for human amusement. Each year Bohdan sponsors a contest to determine the most unusually dressed cockroach. Winning contestants have created cockroaches outfitted as Batman, a vampire, and a windsurfer. Such celebrity cockroaches as H. Ross Peroach, Elvis Roachley and Marilyn Monroach have also garnered awards. There's even Liberoachi, a dead roach clothed in a sequined costume and seated at a miniature piano topped with a candelabrum.

There's even Liberoachi, a dead roach clothed in a sequined costume while seated at a miniature piano topped with a candelabrum.

A Bug Lover

Bohdan says that his interest in bugs dates back to his childhood, when he maintained an ant farm and also went hunting for insect fossils. At Southern Illinois University, where he majored in zoology and added a minor in entomology, he kept many insects and assorted creatures as pets, not pests. They included a praying mantis, snakes, various bugs, and bats.

"I used to get in trouble when they would get out of the dorm and I'd have to go pick them up at three in the morning," he recalls with a laugh. "I was fascinated with anything that crawled or flew. I've been considered a little eccentric when it comes to animals."

191

Inventive cockroach display

My Cockroach is Bigger Than Yours

Bohdan also hosts a yearly contest to find the largest cockroach in the United States. Recent winners include one that measured around three inches long. Winners have appeared on the *Tonight Show*.

For catching cockroaches to enter in the contest, Bohdan offers this strategy: Take a widemouth jar, cut a sock and fit it around the sides of the jar. Put bananas and dog food in the jar and smear the bottom of the jar with Vaseline. A cockroach will crawl up the sock and into the jar to feed on the food. The bait will be the roach's last meal. The Vaseline will make it so slippery that the roach won't be able to crawl back out.

Roach as David Letterman

Bohdan also hosts a yearly contest to find the largest cockroach in the United States.

192

UFO Enigma Museum AND The International UFO Museum & Research Center

UFO Enigma Museum

6108 South Main Street
PO Box 6047
Roswell, New Mexico 88202-6047

904-825-2389

 9 A.M. to 5 P.M. every day.

 $3.50 adults,
$3 seniors,
$1 children under 11.

From center of town head south on Main Street to McGaffrey Street and bear right on Main for about 4 miles. The museum is on the right hand side.

The International UFO Museum & Research Center

114 North Main Street
PO Box 2221
Roswell, New Mexico 88202

505-625-9495
Fax: 505-625-1907

11 A.M. to 5 P.M. every day.

  Free.

  In downtown Roswell, on Main Street between First Street and Second Street.

I n early July, 1947, something fell out of the sky near Roswell, New Mexico. Residents claimed to have seen a glowing, oval-shaped craft whizzing through the clouds. After a severe thunderstorm, a sheep rancher discovered metal debris scattered across a field. This crash evidence was eventually taken to the Army Air Base in Roswell for investigation.

An initial report in the July 8th edition of the *Roswell Daily Record* said that the army had announced the recovery of a flying saucer. Needless to say, this news made for banner headlines. Within hours of the story being released to news services around the world, however, the army shifted gears. What they had recovered, officials now said, was debris from a downed weather balloon.

If you believe in stories of visitors from outer space, the Roswell incident is a compelling tale. There are crash witnesses, physical evidence and hints of a government cover-up. And yet, nothing definitive. The only certainty about the event is that it remains legendary among UFO believers.

Re-creation of the Roswell incident

194

For years, the curious had flocked to Roswell to experience the sensation of being close to the alleged alien crash site, which is actually a few dozen miles north of Roswell. For that reason, a museum that catered to UFO devotees seemed inevitable. Sure enough, in 1992, two such institutions opened for business.

It's an uneasy co-existence. Workers at each museum keep a wary eye on their rival. They join forces once a year for the town's annual UFO Encounter festival, held during the first week of July. The event features speakers, parades, races and an alien costume contest.

In addition to mounting a few exhibits and screening films and videos, both museums stress their role in supporting continued research into UFOs. They each maintain web sites featuring up-to-the-minute information on the latest sightings, as well as the results of new research into old events. If you're looking for books,

videotapes or UFO souvenir items, both museum gift shops are well-stocked.

Fact or Fantasy?

John Price, who opened the UFO Enigma Museum, has been fascinated by UFO reports since he was a kid growing up in Roswell.

"There was a time when I wanted to believe everything I was hearing," Price says. "I never really had a problem believing that there could be life out there and something could have crashed. But I was exposed to so much tabloid stuff that it didn't make any sense after a while. I thought that I could help separate fact from fantasy."

UFO believers contend that a major obstacle in their search for answers is that the government conspires to cover up the truth about close encounters. They believe, for example, that although the government never

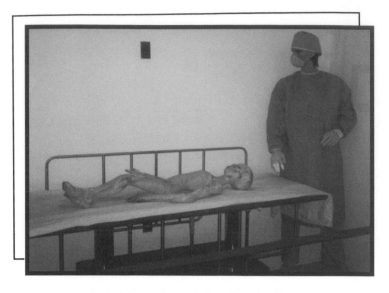

Far left: Mannequin alien seen around the world

revealed this to the public, alien bodies were recovered from the Roswell crash site.

Price says that 95 percent of all claims of alien sightings can be explained away. However, there are some that can't. In one section of the museum there is a display detailing plausible cases of UFO sightings from around the world during the last 60 years.

One of these cases involves Betty and Barney Hill. In 1961 the Hills were driving home late at night when they recall seeing a bright light. They realized later that time had passed and they couldn't remember what had happened. Under psychoanalysis they discovered that they had been abducted by aliens. Price says that while some UFO reports are difficult to believe, this case seems credible.

"There's a lot of

stuff we don't believe. It gets really frustrating at times," Price admits. "You want to throw your hands up and say, 'I'm getting out of it.' We're about at the point where we've had all the testimony we need. We've got to get physical evidence."

Until then, there's always the museum's Blue Room. It features a fiberglass replica of the downed flying saucer that made Roswell famous. The alien craft is represented by two satellite dishes welded together. Four small aliens—gray, ghost-like figures with tear-drop eyes and thin physiques—lay strewn about the saucer. Behind this reproduction is a mural of the crash site.

The museum's 20-seat theater screens several films a day about UFOs. Some are documentaries, and others are fictional accounts. Price thinks that the fictional films are just as vital as the documentaries.

"They're an important part of this. This is what we've all been exposed to," he says. "When the truth comes out, it will be so far away from this that people will be shocked."

Not of this World

The UFO Enigma Museum and The International UFO Museum both claim to have authentic debris from the 1947 crash site. The museums acquired the artifacts in 1996 under similar circumstances. Each museum received an artifact from a third party—not the person who originally found it at the site, but someone to whom it was given years ago.

The UFO Enigma Museum and The International UFO Museum both claim to have authentic debris from the 1947 crash site.

At the UFO Enigma Museum, the debris is displayed. It's a jagged, spiral-shaped piece of silver and brass about four inches long.

"It's a really pretty piece," Price says.

The International UFO Museum's crash debris is a thin strip of metal that contains silver and copper. The museum displays only photos of it. The actual relic is kept in a police station vault.

But you *can* view the mannequin alien used as a prop in the Showtime movie *Roswell*. The four-foot-long figure, covered with a "road rash" from his alleged crash, lies on a gurney with its knees raised. A blue-gowned mannequin wearing a surgical hat and cap and mask stands over the figure.

"Our little alien is quite famous," says museum director Deon Crosby. It's also been featured in other documentaries and newspaper and magazine articles about the Roswell crash.

The museum features about 20 exhibits on various aspects of UFO sightings. Mostly it offers newspaper clippings, photos and texts of testimonials. A recent exhibit dealt with the mysterious crop circles that have appeared in fields in England.

"Our little alien is quite famous..."

The Mayan image of the Palenque Astronaut (400–600 A.D.) is often offered as proof that the ancient people were visited by aliens

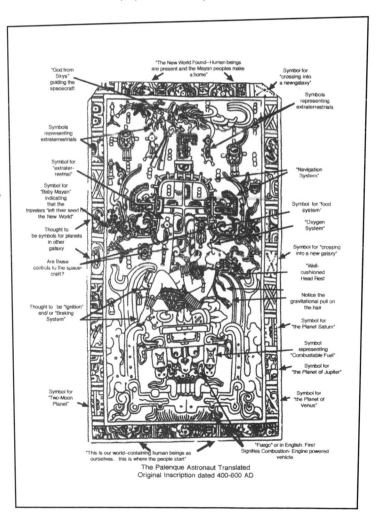

"God from Skys" guiding the spacecraft

"The New World Found--Human beings are present and the Mayan peoples make a home"

Symbol for "crossing into a new galaxy"

Symbols representing extraterrestrials

Symbols representing extraterrestrials

Symbol for "extraterrestrial"

"Navigation System"

Symbol for "Baby Mayan" indicating that the travelers "left their seed in the New World"

Symbol for "food system"

"Oxygen System"

Thought to be symbols for planets in other galaxy

Symbol for "crossing into a new galaxy"

"Well-cushioned Head Rest"

Are these controls to the spacecraft?

Notice the gravitational pull on the hair

Thought to be "Ignition" and/or "Braking System"

Symbol for "the Planet Saturn"

Symbol representing "Combustable Fuel"

Symbol for "the Planet of Jupiter"

Symbol for "Two-Moon Planet"

Symbol for "the Planet of Venus"

"This is our world--containing human beings as ourselves.. this is where the people start"

"Fuego" or in English: Fire! Signifies Combustion- Engine powered vehicle

The Palenque Astronaut Translated
Original Inscription dated 400-600 AD

I CRASHED IN ROSWELL, NM

UFO JULY 2, 1947 UFO ENIGMA MUSEUM

Soukup & Thomas International Balloon and Airship Museum

700 North Main Street
Mitchell, South Dakota 57301

 605-996-2311

 8 A.M. to 8 P.M. daily (Memorial Day to Mid-September). Off-season: 9 A.M. to 5 P.M. Monday to Saturday, 1 P.M. to 5 P.M. on Sunday. Closed in January.

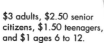 $3 adults, $2.50 senior citizens, $1.50 teenagers, and $1 ages 6 to 12.

 Follow I-90 to Mitchell. Take the Burr Street exit to 7th Street and make a left. The museum is on the northeast corner of 7th and Main Streets, one block north of the Corn Palace.

In 1783, when Pilâtre de Rozier and the Marquis d'Arlandes announced plans to attempt the world's first flight in a hot air balloon, their king, Louis XVI, had a better idea.

Why not, he suggested, send two condemned prisoners up in the flying contraption instead?

The king's gesture was sincere and practical. For centuries men had attempted to soar into the air by various means. Broken bones and sometimes death had been their reward, not flight.

But the two Frenchmen were adamant and confidently set up their launch on the afternoon of November 21st. Hot air produced by the burning of dry straw over an iron grate filled their 70-foot high balloon. The balloon, decorated with zodiac signs, lifted them skyward. Although they landed abruptly hours later, with an unceremonious crash as the balloon deflated, they recorded aviation's first documented flight.

Ten days later another balloon, this time filled with hydrogen, drifted toward the heavens above Paris. Flying was no longer just a dream.

Rozier and D'Arlandes are not as well known as the Wright brothers, yet their contributions to aviation are just as significant. They are certainly not overlooked at the Soukup & Thomas International Balloon and Airship

An array of modern balloons ready for launch

Interior view of the museum

Ballooning became such a popular fascination that balloon motifs began appearing on jewelry, snuff boxes, dinnerware, furniture and other items...

Table setting from the doomed airship

Museum. Using artifacts, photos, texts, videos and many examples of historic and modern balloon ships, the museum tells the history of balloon and airship travel from its crude beginnings in the 18th century to the globetrotting, sophisticated crafts of today.

The museum opened in 1989 with the collection of balloonists Jacques Soukup and Kirk Thomas. The artifacts they assembled range from the dining room service from the ill-fated Hindenburg airship to the submarine-like Zanussi balloon capsule, which in 1978 fell just 100 miles short in its attempt to become the first balloon to complete a trans-Atlantic crossing.

Uplifting Development

Opening exhibits document the excitement generated by the onset of balloon travel in the 18th and 19th centuries. There are letters written by witnesses to the first balloon flights, as well as etchings and other artwork commemorating the achievement.

Ballooning became such a popular fascination that balloon motifs began appearing on jewelry, snuff boxes, dinnerware, furniture and other items, and the

museum showcases examples of these.

Small-scale balloons intended for home enjoyment were also popular during the 19th century. These balloons were held over a small fire and made buoyant, and then released into the air. The museum has a stunning example of this kind of a device in the form of a terrestrial globe produced in Germany in 1840. Four feet in diameter, the balloon is made of linen laid over paper, and is covered with a map of the world as it was known at the time.

Throughout the 19th century balloons were often used to attract crowds at events such as fairs, concerts or theater performances. To illustrate this marketing trend the museum offers many examples of 19th century advertising posters for various events that promoted balloons as a featured attraction.

End of the line for the Hindenburg

The Hindenburg

Visitors learn about the evolution of giant airships by reading the original letters of Count von Zeppelin, which date back to 1897 and describe his ideas about air passenger travel and the potential for using airships as military weapons.

It would be impossible to cover the history of airships without mentioning the Hindenburg, fated to a spectacular

Hot air balloons "Uncle Sam" and "Chic-I-Boom"

The Blimps at War

Throughout the history of balloon travel, military leaders have been in-trigued about their use during war. Although they were never proven to be effective, and their crews often suffered heavy casualties because of their slow speed, balloons and airships have been deployed by many combat forces through the years.

"Balloons at War" is an exhibit featuring dioramas that trace the use of balloons and airship in wars ranging from the Civil War to World War II. You can also inspect letters representing the first use of air mail, flown

and horrible end when it exploded while mooring at Lakehurst, New Jersey in 1937.

Items displayed from the German airship reveal the luxury in which passengers traveled. Included are an officer's casserole dish with Nazi insignia, china plates, crystal goblets, a little mustard pot and small bowl. Also on view are the passenger list, airship stationary, a luggage sticker and several of the German Zeppelin flags.

Round-trip tickets from Germany to the United States cost $720 on the Hindenburg. The horrifying crash, which killed 35 of the airship's 96 passengers and crew, marked the end of the Zeppelin era. Visitors to the museum can look at photos and a video depicting the crash.

A balloon named "Chesty"

by balloon during the Siege of Paris in 1870–71. Displayed as well are a French balloon basket and a U.S. Army observation balloon from World War I.

Another balloon exhibited here was vital to one family during a time of strife. It's a homemade balloon built by a Czech family in 1983 and used for their flight to freedom from the communist-led government.

Another balloon exhibited here was …built by a Czech family in 1983 and used for their flight to freedom from the communist-led government.

The Zanussi

Once the initial flight was accomplished, balloonists began racing to achieve a host of other firsts in balloon flying. A popular attraction here is the Zanussi balloon capsule, which in 1978 almost became the first lighter-than-air craft to fly across the Atlantic Ocean.

Museum director Rebecca Pope says the Zanussi is a big hit with kids, who think it looks like a purple submarine. The capsule weighs one ton and is 10 feet long. It flew by way of a hybrid system of helium gas and hot air.

After the Zanussi fell short of its goal, the Double Eagle II nabbed the record a month later.

"I'll get you my little pretty… and your little dog too!"

Madison Museum of Bathroom Tissue

305 North Hamilton Street
Madison, Wisconsin 53703-1565

608-251-8098

Irregular; best to call first.

25 cents with suggested donation of one toilet paper roll.

A five-minute walk from the state capitol building along Hamilton Street.

Every roll tells a different story

Stacked floor to ceiling on shelving in the front living room of a Madison apartment are more than 3,000 rolls of toilet paper.

The collection reflects a quirky obsession shared by the founders of the Madison Museum of Bathroom Tissue, who also happen to live here.

They, or their representatives, have raided hundreds of bathroom stalls in a determined quest to obtain sample rolls from sites all over the world. The acquisitions process is a sensitive subject; museum staff will only make sly references to "liberating" the rolls.

Everything is presented in lighthearted fashion. The artifacts are stacked up in improbable black-and-white towers that appear ready to topple. Written on each roll in black marker pen is information about where each was acquired.

They range from a tiny roll removed from a dollhouse set to a colossal spool lifted from, as the reference says, "Some Damn Gas Station on Route 66." The most revered rolls are protected in plastic sandwich bags.

Just One Roll at First

The impulse for the collection began with the need for just one roll. A group of friends on a trek to discover small towns around Madison went into a bar in Lodi called the Trophy Room. They asked the bartender for

The museum often hosts parties with more than 150 guests

Literature produced by the museum is usually of the tongue-in-cheek variety. Promotional brochures include somewhat lukewarm endorsements of the museum from collectors of toilet paper rolls. One man is quoted as saying that the museum "isn't all bad. I'm sure there are some people who would benefit by it."

Teaching Through Tissue

Perhaps sensitive to the issue of the museum's relevancy, the staff has organized several educational displays to accompany the presentation of their toilet paper souvenirs.

In the "History of Toilet Paper," the museum presents different items that have been used for the ignoble wiping function, including grass and leaves, sand and catalog pages. Each example is displayed in a large plastic bag and taped to a wall display.

A manufacturer's collection offers samples from makers of bathroom tissue who answered a request by the museum for examples of their work.

There are also temporary exhibits. A recent one featured toilet paper rolls from parents of museum staff and associates.

"It's kind of a homey display, something very family-oriented," Kolb says.

In the "History of Toilet Paper," the museum presents different items that have been used for the ignoble wiping function...

a spare roll of toilet paper that they could use at home. The bartender complied, and with that first roll, plans for the museum started to unfold.

"The next day the roll was left over in the car and we thought we should write on it where it was from so we could have a souvenir of our trip to Lodi," recalls Carol Kolb, the museum's curator.

As they traveled around they began collecting other rolls as mementos. Friends heading abroad were assigned to bring back foreign toilet paper samples. Soon the collection numbered more than 1,000 and plans for a museum began.

Museum or Performance Art?

Sometimes the museum functions more as a performance art space. Parties with over 150 people are held in the room, as guests mingle amid the stacks of bathroom tissue. The roommates will sometimes open up late at night for the benefit of the bar crowd spilling out from a nearby lounge. Perhaps a slightly inebriated state is the best way to see the museum.

Kolb says that the museum is more than just a conversation piece.

"We don't feel very small. We feel that we're a very important museum," she insists.

The roommates will sometimes open up late at night for the benefit of the bar crowd spilling out from a nearby lounge.

One of the many foreign displays

Museum Highlights

The museum has examples of toilet paper from every state in America. For a while, North Dakota wasn't represented, but news of the museum's plight reached a woman in that state, and she sent along a roll by mail. "She made a nice covering for it too," Kolb recalls, obviously impressed. There are many rolls from foreign locations, including the Vatican, and special exhibit areas such as the African Holdings and the Mexican Collection.

Closer to home, favorites include rolls taken from Ellis Island, the Alamo, the Statue of Liberty and one from Lambeau Field, secured during a game in which the Green Bay Packers defeated the Atlanta Falcons, 37–20.

Kolb says she likes to collect samples from "our fellow museums." Rolls from the Guggenheim, the Metropolitan Museum of Art and the San Francisco Museum of Modern Art are proudly displayed.

The museum staff believes it hit the jackpot with a roll taken from Caesar's Palace in Las Vegas. While some people can boast of having a first-day cancellation Elvis Presley stamp from Graceland, the museum treasures the roll it "acquired" from Graceland on that same day.

In most cases the rolls on view are less significant than the efforts that went into acquiring them. Because of this, the museum keeps a journal that records how each artifact was collected.

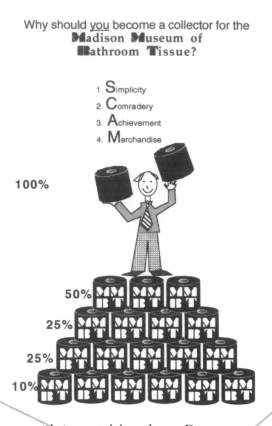

Why should you become a collector for the **M**adison **M**useum of **B**athroom **T**issue?

1. **S**implicity
2. **C**omradery
3. **A**chievement
4. **M**erchandise

100%

50%

25%

25%

10%

Questionable Acquisitions Policy

"When we're going on an expedition, we don't always ask the owner of an establishment if we can have their toilet paper," Kolb admits. "We feel that anyone would be honored to have their toilet paper included in our collection. We are more like archeologists. We take relics. We are not stealing them. We are lifting them up to their rightful purpose so that they can be studied by others."

Curator Carol Kolb, engaged in the acquisition process

...favorites include rolls taken from Ellis Island, the Alamo, the Statue of Liberty and one from Lambeau Field...

"We feel that anyone would be honored to have their toilet paper included in our collection."

Holes in the Collection

As complete as the collection may appear, there are still gaping needs, Kolb sighs. Included in the wish list, in case anyone wants to become an instant museum contributor, are rolls from the following locations: The Pentagon, Alcatraz Island, Kennedy Space Center, Motown, Oregon Trail, Library of Congress, The U.S. Supreme Court, Wrigley Field, The White House, and any maximum security prison.

HOW TO SEND YOUR TOILET PAPER TO MMBT

1. 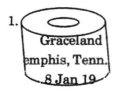 Label your toilet paper with location, city, and date of acquisition in magic marker.

2. Wrap in postal-service-friendly heavy paper or an auto chamois <u>or</u> slip inside a manila envelope.

3. Address and affix postage (or send postage due--we'll welcome it just as happily).

   Madison Museum of Bathroom Tissue
   305 N. Hamilton
   Madison, WI 53703-1565

205

Marvin Johnson's Gourd Museum

PO Box 666
Fuquay-Varina, North Carolina 27526

919-639-2894

Daylight hours, daily.

Free.

The museum is south of the Raleigh-Durham area on Highway 55. Heading south, look for Kennebec Airport on your left and turn right just past the pond at the museum sign.

Marvin Johnson has a few theories about gourds. Selling them, he believes, is bad luck. But giving them away can bring you good fortune.

Through the years he's handed out many gourds to friends and family, but kept dozens of other unique samples to put on display in his Gourd Museum.

Gourds, relatives of the squash and pumpkin families, have been used by many cultures in a variety of ways throughout history. They're handy vessels, adaptable as musical instruments, and can be carved or painted and then admired for their artistic beauty.

Growing up on a farm, Johnson watched his mother use several gourd varieties around the house, sometimes for dipping water out of a well or as containers in the kitchen. Johnson remembers binding several gourds and using them as a float for swimming in a nearby pond.

He worked as a math teacher and retired in 1941 to take care of his ailing parents. While living back at home he sprinkled gourd seeds across a field. To his surprise, hundreds grew, so many that he began giving them away. Some people crafted them into artworks and presented them to Johnson as gifts.

Gourds as works of art

Gourd Father
Marvin Johnson

*It didn't take long
before Johnson was
known around
these parts as the
Gourd Father.*

It didn't take long before Johnson was known around these parts as the Gourd Father. Not only did he have an impressive collection of artistic gourds, but he became a master grower who regularly snatched the blue ribbon at the North Carolina State Fair.

Many craft artists known for their work with gourds have donated some of their creations to Johnson. These gallery-quality art pieces take their place along side more homespun gourd works made by local schoolchildren.

Gourd Overload

When his gourds began to overwhelm the ranch style home he shared with his wife, Mary, he built a white cinderblock structure behind the house to display his collection. The museum opened in 1965.

Johnson still lives in the house. His wife, Mary, died in 1986. Ten years after this, at age 91, Johnson is still open for business, as long as visitors drop by before it gets dark.

There is only a small sign from the road, but you'll know you've arrived when you see Johnson's blue Cadillac in the driveway. The license plate reads, "Gourds," and bumper stickers proclaim, "Gourd Power" and "Gourds Must Predominate."

A Brief History of Gourds

There are hundreds of gourd varieties. Johnson cultivates about 200 of them, and has many more represented in his gourd art collection.

Gourd varieties are often named for their shape. Hence there are the snake, apple, dipper, cannonball and penguin varieties. A common trait is a hard outer shell that easily absorbs paints and stains. Once dried, they last as long as woods. Gourds have often been used as utensils and containers. Johnson says they are like prehistoric Tupperware.

They have been used to make musical instruments such as rattles or miniature pianos, which Johnson exhibits. In some cultures, gourds are used as masks and instruments in religious ceremonies. They come in a variety of sizes. At the museum you'll see examples that range from Japanese plum-sized peace gourds to a 2-foot wide African variety. In Africa, in fact, large gourds have been used by some tribes as boats to cross rivers.

The gourd has gained stature in the art world in recent years as many craft and folk art galleries, especially in the southwestern United States, have begun carrying decorative gourd items.

Gandy Gourd Girl
in all-gourd garb

Gourd Dioramas

The museum has several examples of gourds sliced open and their dried-out shells used as display cases for dioramas. Many of these contains religious scenes, while others are filled with cute doll figures. Some feature Christmas scenes including carolers singing by a lamppost. Others depict generic winter scenes such as one gourd diorama with tiny ice-skaters dancing on a frozen pond.

Other Museum Highlights

Some of the unique art items on display include a globe-shaped gourd painted to look like the world, and a sculpture of a Ferris wheel that has gourd gondolas. There is also a train engine carved from a gourd and one shaped like the Liberty Bell, infamous crack and all. A gourd lamp has a rounded gourd base and is topped with a plain white shade. There are gourds that resemble Fabergé eggs, and others shaped like animals such as swans, dogs, horses, cats and birds.

Johnson exhibits several gourds that have been painted to accent their resemblance to the penguin. They have long, slender necks, mak-

There is also a train engine carved from a gourd and one shaped like the Liberty Bell, infamous crack and all.

A Chirping Good Luck Charm

Giving away gourds is not the only way that the vegetable is believed to bring good fortune. The museum showcases an unusual piece from China. It's a gourd with a wooden top that's traditionally used to carry a cricket in the house. The reason? Good luck, of course!

ing them attractive, abstract representations of the cold-weather birds.

A relative of the gourd, the luffa, has also been used as vegetable art. There are several figures carved out of luffas on display, including ones that look like Benjamin Franklin and Paul Revere.

Tribute to His Alligator

Visitors used to be treated to a bonus attraction in the form of Johnson's pet alligator, who lived in a nearby pond. Johnson fed the gator hot dogs by hand, and encouraged brave visitors to do the same. He says that the gator never bit anybody. It lived by the museum for 19 years until it was shot by hunters.

Now you can gaze at a picture of Johnson feeding the gator, painted on the side of a gourd as a memento.

Gourds...

...and more gourds!

The Country Doctor Museum

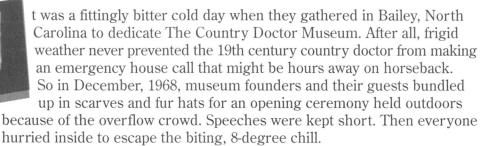

6642 Peele Road
PO Box 34
Bailey, North Carolina 27807

919-235-4165

10 A.M. to 4 P.M.
Tuesday through
Saturday, 2 P.M. to
5 P.M. on Sunday.

$2 adults,
$1 senior citizens,
$.50 children.

Bailey is located
between Raleigh
and Wilson off
I-264. The
museum is 2
blocks south of
I-264's business
route in Bailey.

It was a fittingly bitter cold day when they gathered in Bailey, North Carolina to dedicate The Country Doctor Museum. After all, frigid weather never prevented the 19th century country doctor from making an emergency house call that might be hours away on horseback.

So in December, 1968, museum founders and their guests bundled up in scarves and fur hats for an opening ceremony held outdoors because of the overflow crowd. Speeches were kept short. Then everyone hurried inside to escape the biting, 8-degree chill.

What they launched that day was a warm tribute to a style of American medical care that faded away in the early 20th century with the arrival of the telephone and automobile.

Tools for bloodletting, a common treatment prescribed by 19th century country doctors

The museum is the inspiration of Dr. Josephine Newell of Bailey, and another local physician, Dr. Gloria Graham. Newell, who retired in 1974, followed six generations of country doctors in her family. One day, Newell and Graham discovered the 1857 office of Dr. Howard Franklin Freeman. Since the door was loose, they ventured in, only to be chased away by a caretaker with a shotgun.

Eventually they convinced the owners of the property to let them have it for the museum. Then they acquired another vintage country doctor's office, belonging to a Dr. Cornelius Henry Brantley.

lasted for days, or until the outcome of the case was settled.

Country doctors were respected as much for their education as their ability to cure illness. They were prominent community figures, and usually were involved in town leadership.

"In the 1800s the physician was probably the most literate person in the community," states museum director Jacqueline Morgan. Often, Morgan says, a family might call in the doctor just to help them with tricky legal documents such as wills or deeds, or sometimes merely just to read or write letters for them.

Pharmaceutical box (a secret panel in the back contained narcotics)

When illness hit, families would often wait until homemade remedies had failed before sending someone out on horseback to fetch the doctor.

Both offices were transported to the museum's present location where they were joined together and restored. This structure now houses the bulk of the museum's collection.

The museum's exhibits cover the period 1790 to 1920. During that era, doctors were on call to handle a variety of rural medical needs. They might be summoned to help deliver a baby, pull teeth or set broken bones. When illness hit, families would often wait until homemade remedies had failed before sending someone out on horseback to fetch the doctor. House calls were common, and sometimes

Bad Blood

The "sickly season" for this region of North Carolina ran from August to October, when almost everyone, especially visitors and newcomers, could expect to suffer at least one illness. Common maladies included smallpox, typhus, malaria or yellow fever.

Prevailing medical science was still mired in the ancient concept of linking illness to the effects of "excessive humors." These humors, including bad blood or bile, had to be drained from the body so victims could recover their proper balance. As museum texts explain, contemporary forms of treatment included the four P's:

purging, puking, plaster or phlebotomy (bloodletting).

It's no wonder, then, that one country doctor, according to an account in the museum's library, complained that residents didn't call for a doctor unless they thought they were going to die.

House Call For the "Little Fellow"

In the museum's library there is an account of a typical house call by a country doctor. The 1852–53 diary of Mrs. Anna Pritchard of Warren County describes an illness suffered by her son.

"The little fellow had a hot fever . . . and difficulty in breathing. We sent for Drs. Macon and Howard. They thought Bob had an attack of pneumonia . . . Dr. Howard applied leeches to the upper part of his back . . . all of this time the little fellow screamed and struggled frightfully. They took blood from him . . . He took medicine sometimes every three, sometimes every two hours— Calomel and opium— antimony and Hives syrup. We kept boiled (hot) corn to him, an ear to each side and one at his feet . . . How my soul poured out in agony unto the only source and help, my God, and he heard me and bore me up and restored my child unto me."

Payment in Oats

For their efforts, country doctors were rarely paid in cash, and many were barely able to survive on their income. A museum exhibit explains that the only country doctors who were wealthy had married rich women. Sometimes payment would be food, such as cabbage heads, butter or chickens, if the doctor was lucky. Other times he might only get oats for his horse. When they were paid in cash, a country doctor could charge 50 cents for a puke or purge, and up to a $1 for a pulled tooth. He would add on a 40 cent per mile charge for travel. Even though most visits required the doctor to journey only a few miles, it was a trip by buggy or horseback that could take an hour or two and sometimes more.

"This was the old school, when medicine was godly. They did what had to be done," Morgan says.

Inhalation therapy devices

Sometimes payment would be food, such as cabbage heads, butter or chickens, if the doctor was lucky. Other times he might only get oats for his horse.

"This was the old school, when medicine was godly. They did what had to be done."

Museum Highlights

Exhibits include an apothecary shop with wooden shelves stacked with antique medicine jars, some containing their original potions. Medical equipment includes pill-rolling machines, scales, surgical tools and bloodletting and purging kits.

There are several handsome examples of authentic portable medicine chests, some featuring a hidden drawer in back where physicians kept secret stashes of narcotics used for treatments. Antique inhalation devices are also featured, including an 1870 Atlas steam vaporizer, a Vapo-cresoline Inhaler from 1879 and a Simplex warm vapor inhaler from 1880. They look like elegant china pieces.

Among the more gruesome artifacts are a variety of bloodletting equipment, including a German-made leech jar from 1900, a brass bleeding bowl, and a small scarifier which had four lancets contained in a silver case.

The Show Globe is a popular exhibit. Filled with colored liquids, it's an example of glass globes that were typically placed in the window of an apothecary shop and lit by candle or lamp. These lighted globes acted as beacons for people searching for medicines. The museum has a particularly handsome example— a burgundy globe with a silver base and top.

Among the more gruesome artifacts are a variety of bloodletting equipment...

Civil War Surgical Tools

The surgical set of Dr. Hunter Holmes McGuire, a Civil War-era surgeon, is well preserved and on display. Its last use was on May 2, 1863, after a battle at Chancellorsville, Virginia. Confederate Army General Thomas Stonewall Jackson was accidentally injured by one of his own men and Dr. McGuire had to amputate the general's left arm.

Another surgeon, Dr. Matthew Moore Butler, recognized the historical value of the surgical tools used in the operation. He preserved them in wax and concealed them in a barrel in a nearby farm. The complete surgical set was kept by Butler's family and presented to the museum when it opened, still encased in the protective wax. The

Surgical tools used to amputate the left arm of confederate Army General "Stonewall" Jackson

A strong horse was a country doctor's most important assistant

set, including saws, forceps, knives and scissors, is displayed in a glass case.

Getting Around

A separate building houses authentic country doctor buggies, surreys, saddle bags and a 1912 Model T Ford Torpedo Runabout, used by a Dr. Shields. The car was donated in 1990 by his daughter, who had kept it preserved in her garage since her father's death in the 1930s.

"She must have worshipped her father," Morgan muses. "She kept her father's car in the garage and kept her own Cadillac in the street. She only drove his car around the block once a year, on his birthday. We saw it in 1970. It took us 20 years to talk her out of it, but she finally gave it to us."

The car has brass headlights and oil lamp running lights on the side.

"It's a beautiful thing," Morgan sighs.

Before using the car in his practice, Dr. Shields relied upon his horse, Frank.

"That horse was his best friend," Morgan smiles. "When he left after a house call, Frank would take him home and he could contemplate his patient's ills and needs as Frank carried him. When he bought the car, Frank became his star boarder."

THE COUNTRY DOCTOR MUSEUM

Jacqueline C. Morgan
Executive Director
Res: (919) 235-3873

P.O. Box 34 · Bailey, North Carolina 27807 · (919) 235-4165

Medicinal Herb Garden

The garden is a replica of the Botanic Garden at Padua, Italy, the oldest existing medicinal garden in the world.

Contains plants used for healing from ancient times to the present.

First sponsored by the North Carolina Wild Flower Preservation Society, the Herb garden at the Country Doctor Museum was designed by Miss Elizabeth Lawrence of Charlotte, North Carolina. Walkways and paths are constructed with 19th century handmade Silas Lucas brick.

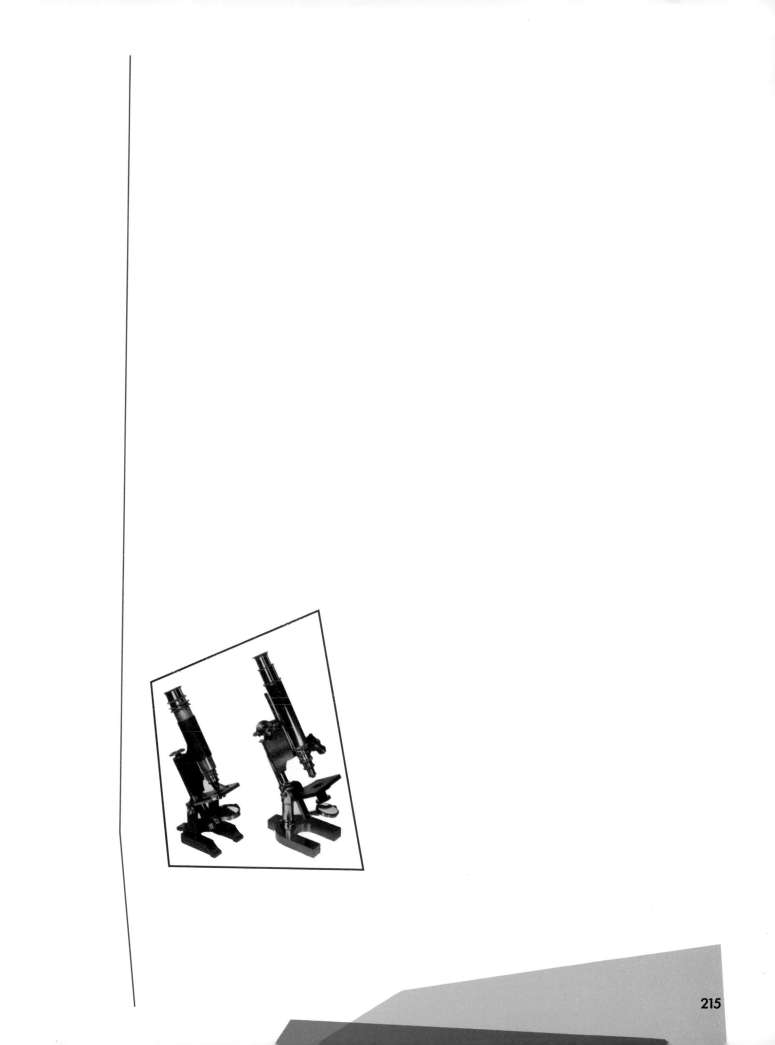

The Mini Cake Museum

Frances Kuyper
The Cake Lady

432 N. Lola Avenue
Pasadena, CA 91107

818-793-7355

Open by appointment.

Free.

From Los Angeles, take the Pasadena Freeway north until it ends and follow the road to Green Street and turn right. At Hill Street turn left and then turn right on Villa Street. Follow Villa Street to Lola Avenue and turn right.

Decorated cakes are often admired for their beauty, especially when made for special occasions such as birthdays or weddings. But then out come the forks and plates, and what is cherished one moment is quickly reduced to crumbs.

As a professional cake decorator for more than 40 years, Frances Kuyper has watched as her most artistic creations were sliced, dished up and then gluttonously consumed. She believed that decorated cakes deserved a longer-lasting tribute. She talked about opening a cake museum for years, but couldn't find sponsors willing to support the concept.

Kuyper went ahead anyway, and in 1994 opened the nation's first Mini Cake Museum. Why "Mini" Cake Museum? Because, as Kuyper explains, "the museum is small."

She saw it all in her head before construction started, much like she envisions her cake decorations before whipping up the frosting. In a quaint Pasadena neighborhood where she lives with her husband, Frank, she converted a second residence into a museum honoring decorated cakes. The converted two-story home is easily spotted by its towering mailbox shaped like a three-tiered wedding cake. Atop the cake is the figure of a cake decorator wearing a baker's hat and a long blue dress.

Cake mailbox

Step inside the museum and you discover tall glass display cases containing more than 150 decorated cakes. The cakes have been designed by top decorators from around the world, and illustrate international styles of cake adornment. Mouth-watering international exhibits range from small-portioned greeting cakes popular in New Zealand to wedding cakes made in South Africa, Japan and England. American frosting techniques are also amply represented with dozens of holiday and special occasion cakes, ranging from Thanksgiving to bar mitzvah cakes. In addition, you can view sugar eggs traditionally made for Easter, gingerbread houses, and figures made from covered sugar cones.

An upstairs reference library contains more than 1,000 books, magazines and scrapbooks, all dedicated to the art of cake decorating. Visitors seeking more expert advice can plop down into an easy chair in the video room and screen one of 90 short features showing the world's top cake decorators in action. For inspiration, you can gaze at the frosted replica of the Eiffel Tower that's displayed in a corner of the room.

For more hands-on help, the museum offers decorating classes in its working kitchen, which is stocked with Kuyper's cake molds and other baking equipment.

Frances Kuyper
"The Cake Lady"

Class topics range from cocoa painting to the craft of making the perfect butter cream flower.

From Vaudeville to Icing

Kuyper was driven to cake decorating after she dropped out of an early show business career. From 1935 to 1946, Kuyper and her sister, Charlotte, were touring performers on the vaudeville and supper club circuit. They dressed as a Danish boy and girl and sang and danced.

Charlotte tired of being on the road and got married, forcing Frances to retire. Eventually, she also got married, settling in California.

Frances turned to cake decorating to earn extra money for her family. At first she practiced decorating techniques using Crisco oil as a substitute for icing. She mowed lawns to get money to buy baking equipment. Cake decorating as a career, however, wasn't her idea of having your cake and eating it, too.

"Who wants to get in front of an oven all day? I fought it as long as I could," Kuyper recalls. "What's funny is that I never wanted to be a cake decorator."

But Kuyper was too creative for her own good. Right away, she began in 1950 by crafting delectable, three-dimensional party cakes for neighbors. They created a sensation. Soon she was staying up all night baking, and then icing all day long.

A local bakery took notice of Kuyper's work and she landed her first professional job. Her reputation grew in the 1960s and 1970s as she appeared on afternoon television shows hosted by Virginia Graham, Steve Allen, Dinah Shore and others. She became known as "The Cake Lady," an ambassador for cakes preaching the virtues of proper frosting to thousands of American housewives.

"It's a wonderful skill," Kuyper insists. "Once you get the hang of it, you can take a cake to a party and all of a sudden you're the star. It really helps with your ego."

Airbrush Wizard

Kuyper's career has been marked by innovation and self-promotion. She continues to teach classes and offer programs in cake decorating. In one classic demonstration, she shows the flair of her early vaudeville career by offering tips on decorative icing while playfully stripping off her apron as she sings: "There'll Be Some Changes Made."

Kuyper has pioneered the use of the airbrush in cake decorating. When she first tried to use an airbrush to decorate a cake, the air pressure was so strong that it blew the icing right off the cake. But Kuyper was convinced that it could be an effective tool, so she worked with the manufacturer to design one with a gauge that regulates the brush's power. Using this refined tool, she's been able to perfect the art of portrait cakes—treats coated with decorative icing that resembles a person's face. Kuyper has received publicity for making cakes that feature famous mugs such as former President Ronald Reagan, Oprah Winfrey, Barbra Streisand, and former Los Angeles Mayor Tom Bradley. Several of these airbrushed portrait cakes are on display in the museum.

Museum Highlights

The oldest item in the museum is an egg mold from 1930. Traditionally made for Easter, these hollowed out egg molds were decorated on the outside with colorful scenes of nature. Peer inside the museum's egg, and you can see tiny birds and flowers made of icing. Theme cakes include an edible

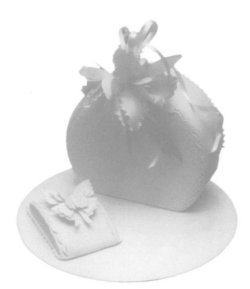

Surprise

"People are always asking me, 'I love cake, but can you take the calories out of it?'" Kuyper laughs. No, she hasn't figured out a way to do that. But she has mastered the art of taking the cake out of the cake. Kuyper specializes in making "surprise cakes"—hollowed out cake molds that consist of an outer layer of icing with no cake underneath. The museum displays one shaped like an Easter bonnet. Kuyper says its fun to place gift items under the icing to enhance the cake's surprise effect.

Mickey Mouse and a colorful, frosted version of Australia's Great Barrier Reef. The reef cake is all edible, Kuyper insists, and includes coral and swimming fish.

A prime example of a wedding cake is "Precision Work," by Graham Haddock, a decorator who made intricate measurements on paper before turning his designs into cake. The high-rise cake features geometric patterns and trimmings as well as a conical dome. Another wedding cake on display is shaped like a castle, with golden towers and newlywed figures positioned under an intricate doorway.

For children, there are Raggedy Ann cakes, a Cinderella cake and a sugared dinosaur with a gaping mouth and long pink tongue.

Merry Christmas from the Kuypers!

The Cake Lady's Favorite Butter Cream Icing Recipe

6 oz. hot water
1/2 tsp. salt
1 lb. 12 oz. SWEETEX
(hi-ratio shortening)
4 oz. Pet evaporated milk
2 lbs. 8 oz. powdered sugar
Flavor to taste

Blend water, sugar, salt and flavor in mixer bowl. Using wire (paddle will also work), whip until completely dissolved. Mix for one minute on high speed. Reduce speed of mixer and add shortening steadily in small amounts. Add milk slowly while mixer is still running.

Scrape bowl. Continue mixing on medium speed, for about eight minutes. Note: In hot weather you may have to decrease liquid by a small amount.

Her biggest customer for surprise cakes is her own granddaughter, who only likes frosting. But the biggest surprise of all may be that the granddaughter of The Cake Lady doesn't like cake at all!

Exotic World Burlesque Hall of Fame

When Dixie Lee Evans performed as a burlesque dancer, she was never in a hurry to shed her clothing. Why would she, when she was usually decked out in a glamorous, expensive outfit that attracted as much attention as the promise of what lay underneath? Complete nudity was rare when Evans and other exotic dancers slinked across stages from the 1940s to the 1960s. Strip*tease* was just that.

Burlesque shows had evolved from vaudeville into a popular form of entertainment that featured musicians, comics and, of course, dancers who spent years crafting their own brand of bawdy but artistic entertainment. They tantalized bug-eyed audiences by seductively hiding behind fans, boas, pasties, G-strings and other exotic props.

It was, Evans says, good theater and great value for your entertainment dollar. Some burlesque dancers made the leap to more traditional arts, such as the stage or movies. But even if they didn't, it was a good life and one Evans doesn't regret.

"I ventured into burlesque and I'm glad I did," Evans insists. "It was solid, steady work. I traveled all over the world and it was wonderful."

Times have changed. Strippers today, Evans notes sadly, don't understand the artistry of the act, and the importance of the tease.

Burlesque legends Blaze Starr and Jennie Lee

Mannequins display vintage burlesque costumes

"Girls today have nothing to take off. They come out and immediately get down and risqué."

"Girls today have nothing to take off," Evans observes. "They come out and immediately get down and risqué. In our era you came out in full dress, with a gorgeous wardrobe and music and you wound up with a shake number."

Those days are gone, she admits. "You can't compare your grandmother's iron skillet to the microwave of today. Society has changed," she sighs.

Tribute to Burlesque

The heyday of the burlesque era is captured with such great detail in the Exotic World Burlesque Hall of Fame that you can almost hear the rimshots echoing throughout the 13 exhibit areas. The museum honors dozens of burlesque queens with displays of historic costumes, photographs, posters and vintage burlesque films. There's also an annual reunion performance featuring old and young dancers.

The museum's original collection was started by dancer Jennie Lee, who late in her career in the mid-1970s operated the Sassy Lassy nightclub in San Pedro, California. She kept

artifacts at a Los Angeles location and occasionally showed them by appointment. Lee's busy schedule made it too difficult to keep the museum open on a regular basis, Evans says.

When Lee became ill she moved out to the desert community of Helendale, where Evans came to nurse her before she died in 1989. The property she had bought was a goat ranch that Evans converted into the museum.

It's proven to be a popular attraction in this retirement community. Many local residents fondly recall the burlesque days of decades past and visit to relive those memories.

Evans says that researchers and the occasional reporter, filmmaker or television producer also stop by out of curiosity or to seek information for various projects.

"Burlesque has not been covered professionally in our history books. They want to sweep it under the carpet and pretend it didn't exist," she says. "Well, it did exist, and it existed in a big way. This was entertainment that was affordable to the working class.

Contestants vie for annual
Miss Exotic World Crown

For 25 cents they could go and see a great show."

There's no such prejudice against burlesque here, where the museum's brochure declares that burlesque is "as American as baseball and mom's apple pie." Entertainers with names such as Brandy Boom Boom, Sheri Champagne, Rita Atlanta and Blaze Starr are given their due, as are burlesque superstars such as Tempest Storm and Sally Rand.

You can also learn about the career of Evans, who was known as the "Marilyn Monroe of Burlesque." She began with a Hollywood act called "Crashing the Movies" in which she strutted onto the stage and slid into a red velvet couch. She then proceeded to portray what a young actress had to do to make it in Hollywood. Eventually this act evolved into doing a burlesque performance built around Marilyn Monroe, which proved to be Evans' trademark.

She would perform ribald versions of Monroe's films, and also act out scenes from her life. Offstage, Evans' life so closely mirrored her subject that

Burlesque
legend Sally Rand

she also attempted suicide.

"I adored her with all my heart," Evans says of Monroe. The feeling wasn't all that mutual as Monroe's lawyers threatened to sue her but ultimately never did.

Breakaway Clothes

The museum displays many costumes from famous strippers of long ago. Included are a silver sequined gown worn by Tempest Storm, Sally Rand's original set of fans, a velvet green dress and coat worn by Gypsy Rose Lee and many outfits that covered the shapely figure of Jayne Mansfield, including a cape. Sheri Champagne, who danced inside champagne glasses and made them a trademark on every part of her clothing, recently donated her entire wardrobe to the museum. There are also many examples of vintage pasties and G-strings.

Thousands of photographs in the museum's collection capture the flavor of the era, documenting the many costumes and the degree of nudity that prevailed during this period of exotic dancing.

Sheri Champagne, who danced inside champagne glasses and made them a trademark on every part of her clothing, recently donated her entire wardrobe to the museum.

Dixie Evans welcomes visitors to her museum

Knute Rockne, football coach of Notre Dame, got the idea for setting up his shifting offensive backfield while watching a chorus line in a burlesque theater.

stage!" Evans laughs. "Now I couldn't do a split when I was 16."

Burlesque Trivia

The museum offers some revealing trivia about burlesque which shows how striptease dancing has meshed with popular culture through the years. Knute Rockne, football coach of Notre Dame, got the idea for setting up his shifting offensive backfield while watching a chorus line in a burlesque theater. The G-string got its name because that's the thinnest string on a violin. Tempest Storm is the only burlesque star to ever perform at Carnegie Hall. After Marilyn Monroe and Joe DiMaggio divorced, the first girl Joltin' Joe dated after the separation was Dixie Evans, the Marilyn Monroe of Burlesque.

When Gypsy Rose Lee toured Yugoslavia in the 1950s, there were only two Rolls Royce cars in the country. One belonged to Gypsy, and the other to Marshall Tito.

Other Museum Highlights

Evans says she has hundreds of films from the burlesque period and screens them daily in a small theater in the museum. These are particularly illuminating to visitors who never experienced the shows firsthand.

Every year the museum provides burlesque stars of old a chance to relive their former glory during a reunion celebration and dance contest. Younger dancers are also invited to perform. A Miss Exotic World is crowned from the younger contestants, and a winner is picked in the Legends category, where some of the dancers may be in their 80s.

In 1995, Evans says that many performers ignored their age and reached back in time to perform their trademark routines. "We had an 85-year-old lady and she did a split on

The front entrance to Exotic World

Glore Psychiatric Museum

3400 Frederick Avenue
St. Joseph, Missouri 64506

816-387-2300 x1141

8:30 A.M. to 4 P.M.
Monday to Friday,
1 P.M. to 5 P.M. Saturday
and Sunday.

Free.

From Interstate 29, exit
at Frederick Boulevard
(Exit 47). Travel about
one mile west. The
museum is located on
the grounds of the St.
Joseph State Hospital.

The screams and wails of agony no longer reverberate through the halls of the state-run psychiatric hospital which houses the Glore Psychiatric Museum. But the exhibits speak for themselves. They tell the horrifying story of centuries of misguided treatments for the mentally ill.

From a modern day perspective, the exhibited devices once used on psychiatric patients seem more appropriate as instruments of torture. There are metal straightjackets, restraint cages, dunking tubs, immobilizing chairs, "fever cabinets," and swings designed to induce vomiting and vertigo.

One device, the "Bath of Surprise," has a pleasant enough sounding name. But its purpose was far more sinister. Unruly patients were disciplined by being forced to stand upon its scaffolding. Then they were dropped through a trap door into a tub of cold water to make them calmer and more manageable.

The Bath of Surprise

As curator George Glore points out, these devices stem from an era of psychiatric care that preceded the development of psychotropic medications and tranquilizing drugs. Before these were available, a tranquilizer might have been a club or a blackjack. "These old devices were used to shock the person and to alter that person's behavior. By keeping them calm and immobile you could

The Tranquilizing Chair was prescribed for unruly patients

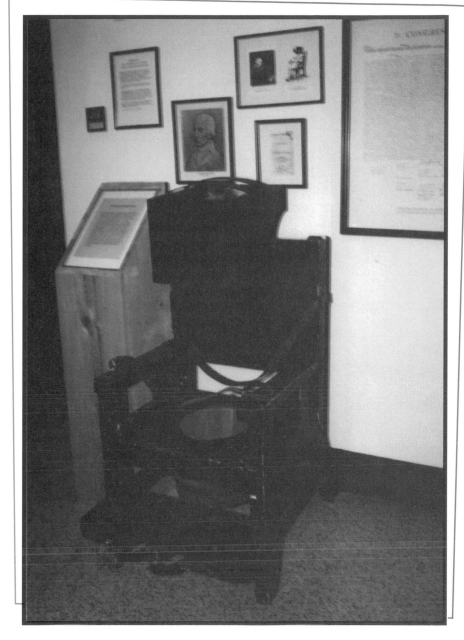

Many early treatments were based on the concept that mental illness stemmed from devil possession or bad blood in the system.

break the spirit of strong-willed patients who were causing trouble on the ward," Glore explains.

Many early treatments were based on the concept that mental illness stemmed from devil possession or bad blood in the system. "There was a belief that by making the body uncomfortable and causing it great pain, you might drive out those evil spirits. Some physicians recommended daily flogging of patients," Glore says.

The museum dates back to an open house held in 1967 by the hospital, a venerable institution that has been treating the mentally ill since 1874. Hospital staff exhibited a few antique treatment devices held in storage, thinking they would make good conversation pieces. They did. So much so that the displays became a permanent museum later that year.

While the exhibits clearly show the cruelty of bygone methods of treatment, the intent, Glore insists, is for visitors to walk away with an appreciation of modern psychiatric care. "We've had people who were certainly concerned and a bit upset that patients had been treated in such an inhumane manner," Glore admits. "But most people come out breathing a sigh of relief."

On a more positive note, the museum

exhibits other artifacts from the hospital's history including antique implements from its farm, dairy, cannery, furniture factory and blacksmith and clothing shops. Patient artwork is also displayed, and some of it is available for sale in the gift shop.

Museum Highlights

The Benjamin Rush 19th century Tranquilizing Chair is a replica of a once common restraining device that has binds for the arms and legs. A disturbed or difficult patient was strapped into the chair and kept there for prolonged periods, sometimes up to six months. A crude toilet fixture, often no more than a bucket, was placed under the chair.

Sometimes a patient's feet were immersed in scalding water and ice packs applied to his head. This was done, Glore explains, to eliminate "brain congestion."

"It had a canopy-like affair that came down over the head to prevent the patient from observing what was happening around him. That was supposed to have a calming effect," Glore continues. Attendants would apply bloodletting instruments to the patient while he was immobilized in the chair.

The Lunatic Box is a coffin-like case in which the patient was placed and forced to remain in a standing position until he became calm. A wooden piece could be dropped over the front opening, keeping the patient in total darkness. During the time of

Left: Embroidery work by a chronic schizophrenic

Sometimes a patient's feet were immersed in scalding water and ice packs applied to his head. This was done, Glore explains, to eliminate "brain congestion."

Patients were forced to run inside the windowless Hollow Wheel for up to 72 hours at a time

O'Halloran's Swing sent patients confined to a bed or chair into a violent orbit, sometimes spinning them at 100 revolutions a minute.

Right: A patient's collection of over 100,000 cigarette packs

confinement, the patient stood in his own waste and was fed only gruel. Sleep could only come in a distorted position.

The Fever Cabinet sealed the patient in a box filled with high-intensity light bulbs designed to drive up the patient's temperature to a feverish pitch, usually 105 degrees. The patient would stay that way all day as a cure for syphilis, Glore says.

O'Halloran's Swing sent patients confined to a bed or chair into a violent orbit, sometimes spinning them at 100 revolutions a minute. This was used to make patients more obedient, Glore explains, and also for patients with suicidal tendencies or those suffering from "general madness."

The result of the treatment was sometimes a brain hemorrhage. At the very least, patients usually "lost the contents of their stomach," Glore confides.

Patient Art

In addition to treatment displays, exhibits include those that reflect the mental condition of the hospital's patients. Among these is a huge container filled with more than 108,000 empty cigarette packs. A patient in the late 1960s believed that if he collected more than 100,000 cigarette packs he could redeem them for a new wheelchair for the hospital.

"We don't know where he got that

O'Halloran's Swing

information. We kind of assumed that someone did it as a joke and laughed about it," Glore shrugs. However, when the hospital's staff found out, they bought a new wheelchair anyway, and told the patient that his effort hadn't been in vain.

Another exhibit shows hundreds of pieces of paper crammed into the back of a television set. This exhibit depicts the 1971 discovery of a patient caught stuffing a note through a back slot in a television. When the set was taken to the hospital's electrical shop, 525 notes were recovered buried in its guts. Doctors theorize that the patient thought the television was a mail slot.

"The messages referred to box cars. He used to work for the railroad and he believed that the hospital had locked away his knowledge in a box car," Glore says.

The museum also displays the contents of a patient's stomach that were recovered after surgery in 1929. A total of 1,446 pieces were removed during the surgery, including nails, screws, nuts, buttons, thimbles and other non-food items.

A partial breakdown of the total includes: 7 broken coat rack hooks, 70 large beads, 148 grape and other small seeds, 5 bent teaspoon handles, 3 salt shaker tops, 105 safety pins, 52 carpet tacks, 136 common pins and 1 nail file.

Now that's one mean case of heartburn.

Offbeat Museums by State

California

Exotic World/Burlesque Hall of Fame
29053 Wild Road
Helendale, California 92342
619-243-5261

International Banana Club® and Museum
2524 El Molino Avenue
Altadena, California 91001
818-798-2272

The Mini Cake Museum
432 N. Lola Avenue
Pasadena, CA 91107
818-793-7355

The Museum of Death
548 Fifth Avenue
San Diego, California 92101
619-338-8153

The Museum of Jurassic Technology
9341 Venice Blvd.
Culver City, California 90232
310-836-6131

Colorado

Nikola Tesla Museum of Science and Industry
2220 East Bijou Street
PO Box 5636
Colorado Springs, Colorado 80931
719-475-0918

Connecticut

The Barnum Museum
820 Main Street
Bridgeport, Connecticut 06604
203-331-9881

The Children's Garbage Museum of Southwest Connecticut
1410 Honeyspot Road Extension
Stratford, Connecticut 06497
800-455-9571

The Menczer Museum of Medicine and Dentistry
230 Scarborough Street
Hartford, Connecticut 06105
860-236-5613

Nut Museum
303 Ferry Road
Old Lyme, Connecticut 06391
860-434-7636

Florida

Tragedy in U.S. History Museum
7 Williams Street
St. Augustine, Florida 32084
904-825-2389

Illinois

Grandpa Moses' Traveling Museum
Various locations throughout Chicago, Illinois.
708-848-0982

International Museum of Surgical Science
1524 North Lake Shore Drive
Chicago, Illinois 60610-1607
312-642-6502

The Time Museum
7801 East State Street
PO Box 5285
Rockford, Illinois 61125-0285
815-229-4199

Maryland

The Great Blacks In Wax Museum
1601-03 East North Avenue
Baltimore, Maryland 21213
410-563-3404

Havre de Grace Decoy Museum
PO Box A
215 Giles Street
Havre de Grace, Maryland 21078
410-939-3739

The Museum of Menstruation
PO Box 2398
Landover Hills Branch
Hyattsville, Maryland 20784-2398
301-459-4450

The National Cryptologic Museum
National Security Agency
Fort George Meade, Maryland
301-688-5848/9

The National Museum of Dentistry
31 South Greene Street (at Lombard)
Baltimore, Maryland 21201-1504
410-706-0600

Minnesota

The Museum of Questionable Medical Devices
201 South East Main Street
Minneapolis, Minnesota 55414
612-379-4046

Missouri

Glore Psychiatric Museum
3400 Frederick Avenue
St. Joseph, Missouri 64506
816-387-2300 x1141.

Leila's Hair Museum
815 West 23rd Street
Independence, Missouri 64055
816-252-4247 (HAIR)

Iowa

The National Farm Toy Museum
1110 16th Avenue SE
Dyersville, Iowa 52040
319-875-2727

Kansas

Kansas Barbed Wire Museum
120 West 1st Street
La Crosse, Kansas 67548
913-222-9900

The Martin and Osa Johnson Safari Museum
111 N. Lincoln Ave.
Chanute, Kansas 66720
316-431-2730

Louisiana

New Orleans Historic Voodoo Museum
724 Rue Dumaine
New Orleans, Louisiana 70116
504-522-5223

Massachusetts

American Sanitary Plumbing Museum
39 Piedmont Street
Worcester, Massachusetts 01610
508-754-9453

Nevada
The Liberace Museum
1775 East Tropicana Avenue
Las Vegas, Nevada 89119
702-798-5595

New Mexico
American International Rattlesnake Museum
202 San Felipe NW, Suite A
Albuquerque, New Mexico 87104-1426
505-242-6569

The International UFO Museum & Research Center
114 North Main Street
PO Box 2221
Roswell, New Mexico 88202
505-625-9495

The National Atomic Museum
Kirtland Air Force Base
PO Box 5800
Albuquerque, New Mexico 87185-1490
505-284-3243

UFO Enigma Museum
6108 South Main Street
PO Box 6047
Roswell, New Mexico 88202-6047
505-437-2275

North Carolina
The Country Doctor Museum
6642 Peele Road
PO Box 34
Bailey, North Carolina 27807
919-235-4165

Marvin Johnson's Gourd Museum
PO Box 666
Fuquay-Varina, North Carolina 27526
919-639-2894

Ohio
Warther Carvings
331 Karl Avenue
Dover, Ohio 44622
330-343-7513

Oklahoma
National Lighter Museum
107 South 2nd Street
Guthrie, Oklahoma 73044
405-282-3025

Oregon
Kam Wah Chung & Co. Museum
N.W. Canton Street
John Day, Oregon 97845
541-575-0028

Pennsylvania
Mister Ed's Elephant Museum
6019 Chambersburg Road (US Route 30)
Orrtanna, Pennsylvania 17353
717-352-3792

The Mütter Museum
College of Physicians of Philadelphia
19 South 22nd Street
Philadelphia, PA 19103-3097
215-563-3737

The Shoe Museum
Pennsylvania College of Podiatric Medicine
8th and Race Streets
Philadelphia, Pennsylvania 19107
215-625-5243

South Dakota

The Shrine to Music Museum
The University of South Dakota
414 East Clark Street
Vermillion, South Dakota 57069-2390
605-677-5306

Soukup & Thomas International Balloon and Airship Museum
700 North Main Street
Mitchell, South Dakota 57301
605-996-2311

Texas

American Funeral Service Museum
415 Barren Springs Drive
Houston, Texas 77090
281-876-3063 Fax: 281-876-2961

Barney Smith Toilet Seat Art Museum
239 Abiso Avenue
San Antonio, Texas 78209
210-824-7791

Cockroach Hall of Fame
2231-B West 15th Street
Plano, Texas 75075
972-519-0355

The U.S. Border Patrol Museum
4315 Transmountain Road
El Paso, Texas 79924
915-759-6060

Washington

Don Brown Rosary Collection
The Columbia Gorge Interpretive Center
990 SW Rock Creek Drive
PO Box 396
Stevenson, Washington 98648
509-427-8211

Wisconsin

Hamburger Hall of Fame
126 North Main Street
PO Box 173
Seymour, Wisconsin 54165
414-833-9522

Houdini Historical Center
330 East College Avenue
Appleton, Wisconsin 54911
414-733-8445

Madison Museum of Bathroom Tissue
305 North Hamilton Street
Madison, Wisconsin 53703-1565
608-251-8098

Spinning Top Exploratory Museum
533 Milwaukee Avenue
Burlington, Wisconsin 53105
414-763-3946

Permissions

Santa Monica Press gratefully acknowledges the following individuals and institutions for allowing their photographs and illustrations to be used in this book:

Pages 8–11: Photos and Illustrations courtesy of the International Banana Club® and Museum

Pages 12–17: Photos and Illustrations courtesy of The Mütter Museum

Pages 18–23: Photos and Illustrations courtesy of The Museum of Menstruation

Pages 24–29: Photos and Illustrations courtesy of The Museum of Questionable Medical Devices

Pages 30–33: Photos and Illustrations courtesy of the Barney Smith Toilet Seat Art Museum

Pages 34–37: Photos and Illustrations courtesy of The National Atomic Museum

Pages 38–41: Photos and Illustrations courtesy of The Shoe Museum, Pennsylvania College of Podiatric Medicine

Pages 42–45: Illustrations courtesy of the Hamburger Hall of Fame; Photos by Countryside Photographers, Seymour, WI

Pages 46–49: Photos and Illustrations by Bradley Penka, courtesy of the Kansas Barbed Wire Museum

Pages 50–53: Photos and Illustrations courtesy of the New Orleans Historic Voodoo Museum

Pages 54–57: Photos and Illustrations courtesy of The Menczer Museum of Medicine and Dentistry

Pages 58–61: Photos and Illustrations courtesy of the Nikola Tesla Museum of Science and Industry

Pages 62–65: Photos and Illustrations courtesy of Grandpa Moses' Traveling Museum

Page 65: Photo of Grandpa Moses and fan courtesy of Geoff Loren

Pages 66–69: Photos and Illustrations courtesy of The Children's Garbage Museum of Southwest Connecticut

Pages 70–73: Photos and Illustrations courtesy of the National Lighter Museum, Ted and Pat Ballard Collection

Pages 74–77: Photos and Illustrations courtesy of the International Museum of Surgical Science

Pages 78–83: Photos and Illustrations courtesy of The Barnum Museum, Bridgeport, CT

Pages 84–87: Photos and Illustrations courtesy of Leila's Hair Museum

Pages 88–91: Photos and Illustrations courtesy of The National Farm Toy Museum and Bob Wilhelm. These photos are representations of toys on display in The National Farm Toy Museum

Page 90: Photo of toy tractor courtesy of Schmitz Photography. This photo is a representation of a toy on display in The National Farm Toy Museum

Pages 92–97: Photos and Illustrations courtesy of the Sidney H. Radner Collection—Houdini Historical Center, Appleton, WI

Pages 98–101: Photos and Illustrations courtesy of the Havre de Grace Decoy Museum

Pages 102–105: Photos and Illustrations courtesy of The Museum of Death

Pages 106–111: Photos and Illustrations courtesy of The Museum of Jurassic Technology

Pages 112–115: Photos and Illustrations courtesy of the Kam Wah Chung & Co. Museum

Pages 116–119: Photos and Illustrations courtesy of The Liberace Museum

Pages 120–125: Photos and Illustrations courtesy of The National Cryptologic Museum

Pages 126–129: Photos and Illustrations courtesy of The U.S. Border Patrol Museum

Pages 130–135: Photos and Illustrations courtesy of The Martin and Osa Johnson Safari Museum

Pages 136–139: Photos and Illustrations courtesy of The Shrine to Music Museum

Pages 140–145: Photos and Illustrations courtesy of the Tragedy in U.S. History Museum

Pages 146–149: Photos and Illustrations courtesy of the Spinning Top Exploratory Museum

Pages 150–153: Photos and Illustrations courtesy of the American Sanitary Plumbing Museum

Pages 154–157: Photos and Illustrations courtesy of Mister Ed's Elephant Museum

Pages 158–161: Photos and Illustrations courtesy of Warther Carvings

Pages 162–165: Photos and Illustrations courtesy of The Great Blacks In Wax Museum

Pages 166–169: Photos and Illustrations courtesy of The National Museum of Dentistry—Bob Creamer, photographer

Pages 170–173: Photos and Illustrations courtesy of the American International Rattlesnake Museum

Page 173: Photo of Bob Myers with rattlesnake skeleton courtesy of Randy Clarke

Pages 174–177: Photos and Illustrations courtesy of the Nut Museum

Pages 178–181: Photos and Illustrations courtesy of the American Funeral Service Museum

Pages 182–185: Photos and Illustrations courtesy of the Skamania County Historical Society

Pages 186–189: Photos and Illustrations courtesy of The Time Museum

Pages 190–193: Photos and Illustrations courtesy of the Cockroach Hall of Fame

Pages 194–197: Photos and Illustrations courtesy of the UFO Enigma Museum and The International UFO Museum & Research Center

Pages 198–201: Photos and Illustrations courtesy of the Soukup & Thomas International Balloon and Airship Museum

Pages 202–205: Photos and Illustrations courtesy of the Madison Museum of Bathroom Tissue

Pages 206–209: Photos and Illustrations courtesy of Marvin Johnson's Gourd Museum

Pages 210–215: Photos and Illustrations courtesy of The Country Doctor Museum

Pages 216–221: Photos and Illustrations courtesy of The Mini Cake Museum

Pages 222–225: Photos and Illustrations courtesy of Exotic World/Burlesque Hall of Fame

Pages 226–229: Photos and Illustrations courtesy of the Glore Psychiatric Museum

Thank you one and all!

Books available from Santa Monica Press

Offbeat Museums
The Curators and Collections
of America's Most Unusual Museums
by Saul Rubin
240 pages $17.95

Heath Care Handbook
A Consumer's Guide to the American Health Care System
by Mark Cromer
256 pages $12.95

The Book of Good Habits
Simple and Creative Ways to Enrich Your Life
by Dirk Mathison
224 pages $9.95

Helpful Household Hints
by June King
224 pages $12.95

How to Win Lotteries, Sweepstakes, and Contests
by Steve Ledoux
224 pages $12.95

Letter Writing Made Easy!
Featuring Sample Letters for Hundreds of Common Occasions
by Margaret McCarthy
224 pages $12.95

How to Find Your Family Roots
The Complete Guide to Searching for Your Ancestors
by William Latham
224 pages $12.95

Order Form

1-800-784-9553

Offbeat Museums _____

Health Care Handbook _____

The Book of Good Habits _____

Helpful Household Hints _____

How to Win Lotteries, Sweepstakes, and Contests _____

Letter Writing Made Easy! _____

How to Find Your Family Roots _____

Subtotal _____

Shipping and Handling (see below) _____

CA residents add 8.25% sales tax _____

Total _____

Name_____

Address_____

City_____ State_____ Zip_____

Card Number_____ Exp_____

○ Visa   ○ MasterCard

Signature_____

○ Enclosed is my check or money order payable to:

Santa Monica Press
P.O. Box 1076
Dept. 4646
Santa Monica, CA 90406
1-800-784-9553

Shipping and Handling:
1 book—$3.00 • 2–3 books—$4.00 • Each additional book is $.50